Created in His Image with a Unique Purpose

SCIENCE AND BEYOND

DR. RODICA MALOS

Trilogy Christian Publishers
A Wholly Owned Subsidiary of Trinity Broadcasting Network
2442 Michelle Drive
Tustin, CA 92780

All Scripture quotations, unless otherwise noted, taken from THE HOLY BIBLE, NEW INTERNATIONAL VERSION®, NIV® Copyright © 1973, 1978, 1984, 2011 by Biblica, Inc.® Used by permission. All rights reserved worldwide.

Scripture quotations marked (KJV) taken from *The Holy Bible, King James Version*. Cambridge Edition: 1769.

For information, address Trilogy Christian Publishing
Rights Department, 2442 Michelle Drive, Tustin, Ca 92780.
Trilogy Christian Publishing/ TBN and colophon are trademarks of Trinity Broadcasting Network.

For information about special discounts for bulk purchases, please contact Trilogy Christian Publishing.

Manufactured in the United States of America

Trilogy Disclaimer: The views and content expressed in this book are those of the author and may not necessarily reflect the views and doctrine of Trilogy Christian Publishing or the Trinity Broadcasting Network.

10 9 8 7 6 5 4 3 2 1

Library of Congress Cataloging-in-Publication Data is available.

ISBN 978-1-64773-582-1 (Print Book)
ISBN 978-1-64773-583-8 (ebook)

Disclaimer

This book is not a substitute for professional medical diagnosis and treatment. It is a book that solely must be used for informational and educational purposes. It contains the author's ideas and opinions about the body's health condition that is complex and unique. Before you begin any changes in your lifestyle, nutrition, exercise, fasting, or supplementation program, you should consult a health professional. If you have questions about your health, you definitely must call your primary care provider or a health-care specialist to discuss your health problems. Neither the publisher nor the author shall be responsible or liable for any damage or loss allegedly arising from suggestion and/or any information in this book.

People and names in this book other than those cited authors are composites created by the author from her stories and experiences as a primary care practitioner. Names and details of people's stories have been modified and changed, and any similarity between the stories and names of individuals presented in this book and individuals known by the readers is simply and purely coincidental. The statements about consumable products or food in this book have not been evaluated by the Food and Drug Administration. The instructions in this book are to be followed exactly as written. The publisher or the author is not responsible for your specific health conditions and/or allergy needs that may require medical intervention and supervision. The publisher and the author are not responsible for any adverse reactions and bad consequences to the consumption of food, medicine, products, or activities that have been suggested and/or written in this book. While the author during writing has made every effort to verify and provide accurate internet addresses at the time of writing and publication, neither the author nor the publisher is responsible for changes or errors that occur after writing and publication. Further, the author does not have any control over and is not responsible for third-party websites or their content.

Please note that all information written in this book is for informational purposes only. It is not medical advice for any specific individual, nor is it applicable for specific medical problems of any individual. No information presented in this book is written or intended as a substitute for any professional medical intervention for diagnosing or treating or for medical advice, and the information should not be construed as instruction or medical consultation for a specific person. You should take no action solely on the basis of this book's contents regarding treatment or diagnosis for your own health condition. Readers must talk to a health professional about any problem regarding their own physical or mental condition. The information found in this book is believed to be accurate, based on the author's best judgment. Readers who fail to seek treatment from appropriate health professionals assume risk of potential ill effects and expenses. Please note that this advice is not specific to any individual; it is generic, and before undertaking any medical or nutritional course of action, you must consult with your doctor. Take your medications as prescribed by your medical providers, schedule follow-up appointments, keep your appointments, and seek and follow medical advice for all your conditions.

Endorsements

If you've ever wondered about the dynamic of the human body, with all the sophisticated details built-in and vast connections with feelings and thoughts, then open this book! You will perceive the reality that the human body echoes His Creator; referring to science and medicine, either probing into cells or into functional brain circuits, the author makes it so transparent that His creative self was invested in us when our intricate being was shaped.

Rodica steps further to convey harmony between the visible and the spiritual world. She confidently presents a majestic mind that creates not only beautifully with reason but also the purpose for our very existence, so well outlined through meaningful scriptures.

It is royal fragrance spilled on her pages, divine gleams of hope and joy, enabling you to stay plugged in the reality of who you really are and how you are meant to live wonderfully made in His image!

—Dr. Crina Crisan, MD
urgent care
Vancouver, WA

*****

The wonders of our world and the details of life are truly amazing. Apart from a loving Creator, there is no credible explanation for these infinite observable details. The chances that life occurred apart from a Creator are akin to throwing a garbage heap into the air that lands to the earth as a fully functional 747 airplane!

Dr. Malos combines some of the scientific understanding of these wonders of life and creation with the eternal truths of the Word of God to give an inspirational message of insight and encouragement. Her own life story of growing up as a believer in a Communist country, moving to America, and serving people as a Christian medical doctor illustrates and undergirds the message she brings in this book.

—Dr. Greg Berglund, MD, MDiv
Mayo Clinic Health System Red Wing Specialty Clinic
emergency medicine, MN
pastor and author of *This Mountain: You Shall Say to This Mountain, "Move From Here to There"*

*****

What a great honor it is to endorse Dr. Rodica Malos's second book, *Created in His Image with Unique Purpose: Science and Beyond.*

While reading the manuscript, you can feel the anointing of God that was used in the beginning of creation, just like God is using Dr. Rodica as she wrote this book. She is able to convey His science, His perfect plan in equipping our body, soul, and spirit with unique purpose in both spiritual and scientific ways. We would expect nothing less from this amazing, gifted woman of God. Larry and I have known Dr. Rodica Malos for many years and had the extreme pleasure of watching God use her gifts and talents in many amazing ways. Her gift is used mightily by the Creator through the power of the Holy Spirit to bring before humanity God's amazing and awesome plan in creating human life. This book contains a medical and scientific evidence and an authentic message of God's Spirit at work in the author's life and every human life who receives Him. This book is the greatest tool to bring understanding of human communication and relationship with their Creator, to experience His supernatural power here on earth and to receive eternal life with a great reward in heaven when this life on earth is over. This book brings the reader a great insight and faith demonstrating that the Holy Spirit is real. As you read this book, get ready to experience God's supernatural power in creating you with a unique purpose.

—Pastors Larry and Tiz Huch
senior pastors, founders, and directors
DFW New Beginnings Church, Dallas/Fort Worth
New Beginnings Stream Church, Portland, Oregon
and Global Stream Ministries, Larry Huch Ministries
Global TV, and Media Outreach Network

*****

Dr. Malos takes her faith and her science seriously. She has done significant research for this book and includes personal vignettes along the way. Her writing is informative and encouraging. There is much to learn from her as she shows us God's fingerprints on our physical body, physiology, and brain.

—Dr. David I. Levy, MD
neurosurgeon and author of *Gray Matter: A Neurosurgeon Discovers the Power of Prayer... One Patient at a Time*

*****

Created in His Image with Unique Purpose: Science and Beyond is a must-read in one's life. This masterful work by Dr. Rodica Malos has been used by our Creator to demonstrate how His plan for our lives plays out in His awesome design and how our lives can be fulfilled through His Word.

In reading this book, you will learn of God's plan for your life and the unique role that you have been designed for. Your perspective, knowledge, and guide will change in reading this masterpiece. I endorse it without hesitation

—Shaneen Clarke
London, UK

*****

Unpacking this book, one chapter at a time, is the key to unlocking divine wisdom. "We are fearfully and wonderfully made" (Ps. 139) is a declaration of truth; it is our choice to believe it, receive it, and fulfill our life mission.

As Dr. Rodica clearly outlines, every person is destined accordingly, with the Master's skillful hand, even before we ever were! Every neuron, every synapse, every muscle, tendon, bone, and cell, our five senses, mobility, thinking capacity is made in His image, for His glory and His pleasure.

Be enraptured with this masterful concept of being personally sculpted, each attribute mirroring a loving Father God. Let this limitless love sink into every fiber of your being and give you strength for all your days.

—Kay E. Metsger RN, BSN
former cardiac operating room nurse manager

*****

Dr. Rodica Malos proclaimed her commitment to the Word of God, and her life reflects God's blessings in so many ways.

In a marvelous way, she is able to unraveled the positive manifestation of God's miracles hidden in plain sight—within His Word and promises—within each of us.

Thank you for yet another inspiring proclamation of God's power.

—Dr. Emilia Arden, DO, cardiologist, FACC
Medford, Oregon

*****

In her book, *Created in His Image with Unique Purpose: Science and Beyond*, Rodica Malos has masterfully painted a beautiful picture of creation and how our heavenly Father God has strategically—intentionally—and purposefully created each one of us for His Glory, for His Purpose, and in His unique fashion.

Strategically, because of His vast wisdom in creating each one of us in our own uniqueness!

Intentionally, because of the specificness of every cell, tissue, organ, and body part intentionally designed with the intent to make us "like Him!"

Purposefully, because we have been created with one purpose...to be imitators of our heavenly Father God...as His "beloved children!"

The Trinity is well presented throughout each page of this amazing book!

To God be the glory!

Well done, Dr. Rodica Malos—and well presented!

—Pastor D. Robinson
network director of pastoral care, TBN

*****

The human body is entangled with God's influence as a Creator like the two chains of the DNA molecule. Rodica Malos, the author, makes a unique, well documented insight into the human body and how every sense, every organ can be used to better ourselves in God's eyes and be a mirror of Him for the world to see, which can only be done with the supernatural help of the Holy Spirit. This book gave me, as a doctor, an interesting new perspective.

—Dr. Bogdan Puscasu, MD
emergency department
Cluj Napoca Hospital
Romania, Europe

*****

Dr. Rodica Malos's latest book is very timely in this time of world-wide disruption, fear, and confusion. Reading it filled me with joy, glorifying God for her Spirit-led insightful reminders from Scripture and the science of the intricate human body. Her book is God's Spirit-filled gift to us, revealing His marvelous design of man and woman as His crowning achievements in all creation, with our ultimate purpose to know Him and commune with Him in love and obedience. Dr. Malos reminds us of our present condition—how disobedience (sin) has distorted our God-given DNA and how we need a Savior, whose work on the cross and whose Spirit restores our spiritual DNA to allow us to fully desire and enjoy communion with God, live lives of joy in His love and in turn, love and bless others for the praise of His glory.

Dr. Robert Sayson, MD, physician
Good News Community Health Center
Portland, Oregon

*****

I am so excited about Dr. Rodica Malos's new book, *Created in His Image with Unique Purpose: Science and Beyond*. It is amazing how she put together the eternal principles of God and how we all need to understand His principles to maintain our health and achieve our purpose and destiny that we were created to glorify the Creator for eternity.

—Dr. Irinel Stanciu, MD, FACE, CCD, ECNU
clinical assistant professor of Medicine
University of Colorado, Anschutz School of Medicine
Department of Medicine, Division of Endocrinology, Metabolism,
and Diabetes
endocrinologist and metabolic bone disease specialist
Colorado Center for Bone Research
Denver, Colorado

*****

In this wonderful book, Dr. Rodica Malos combines the amazing fields of faith and science. She describes how we are fearfully and wonderfully made by our Creator. We are created to lead victorious and prosperous lives here on earth. Read and learn about the amazing resources God has given us to lead abundant, successful, and healthy lives.

—Dr. Oliver Ghitea
anesthesiologist
Portland, Oregon

To my grandsons, Jude and Liam, who through their appearance in this world brought deep insights about God's creation, beholding the most powerful miracles in the entire universe and the most precious gifts from heaven. Since their birth, I have been holding and am looking at God's marvelous work from invisible things bringing into existence the human body, with every single cell functioning based on God's programming through His breath and His Holy Spirit's energy since creation. God created the first DNA that carries hereditary material packed in the genes that give every single person unique features in the "the seed" placed by God from creation with the power to multiply exponentially.

To my faithful husband, Stely (married for almost thirty-five years), and our only daughter, Dr. Andreea Steward (PharmD), and our son-in-law, Jeff, who love God and magnify the Lord Jesus and His Holy Spirit in their lives. I thank God for each one of you. With the Lord on our side, we overcame all the obstacles to be where we are today. I appreciate your huge sacrifices. I love each one of you tremendously.

Contents

Part III

Part IV

◾ Part V

Foreword

I came to Christ in 1996 after the death by suicide of my friend the great photographer Terrence Donovan. Shortly before that happened, we had attended by accident a meeting at the Salvation Army in West London and witnessed a Christian worship meeting. The young lady at the door with others from the Army came to my London office after his death to convey their condolences and to tell me that in Jeremiah 29 verse 11, the Lord had a plan for my life. Following that and a series of events, I came to have my first relationship with Jesus Christ. In my early days as a Christian and for six-month intermittent intervals, I would awake at 3:50 a.m., pray and read my Bible, then return to sleep at 5:30 a.m. Four years later, the lady at the door, Shaneen, became my wife. My life had been transformed.

Shaneen would speak around the world, and on one occasion at New Beginnings Church of family Huch in Dallas, Texas, we were privileged to meet Dr. Rodica Malos and her husband, Stely. Their own story of entering the United States from Romania and their subsequent great commercial success was an incredible and remarkable one. Their love of God and their remarkable achievement was always spoken of by them both as attributable to God. This humble admission spoke volumes to me. Later, Shaneen spoke in their native Romania through their arrangement, and we're mightily blessed through the friendship that ensued.

In 2017, I read the first book of Dr. Rodica, *Beyond Science*, and though it touched me then, I did not fully take on board the power of God's Word and its flow through our lives in real time today. I wondered as a businessman if this was possibly true. Like Thomas the apostle, I had doubt. However, I was moved by the fact that a professional medical doctor related how the Word of God worked through our brain and body. I was reminded how it could possibly not be true. After all, He was the Creator of it; the manufacturer's guide was His Word.

During 2018, I was going through a very difficult time in my life, and I sought the Lord eagerly, looking for His help. I was led to read *Beyond Science* again in that summer of 2018. On the night of the eighth or ninth August, I was awoken again at 3:50 a.m., and I felt led to the book on my desk in the library room. As I started to resume reading the book at page 133, when I read the words "The Holy Spirit is real," my whole body shook as though I was on fire, and great heat came over me, like I was filled with an inexplicable peace. Suddenly, more than ever, I realized that the Holy Spirit was *real*. I felt compelled to immediately contact Dr. Rodica and penned an e-mail, with such a fire and peace in me, with an overwhelming wish to thank her. The e-mail left at 4:14, and I stayed in my library that morning, knowing that something mighty had happened. Five months later, my trouble left my house. I had remained obedient to His Word, held fast, and He performed what could only have been a miracle.

As I had written op-ed articles for *Charisma* magazine, I felt led, if not instructed, to write to its founder-chairman, Dr. Steve Strang, to tell him that *Beyond Science* was a must-read and that it was the best Christian book that I had ever read. I did not realize that he would act upon that recommendation and republish the book with the global reach of his Charisma Publishing House. Clearly, God had also spoken to him also.

When Dr. Rodica invited me to write the foreword to her second book, *Created in His Image with Unique Purpose: Science and Beyond*, I felt a great honor bestowed upon me. As I read her draft manuscript, something again happened to me. I felt the anointing of God upon her text, and what sprung to my mind was that God was again using Dr. Rodica to convey His science, His perfect plan in our Creation, and that her gift would bring her before men and women to show them His awesome way and His plan through His creation in and for our lives. The book is both a textbook, a medical encyclopedia, and most of all, a message of who God is and that His Holy Spirit is real.

The comfort that this book brings, coupled with the assurance that as believers we have, is in my opinion an unarguable case and perhaps the best evangelical tool that will bring others into a relationship with the living God, Creator of the heavens, the earth, and you, the reader of this book. I write this foreword with great gratitude to God and for calling me to wake at 3:50 that summer night in 2018, as He had done before and doubtless will do again. I write this foreword to thank Him for the life of the author of this book, Dr. Rodica Malos, about life's great author, as we read in Hebrews 12:2 King James Version (KJV): "Looking unto Jesus the author and finisher of our faith; who for the joy that was set before him endured the cross, despising the shame, and is set down at the right hand of the throne of God."

Be touched, be blessed, and be ready to receive. He's Real.

Martin Clarke
London, England, 2020

Preface

The human body is built with the most sophisticated, detailed built-in features and extremely complex connections of body, soul, and spirit with thoughts, emotions, and feelings! By reading this book, your eyes will be open to see God's fingerprint in the human body's functions and composition, and your ears will be tuned to hear God's voice decodified by the Holy Spirit speaking to you through His divine intervention in your complex being. Science and medicine, by studying the human body, prove from the microscopic, minuscule cells and molecules through the function of the brain circuits controlling the functions of all systems, showing God's investment in shaping every human being and creating us in His image with unique purpose.

God created our human body, soul, and spirit in His eternal image, while on earth to be able to have dominion over God's creation. God created mankind with mental capabilities to think, to learn, to memorize, to consolidate memories, and to recall information from memory as needed for daily functions and for advanced achievements, to fulfill the purpose of creation. Man was created with executive functions to solve problems and, with healthy cognition, to control behaviors and the like. God created humankind with mental ability to be creative to sustain itself and to subdue the earth and have dominion over every living thing.

The Creator of the universe created humans with the most perfect means for connection between our visible human body and His spiritual realm through the power of the Holy Spirit. God's majestic mind created humans' very existence with unique purpose. It is God's royal fragrance spilled over His creation through the power of the Holy Spirit that enables us to become like Him, to bring hope and joy to a broken world. By reading this book, you will find out who you really were created to be and to live in His own image.

Our body's function is programmed by God's breath, the energy that is in every cell's DNA, in the mitochondria, which keeps the body alive throughout our life. Our body starts with one DNA (half of the cell from the father and half from the mother), with hereditary material packed in the genes that give every single person unique features. "Every person has two copies of each gene, one inherited from each parent," and "a gene is the basic physical and functional unit of heredity. Genes are made up of DNA." I like to believe that the DNA is "the seed" placed by God in His creation with the power for exponential multiplication with unique purpose.

Acknowledgments

Millions of thanks to the Creator of the universe, who gave us Jesus Christ, the Lord and Savior of the world, the Lamb of God (to save the world from sin and to give the joy of salvation, hope, and peace to guard our mind, spirit, and body), and the Holy Spirit to give knowledge, wisdom, revelation, inspiration, and discernment to live a life that matters for eternity. Many thanks to TBN Trilogy team for working hard to make this manuscript and other enjoyable projects that will bless the readers with great insights about God's creation in us all.

Many thanks to my beloved husband, who was by my side the whole time, taking care of many things during our life, and my sweet daughter and her husband and their precious gifts, two adorable boys created in God's image, given by God for us to enjoy forever.

Introduction

Man was created with a unique purpose, to love, to be fruitful, and to multiply through the "seed" placed in human DNA by the Creator in every human being, to continue God's creation exponentially and to bring Him glory. God created our human body, soul, and spirit in His eternal image to carry His breath of life, which He breathed in human DNA. God is Spirit and is eternal, and He wants men and women, His creation, to be eternal as well. Every human's purpose is to carry the characteristics of the fruit of the Holy Spirit. God's creation, humans, is created in God's image, with a physical body with a brain, a conscious mind to understand what is spoken, with eyes and ears to be able to communicate and develop relationships with its Creator and His creation.

Through the eyes to see God's creation, through the ears as mechanical instruments to hear the sounds and decodify them in intelligible and understandable language. Man was created with mental capabilities to think, to learn, to memorize and to consolidate memories, and to recall information from memory as needed. Man also needs executive functions to solve problems, and healthy cognition to control behaviors and the like.

We carry His eternal spirit in our temporary body. In our body's every single cell, function is programmed by God's breath and His Holy Spirit's energy since creation. God created first DNA with the program for life. We have fingerprint in our DNA. Our body starts with one DNA (half of the cell from the father and half from the mother), with hereditary material packed in the genes that give every single person unique features.

God programmed the human DNA from creation to release neurochemicals, "the love hormones" (oxytocin), to feel love, Eros, and the pleasure hormone (dopamine) to feel pleasure and physical affection to reproduce, to be fruitful, and to multiply. God made man and woman to belong to each other in a purpose. He created male and female with purpose for connection and relationship. The brain is wired in a way that it can decodify the voice of God through the power of the Holy Spirit so we can communicate with our heavenly Father each time we open our heart for His Spirit to speak to our spirit.

We have carried His breath in us since creation. After learning about God and experiencing the power of the Holy Spirit, I have had a deeper understanding of us being created in His image and carrying His breath in our lungs and His plan for our life and His language in our DNA since creation. I can make the assertion that God's Spirit is demonstrating the fruit of the Spirit and His godly character in us when we are born again and receive the promised power of the Holy Spirit, becoming a new creation in Christ. He wants us who are created in His image to become like Him, to be imitators of Christ, with the same character to possess the fruit of the spirit to be changed from glory to glory through the power of the Holy Spirit until we enter in His eternal glory to shine as stars forever and ever.

The Holy Spirit hovering on the face of the earth came with strong anointing in the Old Testament, culminating with Jesus Christ's birth miraculously, to reveal the love of the Father, our Creator, to humanity, to represent Him to His creation, to do on earth what He saw His Father in heaven doing, and to show us the way to heaven.

Christ, who lives in us through the power of the Holy Spirit, alters the DNA inside of us through the "epigenetic mechanism" and changes our personality to become a "different person" to imitate Christ, to have the image of our Creator. We possess His divine-nature living, led by the Spirit. Christ came into the world to bring us back to the Father's image with characteristics like His, how humans were created before falling in sin. He sent His Word to renew our mind and transform our life physically and spiritually, body, soul, and spirit.

A transformed life and a born-again creation is the best evidence, with outstanding physical and spiritual measurable, continuous proof of God's power at work in human's life on this planet. A born-again Christian with a transformed life is the clearest proof that the Holy Spirit is real and at work in the world, touching humans for a clear purpose and divine assignment to follow the truth that is in the Word of God. Ignoring this truth leads to overwhelming unhappiness, birthing sins, intoxicating our heart, brain, spirit, soul, and body, separating us from God and His eternal purpose for us to become like Him. God wants us to please Him only, and that is through Jesus Christ and His righteousness.

When the Holy Spirit took possession of me, Christ started to live in me and produced much fruit and did not stop growing. Christ lives in me through the power of the Holy Spirit. "I have been crucified with Christ; it is no longer I who live, but Christ lives in me; and the *life* which I now live in the flesh I live by faith in the Son of God, who loved me and gave Himself for me" (Gal. 2:20 NKJV). God gave us His Spirit to understand God's purpose and plan for us and to help us in our weaknesses to live like God's children and to imitate Christ. "Now we have received, not the spirit of the world, but the Spirit who is from God, that we might know the things that have been freely given to us by God" (1 Cor. 2:12 NKJV).

We cannot hide from God's Spirit. God's Spirit is present in the entire universe. "Where can I go from Your Spirit? Or where can I flee from Your presence? If I ascend into heaven, You *are* there; If I make my bed in hell, behold, You *are there. If* I take the wings of the morning, *And* dwell in the uttermost parts of the sea, Even there Your hand shall lead me, And Your right hand shall hold me" (Ps. 139:7–10 NKJV). God, through His Spirit, created everything in the universe, and He renews everything on the face of the earth. "You send forth Your Spirit, they are created; And You renew the face of the earth" (Ps. 104:30 NKJV). The Holy Spirit accomplished the birth of Christ Jesus, the Son of God. "And the angel answered and said to her, 'The Holy Spirit will come upon you, and the power of the Highest will overshadow you; therefore, also, that Holy One who is to be born will be called the Son of God'" (Luke 1:35 NKJV).

Christ is God's Word made flesh to dwell on earth to demonstrate the love of the Father to humanity created in His image. In order to know the Father, we must know Jesus, His Son, who lived on this planet about two thousand years ago. "And the Word became flesh and dwelt among us, and we beheld His glory, the glory as of the only begotten of the Father, full of grace and truth" (John 1:14 NKJV). The Holy Spirit is the breath of the Almighty God, who gives life on earth. "The Spirit of God has made me, And the breath of the Almighty gives me life" (Job 33:4). The Holy Spirit is the power of the most high God that lives in us. "But if the Spirit of Him who raised Jesus from the dead dwells in you, He who raised Christ from the dead will also give life to your mortal bodies through His Spirit who dwells in you" (Rom. 8:11 NKJV).

But worries of this world can occupy your brain to bring oppression and psychological distress. You must be intentional about reading and living the Word of God with eternal results in your life to reprogram your brain to bring it back to the initial phase of creation in God's image. The Word of God in you produces fruit in your life when He is washing us clean and we intentionally let the Spirit of God take control over our thoughts, emotions, feelings, soul, spirit, and body. The fruit of the spirit characterizes a transformed mind and is a measurable outcome of being filled with the Holy Spirit. Living in the realm of faith, you can get in God's spiritual realm and power. Connecting with His spiritual power, your physical body will be affected positively. Faith has power over your mind, soul, and spirit to prepare you in this temporary life for an everlasting life, where you will enjoy your eternity with the Creator and Savior forever. Eternal life matters.

PART I

Human Life: The Most Powerful Miracle in the Entire Universe

■ Holy Spirit's Purpose at Creation

"In the beginning God created the heavens and the earth. The earth was without form, and void; and darkness *was* on the face of the deep. And the Spirit of God was hovering over the face of the waters" (Gen. 1:1–2 NKJV).

We can get deep insights about God's creation when we look at His marvelous work when He commanded invisible things into existence from the beginning. According to Scriptures, through the power of the Holy Spirit, God created the entire universe. Dr. Avery M. Jackson III, in his book *The God Prescription: Our Heavenly Father's Plan for Spiritual, Mental, and Physical Health*, stated that "the so-called 'Big Bang' occurred when God commanded, 'Let there be light!' when the universe in which we live came into existence."[1]

The Spirit of God, the Holy Spirit, was present at creation. God created our human body, soul, and spirit in His eternal image. God is Spirit and is eternal. At creation, God said, "Let Us make man in Our image, according to Our likeness; let them have dominion over the fish of the sea, over the birds of the air, and over the cattle, over all the earth and over every creeping thing that creeps on the earth" (Gen. 1:26 NKJV). To have dominion over God's creation, man was created with mental capabilities to think, to learn, to memorize and to consolidate memories, and to recall information from memory as needed. Man also needed executive functions to solve problems, and healthy cognition to control behaviors and the like.

Man needed to have the mental ability to be creative to subdue the earth and have dominion over every living thing. In order to have those capabilities and competencies, man needed to be created in the image of His Creator. "So God created man in His *own* image; in the image of God He created him; male and female He created them. Then God blessed them, and God said to them, "Be fruitful and multiply; fill the earth and subdue it; have dominion over the fish of the sea, over the birds of the air, and over every living thing that moves on the earth" (Gen. 1:27–28 NKJV).

The purpose of God creating our temporary body to place His eternal Spirit in it is to be able to communicate to God's heart in the spirit every moment of our life without hinders—wirelessly. (Wireless communication was created by God from the beginning, what science discovered only in the last decades.) Your spirit is from God. So you have his breath and His Spirit. You carry His eternal Spirit in your temporary body. In our body's every single cell, the function is programmed by God's breath and His Holy Spirit's energy, since creation. God created first DNA. We have God's DNA. Our body starts with one DNA (half of the cell from the father and half from the mother), with hereditary material packed in the genes that give every single person unique features. "Every person has two copies of each gene, one inherited from each parent," and "a gene is the basic physical and functional unit of heredity. Genes are made up of DNA."[2] I like to believe that the DNA is "the seed" placed by God from creation in His creation with the power to multiply.

Dr. Guillermo Maldonado, in his book *Created for Purpose*, stated, "Almost everything in creation begins in the form of a seed, and each seed represents a potential mature entity that can bear fruit. Furthermore, each fruit that is produced bears its own seeds, so that the original seed is multiplied exponentially."[3] The 7.7 billion people on earth at this time that carry God's breath are the results of exponential multiplication of the "seed" that God placed in the first DNA when He created the first man.

Science discovered that "DNA, or deoxyribonucleic acid, is the hereditary material in humans and almost all other organisms.

Nearly every cell in a person's body has the same DNA. Most DNA is located in the cell nucleus (where it is called nuclear DNA)."[4]

From creation, our Creator placed His language and the programming of hereditary material in this microscopic molecule for life to be continued and to be preserved on earth, placing the DNA in a nuclear envelope as the command center. "The nucleus serves as the cell's command center, sending directions to the cell to grow, mature, divide, or die. It also houses DNA (deoxyribonucleic acid), the cell's hereditary material. The nucleus is surrounded by a membrane called the nuclear envelope, which protects the DNA and separates the nucleus from the rest of the cell."[5]

Psalm 139, written about 3,400 years ago, describes this profound work of God in creating a new human being and the process of life forming in a mother's womb, with all days programmed from the beginning. "For You formed my inward parts; You covered me in my mother's womb. I will praise You, for I am fearfully *and* wonderfully made; Marvelous are Your works, And *that* my soul knows very well. My frame was not hidden from You, When I was made in secret, *And* skillfully wrought in the lowest parts of the earth. Your eyes saw my substance, being yet unformed. And in Your book they all were written, the days fashioned for me, When *as yet there were* none of them. How precious also are Your thoughts to me, O God! How great is the sum of them!" (Ps. 139:13–17 NKJV). God knows the end of each person's life from the beginning.

Our body starts with one DNA (half of the cell from the father and half from the mother).[6]

The Miracle of Life in the Entire Universe

Every human being's life on this planet, including yours, started with one single new DNA formed from a fertilized egg, called zygote, after the sperm and egg united. Your life started with one single new DNA. You exist because of that one single new DNA formed in your mother's womb. Jeffrey Grant, in his book *Creation*, talks about this miracle of conception of the new human life. Simply put, from over

40–150 million sperms released from the father (when the Eros love is expressed by both parents to fulfill God's purpose for creation to multiply), only one penetrates the mother's egg and fertilizes the ova (half the size of a grain of salt), which descends from the woman's fallopian tube during ovulation. The fluid from the Cowper's gland in the male neutralizes the natural acidic environment encountered in the female reproductive system (programmed to prevent infection) so the sperm is not damaged. The ova release special chemicals to dissolve the protective layer from the head of the sperm, which in turn penetrates the ova by dissolving the protective membrane that covers the ova.[7]

The fertilized egg's surface is changing so there will be no other sperms trying to fertilize the same egg. The DNA of the sperm from the father instantly combines with the DNA from the ova from the mother, forming the first new DNA with life programmed for the new baby, with genetic combination from the father and mother. This new zygote, which is only one cell, starts to divide instantaneously to two cells, then the two cells divide into four, then to eight, and so on, reaching astonishing numbers of trillions of cells forming all the organs, tissues, and every system in the new human body that is attached to the uterus in the mother's womb for the first nine months to develop, protected by the amnion liquid in a special sac. Moreover, after birth, the mother produces special milk with natural antibiotics to improve the immune system of the baby and to fight infections during his first days, weeks, and months on this planet.[8]

This is a short description about life development in the mother's womb when the cells in the embryo continue to divide and "the cells begin to become different from each other, and take on special functions (for example, some cells will grow to form the skin, or the stomach or the brain). There are many stages in the development of an embryo, and the names are complicated so I won't list them, but basically things happen to that initial ball of cells roughly in this order: the mouth forms, the gut forms (stomach and anus), the neural system forms (the spinal cord, brain and eyes), the circulatory system forms (blood vessels and a beating heart), lungs form (even though the embryo gets oxygen from the mother and not from its own lungs), and arms, legs, hands and feet begin to develop and eventually bones form within them. At this stage, the embryo looks like a miniature human being and is called a fetus. Each of the new, growing cells are programmed to perform a function and in this way the fetus develops all the things it will need to live once it leaves the mother's womb. All this happens very rapidly."[9]

"Within the first three months after fertilization of the egg! During the next 3 months the fetus continues to grow, the arms and legs get longer and the fingers, toes and face begin to form. In the last 3 months the fetus is still growing but doesn't change much physically. The fetus may become active (kicking, moving its arms, sucking its thumb) and there is evidence that its brain goes though stages of being asleep and awake, just like our brains do. The fetus is now ready to be born and become a baby!"[10]

I believe that the spontaneous breathing that happens at birth is also programmed in that first DNA that God created in the beginning, "the seed" that carries His breath and, through conception, carries information also for the first breath to occur in the presence of the almighty God when the birth takes place. At birth, the baby must be able to breathe by himself outside of the mother's womb. A major miracle takes place when the baby is detached from the umbilical cord from the mother's womb and takes the first breath using the baby's lungs to get oxygen.

> This is the picture of our grandson Jude at four hours after birth on this planet, on September 29, 2018.

New mothers are amazed at the miracle of the first breath of their newborn baby that is detached from the mother's blood supply for the first time. The Bible states that we are made by God and His breath gives us life. "The Spirit of God has made me; the breath of the Almighty gives me life" (Job 33:4 NIV). The Holy Spirit gives life. According to John 6:63 (NIV), "The Spirit gives life; the flesh counts for nothing. The words I have spoken to you—they are full of the Spirit and life." We see that in medicine and in our life in general, when someone is dead, and if the body has no soul and spirit, it counts for nothing. The soul manifests through the body, and the Spirit manifests too. I believe that through the power of the Holy Spirit, we have the breath of God that is programmed in our first DNA. He placed a program in our DNA, "the seed," at creation when to turn on to get our first breath on earth and when to turn off to have our last breath.

God's supernatural love created the entire universe and human beings with a divine program to be fruitful and multiply through love. We see the results of the multiplication program and the multiplication seed in human DNA today on the planet Earth, where humans have multiplied, arriving, as in 2020, to over 7.7 billion. Each person is the result of love, Eros (*Eros* refers to "passionate love" or "romantic love"), of a heart with desire and longing to fulfill God's purpose from creation.[11]

Man Is Purposefully Made in God's Image for His Glory

Man was created with the purpose to love, to be fruitful, and to multiply in order to continue God's creation and to bring Him glory. The power to create is built in every human being through Eros love. When this kind of love is perverted by Satan, it becomes sin in the human heart. Through Eros love, attraction between a man and a woman is made possible for further multiplication and creation. God placed in people's heart the features to long and to desire, which are very important for monogamous marriage, for family to conceive and to raise children from generation to generation. It is a precious gift from God that man and woman experience pleasure (as the reward system is activated); Eros love brings them together in their marriage to be fruitful and to multiply to fulfill their purpose on this planet and God's plan.

God programmed that in the human DNA from creation to release neurochemicals, "the love hormones" (oxytocin), to feel the love, Eros, and the pleasure hormone (dopamine) to feel pleasure and physical affection to reproduce. God made man and woman to belong to each other in a purpose. He created male and female with purpose for connection and relationship. He said it is not good for man to be alone. "Then the Lord God said, 'It is not good that the man should be alone; I will make him a helper fit for him'" (Gen. 2:18 ESV).

God knows that loneliness is painful emotionally and creates isolation and disconnection, causing mental condition and depression with all consequences for further decline. That was exactly the reason He created male and female for perfect relationship, for love, for joy and happiness. He commanded them to become fruitful, to multiply, to further promote connections and relationships, to fill the earth with His glory. The prophet Isaiah confirms that in chapter 6 verse 3: "And one called to another and said: 'Holy, holy, holy is the LORD of hosts; the whole earth is full of his glory!'" Everything we see on this planet reflects God's purpose for humankind to multiply and bring fruits that nobody could ever imagine through the new ideas, new concepts, inspiration, wisdom, revelation, knowledge to develop advanced technology, science, in every area of life, to fill the earth with God's glory.

The need for connection and relationships is in "the seed" in human DNA that carries humans' characteristics for reproduction and connections from generation to generation, preparing the way for eternity. Each person on earth has built-in thoughts of eternity. "He has made everything beautiful in its time. Also He has put eternity in their hearts, except that no one can find out the work that God does from beginning to end" (Eccles. 3:11 NKJV). The reason that Satan is continuously after the family is to destroy it and to pervert the love, Eros, in family, the attraction between husband and wife, leading to separation and divorce. We are called to nurture Eros love and to love unconditionally and to not let our marriage to be vulnerable to destruction. The devil is at work to pervert the human heart's desires and longing to prevent God's purpose in His creation to glorify His name. We can block the devil's plan through the power of prayer and obedience of His Word. If there are problems in family, go to God for counseling. He is the most powerful counselor for marriage.

God created man and woman for marriage from the beginning. He knows your physical and spiritual needs in your marriage. You are created in His image. He placed your identity in your DNA and the power to produce physical and spiritual fruits. The breath of God lives in you. God's qualities are seen in the characteristics of the fruit of the Spirit that is required from all human beings created by God. God is love. God's quality of love is seen in the entire Bible and is the best evidence of the Spirit of God living in born-again Christians. The love of God is supernatural.

The Purpose of the Human Body

The purpose of God for the creation of humankind is greater than our mind can perceive, understand, and comprehend. Everyone has a destiny, with gifts and potential inside, with a purpose. Our destiny is built in our DNA by our Creator to be in the image of His Son and is activated by His Spirit as we allow Him to intervene and to work in our life. "For whom He foreknew, He also predestined *to be* conformed to the image of His Son, that He might be the firstborn among many brethren" (Rom. 8:29 NKJV). We were created at this time, at this point in history, with a purpose, to make the most difference in His kingdom to glorify His name. God used many generations to carry the seed in every DNA to reproduce from generation to generation to get you in this time of history for such a time as this.

Created from Dust

He created human beings with the body composed of multiple systems from the beginning of creation to be able to think, to love, to walk, to function, to talk, to eat, and to eliminate residuals from the body. He created our eyes, ears, mouth, and brain with the highest computation power to see and communicate the glory of God in His creation on all the earth and to praise His name forever. He created us also with tasting capability to taste His goodness. He created us with physical and spiritual taste to taste and to see that the Lord is good. "Oh, taste and see that the LORD *is* good; blessed *is* the man *who* trusts in Him!" (Ps. 34:8).

God could make us not need food or water. But He created water and all physical food that comes from the ground with the same chemistry that our body is made of. All the vegetables and fruits that come from the ground, created for us to ingest, are rich in all the nutrients needed for our body to grow and to be sustained and to function in divine health our entire lives to accomplish our tasks and the purpose we were created for. Dr. Scott K. Hannen stated in his book *Stop the Pain: The Six to Fix: A Complete Six-Step Approach to Detect and Correct the Cause of Chronic Pain and Suffering* that "God made you a body that heals itself! It just has to be given what is needs. You cannot expect it to do a job if it does not have the right tools. However if you give the body everything it needs to do its job, I am thoroughly convinced that there is almost nothing that it can't cure."[12]

First, God created the earth with everything in it. We know now that the dust God used to create man contains all the resources the human needs to live on this planet. Science discovered that "soils (including clay) contain dissolved minerals which are incorporated and stored by plants for our consumption or eaten by an animal that we later consume. The most abundant elements in the Earth's crust are oxygen (46.6%) and silicon (27.7%). Minerals that combine these two elements are called silicates, which are the most abundant minerals on the Earth. Eight main elements account for more than 98 percent of the crust's composition. The earth's crust contains most of the mineral nutrients our body requires. Oxygen is the most abundant element in both the human body and the earth's crust. The human body is made up almost entirely of 13 elements. Oxygen, carbon, hydrogen, and nitrogen make up 96% of our body's mass. The other 4% of body weight is composed almost entirely of sodium, potassium, magnesium, calcium, iron, phosphorus, sulfur, chlorine, and iodine. Silicon as an element in the human body (less than one percent) is not as prevalent as it is in the earth's crust; however we require this small amount of silicon for bone development, and it is found in skin and connective tissue."[13]

We know now that approximately 99 percent of the human body weight is made up of carbon, oxygen, hydrogen, calcium, nitrogen, phosphorous, and sulfur.[14]

The dust God used at creation contains all those chemical elements that scientists found in the human body (God created male from the dust of the earth). He also made the body with soul and spirit, needing spiritual food that comes from heaven to satisfy our spiritual needs through the power of His Spirit. We have not only earthly origin, because we are created from dust, but we also have divine origin, because God breathed His Spirit in the body made from dust.

Our human body cannot be explained scientifically through labs and research because of the genetic information and the soul and Spirit that the Creator placed in man and woman from creation. "Genetic information cannot rise spontaneously, nor does matter itself operate itself into organizing itself into higher levels of complexity (functioning systems, tissues, bones, organs). Answers in Genesis online has more information on 'Genetics and Biblical events,' and also the complexity of human DNA. It's not the elements ('dust') that we're made of that makes a human; it's the *way* we're put together, it's not the 'dust' that makes life, but the way it's put together with purposeful design and complex organization."[15]

Moreover, all the micronutrients we need for a healthy body for energy and to live, we get from the colorful and tasteful vegetables and fruits with great aroma from plants and trees growing from the ground that carry the seeds within them to multiply exponentially from creation to be consumed by our body by ingesting them and distributing them to every system, organ, tissues, cells that will extract the right elements so we do not need to eat "dust."[16]

God created a natural pharmacy with antioxidants to prevent oxidation, inflammation, body breaking down, and premature aging. It is worth mentioning that we must eat from these fruits and vegetables (and others) because they contain antioxidants, vitamins, minerals, fibers, and active enzymes with essential micronutrients to improve our immune system to fight diseases, cancer, bacteria, and viruses, infection, and cancer. God knew exactly what we need since creation and created the food we eat, the air we breathe, and the move we make to live on this planet.

Learning About God from All Nature

God's creation is of extreme complexity. We can learn about God's supernatural power from the world around us. "But now ask the beasts, and they will teach you; And the birds of the air, and they will tell you; Or speak to the earth, and it will teach you; And the fish of the sea will explain to you. Who among all these does not know that the hand of the LORD has done this, In whose hand *is* the life of every living thing. And the breath of all mankind?" (Job 12:7–10 NKJV).

In the entire universe, the human body is the crown of the entire creation of God, the superintelligent designer of all creation. In his book *Creation*, Dr. Jeffrey Grant stated that "even those who profess to believe in the theory of evolution are confronted with the greatest challenge to their philosophy when they contemplate the incredible complexity of the thousands of separate but interconnected systems within the human body that are essential for its growth, energy, motion, waste disposal, reproduction, and the brain's awesome mental computational powers."[17]

We cannot have excuses, since the entirety of God's creation is created from invisible things, as physicists have discovered. Phil Mason, in *Quantum Glory*, stated that "the building blocks of complex living beings are cells; the building blocks of cells are molecules. The building blocks of molecules are atoms, and the building blocks of atoms are protons, neutrons and electrons. However as we study matter at smaller and smaller scales we find that the building blocks of protons, neutrons, and electrons are things such quarks and leptons. Anything smaller then this scale is purely theoretical but the most popular contender in the quest for a 'theory for everything' has been string theory."[18] This subatomic world is stipulated to be considered "the buffer zone" between the physical and the spiritual realm. This subatomic world is created from invisible things that compose the microscopic living cell that cannot be seen with the human eyes.

In God's creation, the intracellular activity in the human body is pretty amazing. The program for life lives in every cell through our DNA, which gives instructions to this cell to divide in specialized cells to develop vital organs with specialized functions, such as eyes, ears, nose, mouth, heart, brain, kidney, liver, bladder, intestine, muscles, bones, tendons, ligaments, blood vessels, glands, and all special tissues, to develop and to grow, to multiply, to repair, to restore, to regenerate, and to die.[19]

Here is a very short description of the invisible cell, the building block of life: the microscopic cell with its content and complex function that only the mind of a superintelligent designer could create. We have seen already that all living things are created from trillions of cells that are considered the building blocks of life that form the body structures performing specialized tasks and functions by getting in nutrients, processing and converting them into energy. "Cells also contain the body's hereditary material and can make copies of themselves. Cells have many parts, each with a different function. Some of these parts, called organelles, are specialized structures that perform certain tasks within the cell. Human cells contain the following major parts, listed in alphabetical order: Within cells, the cytoplasm is made up of a jelly-like fluid (called the cytosol) and other structures that surround the nucleus. The cytoskeleton is a network of long fibers that make up the cell's structural framework. The cytoskeleton has several critical functions, including determining cell shape, participating in cell division, and allowing cells to move. It also provides a track-like system that directs the movement of organelles and other substances within cells. This organelle helps process molecules created by the cell. The endoplasmic reticulum also transports these molecules to their specific destinations either inside or outside the cell. The Golgi apparatus packages molecules processed by the endoplasmic reticulum to be transported out of the cell. These organelles are the recycling center of the cell. They digest foreign bacteria that invade the cell, rid the cell of toxic substances, and recycle worn-out cell components. Mitochondria are complex organelles that convert energy from food into a form that the cell can use. They have their own genetic material, separate from the DNA in the nucleus, and can make copies of themselves. The nucleus serves as the cell's command center, sending directions to the cell to grow, mature, divide, or die. It also houses DNA (deoxyribonucleic acid), the cell's hereditary material. The nucleus is surrounded by a membrane called the nuclear envelope, which protects the DNA and separates the nucleus from the rest of the cell. The plasma membrane is the outer lining of the cell. It separates the cell from its environment and allows materials to enter and leave the cell. Ribosomes are organelles that process the cell's genetic instructions to create proteins. These organelles can float freely in the cytoplasm or be connected to the endoplasmic reticulum (see above)."[20]

Our body, created from trillions of cells, is like a "modern city" where God wants to reside to make it perfect instead of chaotic, for a perfect relationship with its Creator to bring Him glory.

Regarding the perfection of God's creation in every cell in our body, Philip Yancey, in *Fearfully and Wonderfully Made*, wrote about Dr. Paul Brand's observation and stated that "Brand wrote, 'I have come to realize that every patient of mine, every newborn baby, in every cell of its body, has a basic knowledge of how to survive and how to heal, that exceeds anything that I shall ever know. That knowledge is the gift of God, who has made our bodies more perfectly than we could ever have devised.' In ninety pages, he expressed that sense of wonder about the human body."[21] This example of the complex function of an invisible cell demonstrates that God's invisible hand is at work in the entire universe, including our planet, to sustain life through His divine power, as is written in Romans 1:20, "For since the creation of the world God's invisible qualities—his eternal power and divine nature—have been clearly seen, being understood from what has been made, so that people are without excuse" (NIV).

The power of God is seen in all nature. The beauty of nature reminds us of the glory of its superintelligent designer (life everywhere, from color changes in leaves and flowers and varieties of small and large animal, to the birth of a child and his or her development, a new, born-again Christian at old age, advanced technology by the mind's conception, and thoughts to travel in space and wireless communication), all created by God.

Mitochondria: The Powerhouse

Amazingly, the Spirit of the living God activates the program placed in your DNA to instruct the mitochondria inside every cell to produce energy, adenosine triphosphate (ATP), to fulfill His plan with His creation. Without the mitochondria, there is no energy for the cell to function. If cells have no energy, there is no life on planet Earth. Science demonstrated that "a small amount of DNA can also be found in the mitochondria (where it is called mitochondrial DNA or mtDNA). Mitochondria are structures within cells that convert the energy from food into a form that cells can use."[22]

Without the mitochondria, life will not exist on this planet. Mitochondria are formed of DNA, ribosomes, F0, F1 complexes, cristae, matrix, inner membrane, intermembrane space, all encapsulated in outer membrane of the mitochondria.[23]

In this marvelous molecule that lives in every cell (the building block of life) of our body, God breathed the breath of life, the energy to continue life on this planet. Science describes just that, stating that "mitochondria are often referred to as the powerhouses of the cell. They help turn the energy we take from food into energy that the cell can use. But, there is more to mitochondria than energy production. Present in nearly all types of human cell, mitochondria are vital to our survival. They generate the majority of our adenosine triphosphate (ATP), the energy currency of the cell. Mitochondria are also involved in other tasks, such as signaling between cells and cell death, otherwise known as apoptosis."[24]

It is my belief that when God did breathe His breath of life, the energy that comes from His breath entered in the human body's cells, especially mitochondria, which were created from the dust. He also did breathe in human's spirit and soul the desire for supernatural and the desire (as the physical hunger and thirst centers in hypothalamus) for the Living Water and for the Bread of Life. He stated, "So He humbled you, allowed you to hunger, and fed you with manna which you did not know nor did your fathers know, that He might make you know that man shall not live by bread alone; but man lives by every *word* that proceeds from the mouth of the LORD" (Deut. 8:3 NKJV). The Word of God is processed in our soul and spirit to give spiritual energy as the food is processed by the mitochondria to give energy to the cells and the body to sustain life on earth. God Himself sustains life through the "spiritual" mitochondria.

Spiritual Mitochondria: The Spiritual Powerhouse

As the physical mitochondrion is the "battery" of the cell in our body, so is the spirit "the spiritual powerhouse" for the human soul. It is the Spirit of God that He breathes in you that is empowering you and is teaching you at unconscious and conscious level to live a godly life. As the physical mitochondria turn the physical food into energy for the body, spiritually you must feed the "spiritual mitochondria," your soul and spirit. The Holy Spirit applied the power and energy to create the universe and also applied the power and energy to the human mitochondria that continue to create the energy and maintain life. You carry His breath in your being if you acknowledge Him or not. Even people who deny His existence have His breath in them. God exists regardless if people believe or not. Dr. Jackson, a renowned neurosurgeon, in his book *The God Prescription: Our Heavenly Father's Plan for Spiritual, Mental, and Physical Health*, stated, "I believe that God created us in His divine image. As a neurosurgeon, I understand how complex we are. I believe that only God could create such intricate beings composed of sophisticated systems working in tandem to keep our hearts beating, our lungs breathing, and our brains functioning for a century or more."[25]

Knowing that God is in control of human life, starting our day with great attitude will increase the energy level in our body through neurochemicals released in our body as a result of our attitude and emotions (as dopamine, endorphin, serotonin, oxytocin, and more at unconscious level), which help us to engage in our daily activities and be motivated to accomplish our daily tasks and assignment to interact joyfully with others. With our activities in the morning, walking, exercising, spending time in prayer, meditating of God's goodness and His amazing grace and love, our heart will be filled with energy and joy.

Stretch your faith that joy comes in the morning. The psalmist, inspired by the Holy Spirit, tells us that praising God and giving Him thanks will bring favors from Him and joy in the morning. "Sing praises to the LORD, O you his saints, and give thanks to his holy name. For His anger is but for a moment, and his favor is for a lifetime. Weeping may tarry for the night, but joy comes with the morning" (Ps. 30:4–5 ESV).

In the morning, we need energy to move. We need to start our day with great joy to be full of energy through the Spirit of God. The Holy Spirit passes the threshold of your mitochondria in your cells through the subatomic world, the buffer zone, to give you physical and spiritual energy for your daily life and to feel God's presence in your physical body, the temple of God, God's dwelling place. You are empowered through joyful attitude by giving God thanks and singing praises to the Lord.

In his book *Quantum Glory*, Phil Mason stated, "There is a threshold at which the experience of God's presence transitions into glory. All who draws near and nearer to God will inevitably cross this invisible threshold. At this point the experience of glory moves beyond something that is spiritual discerned. It becomes physical."[26]

When in our spirit, we pass the threshold of glory in the presence of God, which is always a measurable and a physical manifestation, so much so that we can see it and measure it with our physical eyes and feel with our physical body. That happens when God's Spirit passes our sensory threshold. Moses did see with his physical eyes the manifestation of the glory of God when the cloud hindered him to enter the tabernacle. "And Moses was not able to enter the tabernacle of meeting, because the cloud rested above it, and the glory of the LORD filled the tabernacle" (Exod. 40:35 NKJV).

In our physical body, when we live in the presence of God with great joy, I like to stipulate that the mitochondria in every cell create more energy, helping us to focus and concentrate, improving our deep thinking and the executive decision-making in our prefrontal cortex activity, creating a better thinking. The "superfood" for the brain, soul, and spirit.

The Holy Spirit takes control of our mind and our being. He is all powerful to block out our soul's enemy for that day. He is our healer and restorer every single moment of our life. The program to recover is in our DNA physically and spiritually to be made whole. The supernatural power of the Holy Spirit heals our DNA, according to the prophet Isaiah. "But He *was* wounded for our transgressions, *He was* bruised for our iniquities; The chastisement for our peace *was* upon Him, And by His stripes we are healed" (Isa. 53:5 NKJV). The Holy Spirit is not only the restorer of our health and emotional feelings but is also our spiritual help for spiritual growth.

Your DNA Carries Your Identity

The Creator of the universe is one God in three persons, according to Deuteronomy 6:4, making it clear. "Hear, O Israel: The LORD our God, the LORD *is* one!" (Deut. 6:4 NKJV). God the Father; God the Son, Jesus Christ, who is God's Word; and God the Holy Spirit, who is the power of God hovering in the entire universe and on this planet, supply creation with power and the energy programmed in human DNA at creation and continues today according with His programming. Everything about who you are is placed in this microscopic molecule, DNA, from creation. Our life is programmed by our Creator in our DNA. He placed His language in our DNA through the genetic code at creation with a purpose. "For we are God's handiwork, created in Christ Jesus to do good works, which God prepared in advance for us to do" (Eph. 2:10). Human DNA is the most important molecule in the entire universe because the program for our life is embedded in this microscopic molecule, the structure of deoxyribonucleic acid (DNA) that Watson and Crick discovered in 1953.[27]

You have God's DNA. Sin distorted and altered the human DNA, but through Jesus, through the cross, we got our spiritual DNA back (through His Spirit that lives in us), how it was created in the beginning to live with the joy of salvation, to love with gladness with God's love. God put the hunger for His supernatural in the human DNA. The Holy Spirit alters our old DNA to become a new creation when we are born again of the spirit with new spiritual DNA of the Father, created in His image from the beginning (John 3:3–6). The Spirit of God passes the threshold of our physical DNA in our body and alters its gene expression and its hereditary material of personality and character (it will change the genetic code), and we become a new person with different personality and character, a new creation in Christ. Jesus Christ lives in us. We do not live anymore in the old ways.

Physically, every organ, including the brain, is programmed to work according to information stored in our DNA. There is a program in our DNA with instructions to produce sequences of amino acids, neurochemicals, neurotransmitters that are responsible for our emotions. Likewise, spiritual DNA gives us our identity in Christ, joining our physical DNA, being a new creation, born by the Spirit of God when we receive Jesus Christ in our heart as our Lord and Savior through faith.

When we confess loudly our sins, we are forgiven. Faith increases by hearing, because what we hear triggers our old memories of sin and its consequences, and confession breaks the pattern of our sins and the bad emotions that take many patterns. Lack of faith and negativity have great impact on our emotion, spirit, and body. The Spirit of God, through the powerful Word, alters our old spiritual and physical DNA. From that moment, we think different, act different, behave different. It is great alteration with great measurable outcomes because God's thoughts are instilled in our thoughts. God's thoughts are powerful and give life abundantly. We cannot alter the blueprint, the genetic code, but we can control our gene expression, which controls our genetic potential through the power of faith in the Word.

God's Word addresses the issues of life about what we think about, what we see with our eyes, and what we hear with our ears. People ask questions about God and who He is. The Word answers that pertinent question. The Word reveals the mind of God and who we are and help us know ourselves and our identity. In order to know Who God is in this universe, we must know ourselves and tell the generations after us and those not yet born who God is—the Creator of heaven and earth. "We will not hide *them* from their children, telling to the generation to come the praises of the LORD, And His strength and His wonderful works that He has done. For He established a testimony in Jacob, And appointed a law in Israel, Which He commanded our fathers, That they should make them known to their children; That the generation to come might know *them*, The children *who* would be born, *That* they may arise and declare *them* to their children, That they may set their hope in God, And not forget the works of God, But keep His commandments" (Ps. 78:4–7 NKJV).

The Gift of Understanding

◾ The Gift to Understand the World Around Us

The gift to understand the world around us (through anatomy and physiology) is astonishing in God's creation. The eternal God (our Creator) revealed Himself to humanity through His Word, inspired by the Holy Spirit. He gave us the gift of understanding His Word through our anatomy and physiology of our brain structures, to be able to interpret and understand what we read with our eyes and what we hear with our ears. Purposefully, our superintelligent designer created us with mental ability to reason, to solve problems, to control behavior and with the executive function through the frontal lobe to attain temporary and eternal goals. Scientifically, we know that the "executive functions (collectively referred to as executive function and cognitive control) are a set of cognitive processes that are necessary for the cognitive control of behavior: selecting and successfully monitoring behaviors that facilitate the attainment of chosen goals. Executive functions include basic cognitive processes such as attentional control, cognitive inhibition, inhibitory control, working memory, and cognitive flexibility. Higher order executive functions require the simultaneous use of multiple basic executive functions and include planning and fluid intelligence (e.g., reasoning and problem solving)."[1]

T. D. Jakes, in his book *Instinct: The Power to Unleash Your Inborn Drive*, stated, "I believe that what God has given us is His gift to us. How we utilize what we've been given is our gift back to Him. By shedding fresh light on something profoundly primal but not primitive within us, I've challenged you to consider new paradigms and empowered you to shatter the limitation of fear and frustration blocking your liberation."[2]

The Creator endowed the human body with the most sophisticated organ in the entire universe, the brain, with an amazing computation power of all information received from outside and inside the body and the capability to coordinate all functions of every organ and all systems to keep us alive (beyond our comprehension).[3]

In our daily life, we collect worldly and spiritual information from the external world and from inside the body and brain through our five senses and process that information with our brain structures and our nerve cells, called neurons, that "carry messages in the form of electrical signals called nerve impulses. To create a nerve impulse, your neurons have to be excited. Stimuli such as light, sound or pressure all excite your neurons, but in most cases, chemicals released by other neurons will trigger a nerve impulse. Although you have millions of neurons that are densely packed within your nervous system, they never actually touch. So when a nerve impulse reaches the end of one neuron, a neurotransmitter chemical is released. It diffuses from this neuron across a junction and excites the next neuron."[4]

Recognizing His Presence in Us

Through our brain functions, we understand that the eternal God entered in space and time of humanity to manifest Himself through His presence. We sense His love and His joy through the power of the Holy Spirit passing the threshold of our physical cortex, exciting neurons, becoming electrical impulses, to get in our physical body, mind, and spirit to manifest His power and confirm His Presence in us. Very often we feel the physical manifestation of the Holy Spirit through electrical impulses that overwhelm us with intense heat, tingling sensation, and unspeakable joy to heal our painful emotions from psychological distress and our emotional and physical illnesses. The Holy Spirit, hovering on the face of the earth, came with strong anointing in the Old Testament, culminating with

Jesus Christ's birth miraculously to reveal the love of the Father, our Creator, to humanity, to do on earth what He saw His Father in heaven doing and to show us the way to heaven. Jesus stated, "I am the way and the truth and the life. No one comes to the Father except through me" (John 14:6 NIV).

The Power to Reprogram Your Mind

The program in your mind was altered negatively through epigenetic mechanism and modified the gene expression by disobedience of the first humans in the garden of Eden when they were tempted by Satan, and the human mind carried the burden of sin as a curse. But the Creator created a way to reprogram the human mind through the power of His Word, His letter of love to the humanity, the Bible, stating, "Do not conform to the pattern of this world, but be transformed by the renewing of your mind. Then you will be able to test and approve what God's will is—his good, pleasing and perfect will" (Rom. 12:2 NIV). With a mind renewed by the spirit of the living God, you are able to know His perfect will for your life and the purpose you were created for. You can renew your mind and reprogram your brain by reading the Word of God daily, memorizing scriptures, applying the Word to your life, and obeying the Word with intention to change your behavior.

By reading the Word, memorizing and meditating God's living Word, you can alter your human DNA in a positive way and grow new physical neurons through neurogenesis and can get a completely new mind through neuroplasticity, a process that changes the structure of your brain, getting the mind of Christ to become like Jesus. Christopher Bergland (2017) stated that "new research identifies how the birth of new neurons can reshape the brain." He also wrote in a post that "through neurogenesis and neuroplasticity, it may be possible to carve out a fresh and unworn path for your thoughts to travel upon. One could speculate that this process opens up the possibility to reinvent yourself and move away from the status quo or to overcome past traumatic events that evoke anxiety and stress.

Hardwired fear-based memories often lead to avoidance behaviors that can hold you back from living your life to the fullest."[5]

Worries of this world can occupy your brain to bring oppression and psychological distress. You must be intentional about reading and living the Word of God with eternal results in your life to reprogram your brain. The Word of God in you produces fruit in your life. The fruit of the spirit characterizes a transformed mind and the outcome of being filled with Holy Spirit. Living in the realm of faith, you can get in God's spiritual realm and power. Connecting with His spiritual power, your physical body will be affected positively. Faith has power over your mind, soul, and spirit. You perform in life according to your faith. Faith propels you in your actions, and it puts you beyond logic on a superior position. Through faith you can change your behavior and can change the world around you. Have faith in what God says about you in His Word. God's Word is His letter of love to you to guide your step to become the person God created you to be. Our choice to live in faith determines the outcome of God's instructions and prescriptions for life.

Mapping the Brain

The Word of God affects your brain in a positive way. Your brain contains billions of neurons. Every neuron functions as "a microcomputer" to process all information from the outside world and inside the body. So your brain has billions of "microcomputers" networking at an extremely high speed in connection with one another. And you think sometimes that you are worthless and have no value. I like to reassure people (and you, the reader) that you are a very wealthy person possessing a "company with billions of microcomputers" to use it the way you want. You are God's masterpiece.[6]

The brain is wired in a way that it can decodify the voice of God through the power of the Holy Spirit so we can communicate with our heavenly Father each time we open our heart to His Spirit to speak to our spirit. Jentezen Franklin, in his book *Right People, Right Place, Right Plan: Discerning the Voice of God*, stated that "there are so many voices in the world. There are the voice of God, the voice of the devil, the voice of people, and your own inner voice." He goes on to say that "the way God speaks and leads us is through our spirits. We have to be spirit-conscious in order to hear God's voice and receive His direction."[7]

Wire the Brain with the Right Values from Childhood

The brain must be wired with the right values starting in childhood to fulfill God's purpose. Phil and Diane Comer, in their book *Raising Passionate Jesus Followers*, gives us a comprehensive list of values that are important in life, starting from childhood, to love God with passion and to fulfill one's purpose on earth. The list comprises "fun, organization, efficacy, creativity, respect, healthy diet, strong work ethics, resourcefulness, success, independence, optimism, athleticism, protectiveness, physical fitness, kindness, honesty, education, tolerance, gratitude, peace-loving, generosity, compassion, friendliness, respect for authority, care for animals, good communication skills, love of reading, initiative, ability and willingness to resolve conflict, interest in theology, boldness, leadership, sense of humor, stylishness, frugality, cross-cultural adeptness, desire for justice, sexual purity, confidence, safety, spontaneity, discipline, punctuality, hospitality, concern for creation, family closeness, musical skills or interest, adventurousness, affection, friendship among siblings, responsibilities, artistic skills or interest, learning, intellectualism, competitiveness, political activism, management skills, neatness, analytical thinking, strategic thinking, imaginativeness, empathy, positivity, adaptability, productivity, patience, presence, deliberateness, nostalgia, harmony, critical thinking, loyalty, enthusiasm."[8]

All these values must be taught in childhood, to last one's entire life. The Word of God made it clear to "train up a child in the way he should go, And when he is old he will not depart from it" (Prov. 22:6 NKJV). The Word of God, through faith, has the power to transform you at any age. The brain is programmed with the power to restore abilities but must be activated by our decisions to make the changes that are needed. Jesus, as a man and God on this planet, promoted all those values, as we read in the entire Bible. Those values are included in God's commandment to "love the Lord your God with all your heart and with all your soul and with all your strength and with all your mind; and, Love your neighbor as yourself" (Luke 10:27 NIV). The Holy Spirit coordinates this network in your brain when you receive the power from above. He gives you wisdom and revelation to know Him better, "that the God of our Lord Jesus Christ, the Father of glory, may give to you the spirit of wisdom and revelation in the knowledge of Him, the eyes of your understanding being enlightened; that you may know what is the hope of His calling, what are the riches of the glory of His inheritance in the saints" (Eph. 1:17–18 NKJV).

God's grand design in humanity is to transform one mind at a time through the power of His Word and to accomplish His plan for salvation of humankind through Jesus Christ, who *is* the Word. He stated, "So shall My word be that goes forth from My mouth; It shall not return to Me void, But it shall accomplish what I please, And it shall prosper *in the thing* for which I sent it" (Isa. 55:11 NKJV). He makes a supernatural disclosure to humans relating to human existence. "And this is eternal life, that they may know You, the only true God, and Jesus Christ whom You have sent" (John 17:3 NKJV). God's eternal plan changed the world's temporary agenda with its values and beliefs. God invested through His only Son's sacrifice in humanity to bring it back in relationship with Him for eternity. The Holy Spirit, through its power over our mind and brain's functions, helps us to develop those values that will fill our heart with joy and shape our behavior to fulfill our purpose in our life.

The Holy Spirit will change our value system and manifests Himself in a physical way. We can feel His "wind" passing the threshold of our brain cortex, blowing through the billions of neurons in our brain structures, becoming electrical impulses surging through our body so we can feel His person's divine power, physically touching us through as electricity, intense warmth, and overwhelming emotions of love or unspeakable joy. He presents Himself with audible appearance, "hearing the sound" of His manifestation through indwelling believers. God, as a loving Father, wants us to be aware of His physical presence and to reassure us that we are not alone. The person of the Holy Spirit recognizes our spiritual needs for God's grace and mercy. He activates in us the thought of eternity that God placed in our DNA from creation according to Ecclesiastes 3:11

The Person of the Holy Spirit Passes a Threshold in Our Brain

The Holy Spirit enters from the Father's spiritual realm in heaven in our physical world through a physical threshold. Author Phil Mason, in his book *Quantum Glory*, describes the phenomenon of thresholds' existence in physics as freezing point of water becoming ice and boiling point of water becoming vapor or the sun's beams of light touching electrical panels, creating energy. He went on to state that "just as there are thresholds in all aspect of physics, so there are thresholds in spiritual realm as well. Consider the theme of the presence of the Lord. It is universally understood amongst theologians that God is an omnipresent Being. Omnipresence means that God is everywhere present through the entire Universe. But a human being feels His Presence only when our spirit is cognized of His Presence and passes our physical threshold in our brain. David said, 'Where can I go from Your Spirit? Or where can I flee from your presence? If I ascend into heaven, You are there; If I make my bed in hell, behold you are there' (Psalm 139:7–8 NKJV)."[9]

We must cultivate our spiritual senses to experience the presence of God. Phil Mason stated that "this is what happens in a glory explosion. It crosses the threshold of subjectivity into a powerful physical experience of the glory and the power of God."[10] We must allow the Holy Spirit to pass the threshold of our physical brain with billions of neurons with trillions of connections in our body to join our spirit to become a Spirit-filled person, to experience physically the transforming power of God and sense His glorious presence.[11]

Through billions of neurons, we feel in our physical body His power, His presence, His anointing, which causes a shift in the atmosphere of our brain, mind, and thinking, anchoring our faith in Him, increasing our joy and hope in His promises written for us in His Word, renewing our mind completely, making us a new creation in Christ. He gave the anointing to His disciples in the past and those who ask today to accomplish His work on earth. He comes to dwell in us through the power of the Holy Spirit entering our physical body. "Where can I go from Your Spirit? Or where can I flee from your presence? If I ascend into heaven, You are there; If I make my bed in hell, behold you are there" (Col. 1:27 NKJV). When you are immersed in His Spirit, you become a fountain, and from your heart will flow rivers of living water to affect those around you through His power through His Presence and His anointing to advance the kingdom of God.

The Holy Spirit enters our body, soul, and spirit through the walls of our physical body even though it seems impossible for Him to get inside of us. In John 20:19, we read that Jesus, after resurrection, entered through "door locked of fear" to bring peace. "Then, the same day at evening, being the first *day* of the week, when the doors were shut where the disciples were assembled, for fear of the Jews, Jesus came and stood in the midst, and said to them, 'Peace *be* with you'" (John 20:19 NKJV). He surprised all His disciples, showing up in their midst even if the doors were locked, and spoke to them, saying, "Peace be with you." They were filled with joy when they did see Jesus in their midst.

The same Jesus, through the Holy Spirit, entered "the wall" of your body, soul, and spirit to cast out fear and all emotions of discouragement, loneliness, unbelief, anxiety, depression, bitterness, rejection, and unworthiness. He will replace them all with His lovingkindness, joy, and hope. He enters in your being to restore your peace, which passes all understanding, bringing unspeakable joy. He prepares your heart for greater work. He gives you peace and fills your heart with joy to calm your overactive brain, to increase your faith to speak to the mount of impossibilities to move away from your life to prepare your brain to be able to focus on what is more important and purposeful in life. Only then can you focus to receive forgiveness of all sins. He wants to breathe in you the power of the Holy Spirit as at the day of Pentecost. "You shall receive power" was the instruction given by Jesus to His disciples. When you realize that is Jesus Christ, through the Holy Spirit, touching your body, soul, and spirit, you cannot contain His manifestation through overwhelming joy. We do not see the Spirit, but we feel His presence.

He Is at Work in Us

To illustrate that, I am sharing an experience from my youth when I was in Bucharest in 1977 and when the big earthquake—7.2 on the Richter scale—hit the city and millions of people were in terrible distress and fear. Thousands died that night. It was 9:22 at night, when people were ready to go to bed or were already in bed for the night, and now, because of the big shaking, they were terrified, leaving their houses and apartments in high buildings (in the capital of Romania) in their pajamas, carrying their blankets and gathering in groups outside in the fields, afraid to go back to their homes. I was coming from the evening classes at school and was talking on the phone in a telephone cabin with one of my old friends that I was prompted to call (we did not have cordless phones at that time; no high technology was developed yet). I was prompted by the Holy Spirit to call my old friends just to check in to reconnect after a longer period and see how she was doing. I entered in that telephone cabin without knowing that God, through the power of the Holy Spirit, was directing my steps to that cabin to protect me from falling down when the earth started to shake violently, or to have bricks falling from different high buildings on my head. As I was walking by that telephone cabin, a thought came in my mind to call an old friend to talk and reconnect with her for a few minutes because that was a good hour for her to be home from long hours of work. But God, Jehovah El Roy, who knew everything, dropped that thought in my mind and heart about a phone call to my friend. Nothing is hidden from God's eyes. He knew that a violent earthquake was coming, and He was leading me to that telephone cabin to provide me divine protection.

He is Jehovah El Elyon, the most high and mighty God, who provided divine protection for me in that evening from that disaster in that telephone cabin. The violent shaking started just shortly after I started the conversation on the telephone and lasted for almost one minute (fifty-five seconds), which seemed like eternity at that time. I knew for sure that was the end of the world, because I never had that experience and nobody was talking about earthquakes during that time. When I came out from that cabin and saw the scene displaying despair in people's heart, crying, sobbing, terrified with fear, the Holy Spirit from inside of me started to pray in heavenly language and singing loud enough to suppress any fearful thoughts that tried to grip my mind, and the peace of God was flowing in my heart and soul, surpassing my understanding.

My fear was drowning in His perfect love and joy. My whole body was vibrating under the power of the Holy Spirit as I was walking toward my house on the sidewalk, passing by terrified groups of people, wanting to sympathize with them, trying to feel their pain to identify with them, going through the same turmoil, but my soul was overwhelmed with joy inside of me and I could not hide it. I tried to pray in my native language, but I couldn't. I started to sing in heavenly language all the way home, rejoicing in the Lord. I remembered then that I had a dream one night before that earthquake that I was in an exam room and I was given a white paper for the exam but I could not write anything on that immaculate white piece of paper. God gave me a sign that I had to go through a test but the Holy Spirit would intercede for me. And He did.

Instead of worrying about what happened, even though I thought that was the end of the world, I continued to experience in my soul the unspeakable joy in the Holy Spirit through the night and the next day, singing and rejoicing in the Holy Spirit. I did not understand what happened to me at that time, but as I continue to mature in Christ, I know now that the Holy Spirit was present in my time of need to comfort, to give peace that passes all understanding to glorify God.

Next day at work, Communist people who did not believe in God noticed my joy and peace and were more afraid, asking me questions, why I had so much peace and joy, why I was not afraid or in distress and in despair like they were. When I told them that I was talking on the phone in the telephone cabin exactly at that time when the earthquake happened and I was protected that way from the disaster of the earthquake, they were more afraid to ask me more questions. They were saying that I was in that telephone cabin "to talk to God on the phone" (mocking me again) when I explained to them that nothing bad happened to me and I was protected by God in a telephone cabin. They were right. That night, I talked to God almost all night long. "The telephone line was open" wirelessly for me to communicate with my heavenly Father.

I was praising God for that evening and gave Him glory for the divine protection and for His divine presence, which I felt in my body, soul, and spirit in such a time of need. I wanted to please Him more when I felt the power of the Holy Spirit bringing me joy and peace, contrary to all circumstances. That unspeakable joy was multiplied for weeks and months when people were in psychological distress and major depression due to the aftermath of the disaster. People asked me to pray for them and their families too.

God had the purpose for me to glorify His holy name in front of Communist people in stressful situation. God had a purpose in that fearful event to wake up people to realize that life is not in our hands. He wants His creation to focus on Him and live with eternity in mind. We must change our thinking and think God's way in all circumstances in order to please Him. We must find out God's will and His likes. He likes to change our life according to His will and purpose. His desire for His creation is to bring Him glory and expressive worship and praises. He wants the human heart to be pure so He can have an intimate, holy relationship with you and continue communication. We need to cry out to God for a new and pure heart and for His love to be revealed to us at the deeper level. God is present through the power of the Holy Spirit on this planet to help humanity, who is created for His purpose.

God's Purpose for Your Eyes

Created with Eyes for God's Purpose

"The lamp of the body is the eye. If therefore your eye is good, your whole body will be full of light. But if your eye is bad, your whole body will be full of darkness. If therefore the light that is in you is darkness, how great *is* that darkness!" (Matt. 6:22–23 NKJV).

To be able to see the world around us, to interact with others, to communicate our needs, to develop relationship with God and people, to care for ourselves and for others, we need to have healthy physical and spiritual eyes. The human eye is the most complex and intricate optical system in the entire universe.[1]

Dr. Jefrrey Grant, in his book *Creation*, explains well how this complex organ that is formed in the human body is in the mother's womb. He stated that "when a baby is conceived in its mother womb, the genetic DNA code governing the eye programs the baby's body to begin growing optic nerves simultaneously from both the optic center of the brain and from the eye. A million microscopic optic nerves begin growing from the eye through the flesh toward the optical section of the baby's brain. Simultaneously, a million optic nerves, with a protective sheath similar to a fiber-optic cable, begin growing through the flesh toward the baby eye. Each of these one-million optic nerves must find and match up to its precise mate to enable vision to function perfectly."[2]

Jeffrey grant continues to describe the complexity of the human eye, describing its amazing capability to analyze the images our eyes see in the outside world. Your eye has millions of specialized cells that collect information in your environment and the world and analyzes them at a speed of one million per second, with retina cells making ten billion instantaneous calculations per second to determine the image sent to the eye by the light photons.[3]

The Bible tells us that "the lamp of the body is the eye. If therefore your eye is good, your whole body will be full of light. But if your eye is bad, your whole body will be full of darkness. If therefore the light that is in you is darkness, how great *is* that darkness!" (Matt. 6:22–23 NKJV).

We were created in His image, with physical eye for both physical and spiritual purpose, to be able to see God's creation, to adjust your spiritual vision for your soul to live eternally. Our soul's enemy keeps us in a spiritual darkness, bringing images in our visual field that are poisonous for our soul, spirit, and body. We need to open our spiritual eyes and adjust our vision to see things through God's eyes and God's lenses. You have the power through your prefrontal lobe in the brain to analyze things you see, to use reasoning and logical thinking to decide what you choose to look at throughout the day. The information you allow your eyes to see will feed your brain, which will get the message and will command the glands to release neurochemicals that can heal or destroy your body, soul, and spirit. Your physical eyes are for you to discern how you see things around you, to collect physical information that affects the spiritual vision of your soul and spirit, making your body full of light. William Shakespeare once said, "The eyes are the window to your soul."[4]

All the information we collect by our five senses, including seeing things around us and far away, will become electrical impulses and will activate memories spread throughout our cortex, forming new thoughts and new emotions that will be processed in our brain and our heart, affecting our soul, spirit, and body. What you see with your eyes, you feed your soul and spirit and will affect your entire body. Be careful what you allow your eyes to see. Your soul and spirit, on a daily basis, are stirred up with emotional needs to see physical things with your physical eyes that will quench a spiritual desire deep in your heart. With your eyes you can read a magazine with pictures, newspapers, a book or watch a movie, the internet, your phone, to see things needed to perform your daily tasks, see people around, cars, the sky, the sun, clouds, etc. You have your physical eyes to collect information for spiritual needs to feed your brain with spiritual food for you soul and spirit that will affect your entire being.

Spiritual Eyes of the Soul and Spirits

Do not set wicked things before your eyes so you do not fall away because of the things that Satan brings in front of your eyes. For that reason, the psalmist a long time ago stated, "I will set nothing wicked before my eyes; I hate the work of those who fall away; It shall not cling to me" (Ps. 101:3 NKJV), and further, he saw the need to protect his physical vision that will affect his internal soul and spirit. "Turn away my eyes from looking at worthless things, *And* revive me in Your way" (Ps. 119:37 NKJV).

In the Bible, there are many examples of people that had their spiritual eyes opened because of what they did see with their physical eyes, starting from Adam and Eve seeing their physical nakedness and their spiritual emptiness. Abraham did see the ram in the bushes to be brought as a sacrifice instead of his son Isaac, and with his spiritual eyes, he saw God's provision for his obedience and act of faith. The Bible is full of examples about physical manifestation of God's spiritual power for people to be able to see with their physical eyes, to influence their spiritual vision.

There is a powerful connection between the physical things that we see with our physical eyes and the perception of those things that we see with our spiritual eyes. The Samaritan woman did see Jesus at the well with her physical eyes, talking to her about the "living water," but in her spirit she did see the Messiah, who had to come into the world. She then invited the entire city to come and see "a man" with both their physical and spiritual eyes. When our spiritual eyes are open, and as we see with our physical eyes God's promises in our lives, then "living water" will flow for the thirsty soul. God uses our brokenness in our painful emotions to make us whole and people of influence.

A great example of such a deep spiritual hunger and desire to see Jesus is written in Luke 19:3–10, where the Word of God tells us the story of a tax collector whose desire was activated inside of him to see Jesus physically in His time on this planet for his spiritual hunger and thirst. The burning desire inside of him made him run physically and find a way to see Jesus with his physical eyes. The Scripture says, "Zaccheus was trying to see who Jesus was, and was unable because of the crowd, for he was small in stature. So he ran on ahead and climbed up into a sycamore tree in order to see Him, for He was about to pass through that way. When Jesus came to the place, He looked up and said to him, 'Zaccheus, hurry and come down, for today I must stay at your house.' And he hurried and came down and received Him gladly. When they saw it, they all *began* to grumble, saying, 'He has gone to be the guest of a man who is a sinner.' Zaccheus stopped and said to the Lord, 'Behold, Lord, half of my possessions I will give to the poor, and if I have defrauded anyone of anything, I will give back four times as much.' And Jesus said to him, 'Today salvation has come to this house, because he, too, is a son of Abraham. For the Son of Man has come to seek and to save that which was lost.'"

Zacchaeus internally desired to see Jesus with his temporary physical eyes and received salvation for his eternal soul and spirit. Zacchaeus had a breakthrough because of the desire in his spiritual DNA to see Jesus, the light of the world. He had a prophetic destiny, and God ordained his step to meet Jesus and fulfill his destiny. Each person on earth has a prophetic destiny to receive Jesus, the Messiah, in their heart, to follow Him to the end of their life, to bring God the glory on earth, and to receive eternal life through the death and resurrection of Jesus Christ. You can see Jesus with your physical eyes in His Word on the Bible's pages, which have the power to transform your thoughts and change your destiny forever.

People have the spiritual desire to see Jesus's love and His light. It is the Christians' responsibility to show the world who Jesus *is* and His eternal love and bring the light for people who live in the darkness to see the light in our action with their physical eyes and to feel the love in their soul and spirit. We advertise for our Lord Jesus when we show His love to those around us who live in the darkness. The most powerful advertising organization on this planet for heaven and eternal life through Jesus Christ is the church, the body of Christ. He gave us vision to come to the US to follow His direction in His Word, to live by biblical principles, to be blessed so we could bless others. He indeed blessed us beyond what we could ask or think. He made us rich physically and spiritually by His unmerited grace and favors from God in heaven because our spiritual eyes have been opened. "For you know the grace of our Lord Jesus Christ, that though he was rich, yet for your sake he became poor, so that you through his poverty might become rich" (2 Cor. 8:9 NIV).

So we can be the light for those around us and those far away through our deeds, because where there is light, life is booming. Our actions validated our vision, what we believed, and our faith. Faithfulness is a fruit of the spirit. It flows from the Holy Spirit. When you have an increased faith, you pray at a different level, you take action, and you do visible things to show your invisible faith and your faithfulness. James stated, "Thus also faith by itself, if it does not have works, is dead" (James 2:17 NKJV). The work you do by faith because of your vision inside will give you life experience that will lead to a living testimony that others can see physically. I know God from my experience with Him. Through experience your spiritual eyes are opened. He gave me an experience so I can have a testimony. I have seen God's hands working powerfully in my life in many ways, performing physical work from inside out. Pursue the experience with God from visions that He put in your soul and spirit.

God's Purpose for Your Ears

Created with Ears for God's Purpose

"He who planted the ear, shall He not hear? He who formed the eye, shall He not see?" (Ps. 94:9 NKJV).

God's Word speaks to your soul and spirit, but you must adjust your physical and spiritual hearing to His powerful Word. "The Sovereign LORD has given me a well-instructed tongue, to know the word that sustains the weary. He wakens me morning by morning, wakens my ear to listen like one being instructed" (Isa. 50:4 NIV).

All sound waves become electrical nerve signals after passing through the inner ear, filled with liquid, and are decoded by the cerebral cortex into intelligible sound information. The mechanism of hearing is complex and miraculous.[1] "The hearing ear and the seeing eye, The LORD has made them both" (Prov. 20:12 NKJV). In order to be able to communicate with God and people, we must have ears to hear. Phil Mason, in his book *Quantum Glory*, stated that "the ear is a miracle of sensory perception. It has been intentionally designed and built by the creative genius of God to enable sounds waves to be converted into electrical signals in the nervous system so that they can be decoded by the brain. This process is essential to facilitate audible communication and the perception of sound. Sound waves vibrating through the atmosphere are captured by the radar dish of the outer ear and funneled into the ear canal so that these waves vibrate the ear drum (which is technically called the tympanic membrane)."[2]

We are created in God's image with ears to be able to hear. He gave us ears to hear all sounds around as He hears our cries to Him. "The eyes of the LORD *are* on the righteous, and His ears *are open* to their cry"

(Ps. 34:15 NKJV). God, the Creator of the universe, hears us and sees us. He has eyes to see us and ears to hear us. Therefore, He created us with eyes to see His acts and ears to hear the sounds of His voice.

We are advised to follow God's voice, not your "good idea." He speaks to you regularly. As your vision needs to be adjusted, so does your hearing. In order to hear from God, we must listen to Him. To listen, we must start a conversation by reading His Word and praying. A close relationship with God is needed to hear the sound of His voice when He speaks to our hearts through His living Word. You need to hear God's heart for you. He speaks through visions, dreams, angels in a miraculous way, but most of the time, He speaks through His Word, through your thoughts. You must be very close to God to hear His small voice, which is leading and guiding you. You must have experience with God working in your life.

The voice of God uses different sounds and frequencies. Do not ignore God's voice. Tune in to God's "channel," the Holy Spirit's frequencies, to hear His voice clearly. He is talking about the great reward in heaven. He is preparing you for that reward when He speaks to you. Put God in the center of your life and your life will be filled with hope. Seek the kingdom of God first through prayer and meditation at His Word and you will hear His voice. Prayer is a necessity to communicate with God. Our Father likes communication with His creation. Prayer is God's mystery to connect humans with His spiritual realm and power. That is why He gave us His Word and His Spirit, to keep the line open for communication wirelessly, available twenty-four hours a day, 7 days a week, 365 days a year. You get the point.

People are dissatisfied with all their achievements if they miss communication with the Father and the spiritual aspect and the meaning of life. We have seen wealthy people with great profession and high achievements suffering from depression and being unhappy, which lead to weakness of the body and more illnesses. Their joy is temporary from all the high achievements in the absence of God's presence and lack of communication with our Creator. The Word of God is the greatest success manual for high spiritual achievements that help us succeed physically too and for health promotion and disease prevention through joy and peace, guaranteeing eternal life, relationship restoration, blessings and return of finances, and more when you tune in to hear His small voice.

God's Small Voice

God's purpose for creating humans was to continue to communicate with each one of us and to speak to us regularly. He spoke to Elijah with a small voice. "Then He said, 'Go out, and stand on the mountain before the LORD.' And behold, the LORD passed by, and a great and strong wind tore into the mountains and broke the rocks in pieces before the LORD, *but* the LORD *was* not in the wind; and after the wind an earthquake, *but* the LORD *was* not in the earthquake; and after the earthquake a fire, *but* the LORD *was* not in the fire; and after the fire a still small voice. So it was, when Elijah heard *it,* that he wrapped his face in his mantle and went out and stood in the entrance of the cave. Suddenly a voice *came* to him, and said, 'What are you doing here, Elijah?'" (1 Kings 19:11–13 NKJV).

A strong wind, an earthquake, and a fire may precede the small voice of God when He needs our attention. To hear His small voice is essential for us to be able to sharpen our thoughts, to obey and follow His advice in our relationship with Him. Both your vision and your hearing are the catalysts to give birth to the spiritual fruit of the spirit and develop the sweet aroma through your thoughts, emotions, deeds, expressions, and actions and behavior. What you see and hear feed your spirit and your unconscious mind, which will bring out words and things stored up. To guard your heart and mind are valid and real instructions, because the information that you collect with your eyes and ears are processed in your mind and affect your emotions and your heart. The Holy Spirit can give you the gift of discernment to be selective with what you see and what you hear or listen to.

God's purpose for our eyes and ears is that we are in tune with His heart's desires, to be His musical instrument. He is singing over us. God's desire is to rejoice over you with singing. "The LORD your God in your midst, The Mighty One, will save; He will rejoice over you with gladness, He will quiet *you* with His love, He will rejoice over you with singing" (Zeph. 3:17 NKJV). You must see God's glory, which prompts you to hear His praises in your ears.

Train your ear to hear God's voice. There is a huge competition of millions of voices for your ears. The enemy of your soul, spirit, and body knows that if he will get your attention "roaring to swallow," he will have access to your mind (through deceiving thoughts becoming the electrical impulses), taking residence in your mind and brain, controlling your life, leading you to distraction. That is the strategy of the enemy for your soul. The most outrageous battle in the entire universe is for your neurons. Very often I present a slide with pictures of a neuron, the nerve cell involved in thinking. People are astonished at that picture of a neuron (shown in a later chapter), speaking volumes about the thinking process through the billions of neurons and all information circulating in the human brain. If the enemy can access neurons with the voices of the world, you will be defeated.

With a worldly mind, you are prone to hear the roaring voice of the enemy. You must renew your mind to hear God's small voice. Your thoughts must be cleansed from false beliefs, unhealthy thoughts, and unhealthy feelings. Your thoughts must reflect God's will and His purpose. You must develop the mind of Christ and not conform to the thoughts of the world that are dirty and cluttered with filthy voices. The Word of God is a force and will come alive in you. God speaks through His Word. God instills His thoughts into your mind and soul through His Word to increase your faith and to feel His love. He speaks through visions and dreams, signs and miracles also.

God spoke to Nehemiah's mind and heart when he had a dream, a vision, and a desire to build the wall of the ruined city of God's people. His mind was set on finishing the work to accomplish his task and fulfill his dream and vision for the Jews' city. Nehemiah listened to God's voice inside of him. He tuned in to God's frequency and received the message directly from God. God gave him a strategy and miraculously provided everything he needed to finish the wall in fifty-two days (Neh. 6:15 NKJV). You must hear from God every day and start small achievable steps with small goals. His voice is new every morning to restore your hope every day.

When you hear God's voice through His Word, you have goals in mind and set your mind to work. The qualities of your thoughts are changed, and that influences people around you.

Understand the Word of God and hide it in your hearts; read, memorize, and meditate on the Word. Fill your mind with verses from the Word that will get in your unconscious mind. Your brain is working all the time. Do not speak against your own healing. In my office, I have a big list of physical and emotional verses extracted from the Bible with powerful essence. Each time I pass by those verses, my eyes will scan over and will consolidate those powerful verses in my brain. Through those verses, I hear God's voice speaking to me. The Holy Spirit will remind me when I need them the most. Many times I wake up with a verse in my mind, and other times I wake up singing a song glorifying God. God's Word speaks to my unconscious mind and my spirit even when I sleep.

Learn to discern God's voice from other millions of voice. God will never contradict with His own Word. God wants us to meditate at His Word in any circumstances we encounter to confirm that He is speaking to us. His voice will give us confidence in His powerful supernatural work, which will bring peace, joy, confidence, authority, and reasonableness. The Holy Spirit will put an impression in your heart and mind. Take time to listen to God's voice after you pray. God is still whispering to your ears with a gentle voice to trust in Him in all your ways. "After the earthquake, came a fire, but the LORD was not in the fire. And after the fire came a gentle whisper" (1 Kings 19:12 NIV). Listen to the gentle whisper. Do not let fear grip your heart in the darkest moments of your life. He speaks to you even in that difficult situation.

Set Boundaries and Restraints

"He who has knowledge spares his words, *And* a man of understanding is of a calm spirit. Even a fool is counted wise when he holds his peace; *When* he shuts his lips, *he is considered* perceptive" (Prov. 17:27–28 NKJV). What you hear with your ears and see with your eyes, that will affect your mouth and your actions. Be careful with what you set before your eyes and ears, because violence, tragedies, trauma, adultery, inappropriate behavior in movies, schools, books, etc. are as the devil snares to enslave you and keep you hostage your entire life. John Bevere, in his book *The Bait of Satan: Living Free from the Deadly Trap of Offense*, stated that "Satan, along with his cohorts, is not a blatant as many believe. He is subtle and delights in deception. He is shrewd in his operations…cunning and crafty. Don't forget he can disguise himself as a messenger of light. If we are not trained by the Word of God to divide rightly between good and evil, we won't recognize his traps for what they are."[3]

The ultimate purpose that God created the ear is to hear the trumpet's sounds when Christ returns for His bride. "For the Lord Himself will descend from heaven with a shout, with the voice of an archangel, and with the trumpet of God. And the dead in Christ will rise first. Then we who are alive *and* remain shall be caught up together with them in the clouds to meet the Lord in the air. And thus we shall always be with the Lord" (1 Thess. 4:16–17 NKJV). For that glorious day we must be the sweet aroma for Christ so nonbelievers will see, hear, and smell and be saved. They will flee from the smells of the danger in the world, and their lives will be transformed.

We are called by our Creator to be a sweet aroma by worshipping Him through music and praises. "O praise the LORD, all ye nations: praise him, all ye people. For his merciful kindness is great toward us: and the truth of the LORD *endureth* forever. Praise ye the LORD" (Ps. 117:1–2 KJV). Our ears are involved in hearing the music that is praising the Creator of the universe. We have the preserved ability to sing. There is music inside of you that never stops. Music connects us with heaven. "Oh, sing to the LORD a new song! Sing to the LORD, all the earth. Sing to the LORD, bless His name; Proclaim the good news of His salvation from day to day. Declare His glory among the nations, His wonders among all peoples" (Ps. 96:1–3). Music is good food for the brain. The music sounds and rhythm are preserved inside of you in the brain structure.

Phil Mason, in his book *Quantum Glory*, stated that "all human beings love the sound of music. Music soothes the soul and uplifts the spirit. The love of music and the capacity to sing and make melody is something that reflects the very image of God."[4] Then he goes on to say, "When God created the earth He determined to create a highly unique environment in the universe that could sustain the creation and transmission of the sound of music. Human being are created by God to appreciate the delicate harmonies and blends of sounds of music. It is a universal characteristic amongst human beings everywhere on the planet that we all enjoy music!"[5]

Also, Phil Mason stated that "heaven is filled with music of harps and the song of angelic choirs. There are also trumpets and sounds of thunder and the sounds of rushing waters. Heaven is filled with glorious sounds. It is also filled with the voice of God who sings over is creation. God is supremely happy being who delights over His children with singing" (Zeph. 3:17).[6]

I grew up in a family that loved music. Each time my parents, my brothers, or my sisters met with friends, they played instruments and did sing beautiful Christian songs praising God. All my brothers and sisters played some kind of instruments, except me. I was singing with my voice only. Everybody loved music. My father played every single instrument that he put his hands on. He had a unique gift from God to play musical instruments. I vividly remember as a child growing up on a big farm (that Communists took away by force from my parents and grandparents) and running in the fields, and suddenly, from far away, I could hear my father playing the accordion in the backyard, raising his voice out loud in song of praises. He was not afraid of the Communists that would hear him playing music out loud and arrest him. That musical sound remains with me still today. I remember the sweet aroma of those songs of praises from my early childhood. Music sounds will remain in your memory storage for life. It has an eternal effect on our mind, soul, and spirit.

Now, as a grandma, when I watch my grandson and need to help him with naps, I sing him smooth songs of Jesus, and he goes to sleep peacefully. Music is created by God to capture our ears, our heart, and our brain to bring Him praises and glory. I like to believe that music originated in heaven and will go back to heaven as a sweet aroma for our Creator from His creation.

God's Purpose for the Olfactory System

◼ Created to Be a Sweet Aroma

The fragrance of the fruit of the spirit is desired to bring a sweet aroma. The scent is used in the Bible many times to illustrate the importance of the smell. "But thanks be to God, who always leads us as captives in Christ's triumphal procession and uses us to spread the aroma of the knowledge of him everywhere" (2 Cor. 2:14 NIV).

The olfactory system for smell is created by God with an extreme importance in our physical and spiritual being, body, soul, and spirit, for communication purpose with people around us and our Creator at a deeper level.[1]

Naturally, our body was designed and created with the olfactory system with warning system to be able to enjoy the smell of food, flowers, perfumes and/or to warn us about dangerous toxins close to our body that excite the extremely sensitive olfactory receptors with nerve fibers covered with mucus inside the hollow space of the nose. "When your olfactory receptors are stimulated, they transmit impulses to your brain. This pathway is directly connected to your limbic system, the part of your brain that deals with emotions. That's why your reactions to smell are rarely neutral—you usually either like or dislike a smell. Smells also leave long-lasting impressions and are strongly linked to your memories. The scent of mown grass, for example, might remind you of a childhood summer holiday, and the smell of chocolate chip cookies may make you think of your grandmother."[2]

Limbic System: Connected with the Olfactory System for Smell

Many brain structures as prefrontal cortex, cingulate gyrus, basal ganglia, hypothalamus, amygdala, pituitary gland, hippocampus, thalamus, locus coeruleus, raphe nuclei, and others are involved in the smelling process and are affected by it.[3]

Thousands of smells pass the threshold of our physical nose when they stimulate the olfactory receptors and send impulses through the pathway that connects our limbic system, involved in processing our emotions, consolidating our memories, and dictating our personality. Our emotions dictate our feelings, which determine our actions to spread a pleasant aroma to those around us. In Ephesians 5:2 we read that we need to walk in love, "just as Christ loved us and gave himself up for us as a fragrant offering and sacrifice to God" (Eph. 5:2 NIV). Through our limbic system's function in connection with other brain structures, we understand the love of Christ, His sacrifice for us, and His fragrant offering and sacrifice to our Father in heaven.

We were created to be a sweet aroma, as Christ Jesus's life on earth demonstrated, a fragrant offering to our Creator. In Romania, in a Communist environment, during my schooltime and at work, everybody knew that I was a Christian and I believed God and followed His Word because of the smell of Christ's aroma in my deeds and my attitude. Communists did not like that I was a Christian, but they, for sure, liked my Christian walk, because I let the light of Jesus and His Word shine through me. They liked the flavor of my deeds being the salt, the hope for the hopeless around me. One time, the secretary of the Communist Party organization in the company I had worked for sixteen years in Bucharest asked me to sing a Christian song during our break time, and he did listen with tears in his eyes because the "sweet aroma" from the words full of hope activated his limbic system and he felt those emotions of peace and joy. "But the fruit of the spirit is love, joy, peace, kindness, goodness, faithfulness, gentleness, self-control; against such things there is no law" (Gal. 5:22–23 NIV). Our limbic system is involved in memory consolidation. Through our olfactory system, we are able to store memories of emotions of the characteristic of the spirit of "love, joy, peace, kindness, goodness, faithfulness, gentleness," written in Galatians 5:22–23 as a fragrant and sweet aroma.

The Smell of the Aroma

The smell of the aroma has a great effect on people's brain, memory, and physical body. Kandhasamy Sowndhararajan and Songmun Kim (2016) stated in their study that "in our daily life, several fragrances appear and a sense of smell plays an important role in the physiological effects of mood, stress, and working capacity. Fragrance is a volatile chemical component with a molecular weight of <300 Da that humans perceive via the olfactory system. In the olfactory process, the fragrant molecules in the air attach to the cilia of olfactory receptors in the olfactory epithelium, located in the nasal cavity. Then the guanine nucleotide binding protein (G-protein) coupled receptors (GPCR) are activated and electrical signals are generated. Subsequently, the electrical signals are transmitted to the brain by olfactory sensory neurons via olfactory bulb and higher olfactory cortex. Consequently, these electrical signals modulate the brain functions including memory, thoughts, and emotions. Many studies describe that the inhalation of fragrances highly affect the brain function since the fragrance compounds are able to cross the blood-brain barrier and interact with receptors in the central nervous system. Furthermore, many studies have suggested that the olfactory stimulation of fragrances produces immediate changes in physiological parameters such as blood pressure, muscle tension, pupil dilation, skin temperature, pulse rate and brain activity. Hence, the studies in relation to the role of fragrances in the brain functions of healthy and diseased subjects have significantly increased in the past decades."[4]

Like perfume, you spread the aroma around you. Many times my husband and I visit parks with flowers and admire those beautiful flowers and their diverse smells, and my husband will ask the question, "How can I capture these smells on my camera? Because

I cannot take picture of these fascinating smells!" You cannot take pictures of the smell of the flowers, perfume, fragrance, but you smell it through your nose and will influence your limbic system and your memory. You will remember that smell. What you see in your spirit cannot be recorded (like perfume) but sends messages to your brain through the olfactory neuropathways, influencing neurochemicals to be released and become pleasant emotions. "For we are to God the fragrance of Christ among those who are being saved and among those who are perishing" (2 Cor. 2:15 NKJV).

Your Incense and Aroma

> "May my prayer be set before you like incense;
> may the lifting up of my hands be like the evening sacrifice" (Ps. 141:2 NIV).

In nature, the incenses have effect on memory, thoughts, and emotions in the limbic system and brain. Prophetically, through the revelation received from the Holy Spirit, David asked the Lord to receive his prayers like incense so the Lord would show emotions of mercy, grace, endurance and remember David's cries toward heaven before the King of the universe. "The smoke of the incense, together with the prayers of God's people, went up before God from the angel's hand" (Rev. 8:4).

The prayers of God's people are incense in golden bowls. "And when he had taken it, the four living creatures and the twenty-four elders fell down before the Lamb. Each one had a harp and they were holding golden bowls full of incense, which are the prayers of God's people" (Rev. 5:8 NIV). When you pray and bring incense to the Lord through your continuous prayers, your Father in heaven remembers your prayers, your good deeds, your obedience, your thankful attitude, your gratitude. He remembers when you helped needy people, orphans, widows, the sick, and those in great physical and spiritual need. He will remember when you represented Him to the world, being the salt and the light. You must bring flavor to the world around you because Jesus said you are the salt. That flavor you add to your incense is hope, faith, healing, joy to a suffering world that has a positive effect on people's brain structures, cognition, memory, life, etc.

Walk in confidence, shining your light, and bring flavor to the world because God's anointing is over you and in you and the Almighty God is with you. He knows your name, and He calls you by name. "I will give you hidden treasures, riches stored in secret places, so that you may know that I am the LORD, the God of Israel, who summons you by name" (Isa. 45:3 NIV). You are a treasure in the world because of the blood of Jesus, His fragrance offering for the world. He asks us to take communion in remembrance of Him, "and when He had given thanks, He broke *it* and said, 'Take, eat; this is My body which is broken for you; do this in remembrance of Me'" (Cor. 11:24 NKJV). Through communion we will remember Jesus's sacrifice and sweet aroma to God the Father for the humanity.

He gave us the assignment to be a sweet aroma to the world, to bring comfort, peace, and joy to those around us. God is looking for people He can trust to be His hands, His feet, His mouth, His eyes, His ears, His heart, His mind to function as He is walking again on this planet in each one of us who are willing and able to pour out our life to be the aroma for Christ as we were designed to transform the world for His glory through the power of the Holy Spirit.

Prayers, as incense, allow you to live even longer. The Holy Spirit inside of you helps you to connect with true believers and helps you to meditate at God's promises. The Holy Spirit is present during distractions in life to tell you which direction to walk. When you have a positive attitude, sense of purpose, and enthusiasm, you develop more resilience because you know who you are. You become physically and spiritually stronger because you develop awareness of your place in the world.

For holistic care for body, soul, and spirit in medicine, often patients are encouraged to use meditation. During meditation, the mind sets functions at the highest level. According to Wikipedia, "Christian meditation is a form of prayer in which a structured attempt is made to become aware of and reflect upon the revelations of God. The word *meditation* comes from the Latin word *meditārī*, which has a range of meanings, including 'to reflect on, to study, and to practice.' Christian meditation is the process of deliberately focusing on specific thoughts (such as a Bible passage) and reflecting on their meaning in the context of the love of God. Christian meditation aims to heighten the personal relationship based on the love of God that marks Christian communion. Both in Eastern and Western Christianity, meditation is the middle level in a broad three-stage characterization of prayer: it involves more reflection than first-level vocal prayer but is more structured than the multiple layers of contemplative prayer. Teachings in both the Eastern and Western Christian churches have emphasized the use of Christian meditation as an element in increasing one's knowledge of Christ."[5]

Make a priority to meditate every day at what the Word of God promised to keep being prosperous and successful, to enjoy life, as is written in Joshua, to "keep this Book of the Law always on your lips; meditate on it day and night, so that you may be careful to do everything written in it. Then you will be prosperous and successful" (Joshua 1:8 NIV). It is a clear demonstration that meditation has a huge impact on our success and prosperity. To be successful and to become prosperous, we must be able to have clear thoughts, to have a great memory, ability to learn, and improved cognition, to make well-informed decision. Meditation will enable you to achieve just that. That is possible with healthy neurons, wisdom, and revelation, knowledge through the power of the Holy Spirit to be a sweet aroma to God and to people.

PART II

The Reward System

God's Purpose in Creating the Reward System

> "For You, LORD, have made me glad through Your work; I will triumph in the works of Your hands. O LORD, how great are Your works! Your thoughts are very deep" (Ps. 92:4–5 NKJV).

God created every human being with a reward system and a center for pleasure, to be motivated to follow the Word of God's instructions, to live full of love and joy as we were created to live.

The human being was created with an amazing reward system with the purpose to rejoice in the Lord's salvation. Jesus Christ, the Son of God, had the perfect reward system in His physical body when he was born as a man here on this planet. His reward system was activated by the power of the Holy Spirit of God. Christ rejoices of His work at the Calvary, bringing salvation to the dying world. Jesus's joy for our salvation was activated from the foundation of the world when the Lamb of God was already slain in the Father's heart. "All who dwell on the earth will worship him, whose names have not been written in the Book of Life of the Lamb slain from the foundation of the world" (Rev. 13:8 NKJV).

The reward system in Jesus Christ was kept under divine control to the point of humbling Himself to the point of dying on the cross, to be exalted by the Father, that every knee will bow down at the feet of Jesus and every tongue will confess that He is Lord, as is written in Philippians 2:8–11. "And being found in appearance as a man, He humbled Himself and became obedient to the point of death, even the death of the cross. Therefore God also has highly exalted Him and given Him the name which is above every name, that at the name of Jesus every knee should bow, of those in heaven, and of those on earth, and of those under the earth, and that every tongue should confess that Jesus Christ is Lord, to the glory of God the Father" (NKJV).

Studying the reward system in our brain with the pleasure system and the neurochemicals for pleasure opened my eyes to understand their functions and God's purpose in creating the human brain at a deeper level. I realized that Satan's strategy is to destroy the reward system in our brain so people cannot experience the joy of salvation. It is a great competition for the nucleus accumbens. Science discovered that "the nucleus accumbens definitely plays a central role in the reward circuit. Its operation is based chiefly on two essential neurotransmitters: dopamine, which promotes desire, and serotonin, whose effects include satiety and inhibition. Many animal studies have shown that all drugs increase the production of dopamine in the nucleus accumbens, while reducing that of serotonin. But the nucleus accumbens does not work in isolation. It maintains close relations with other centers involved in the mechanisms of pleasure, and in particular, with the ventral tegmental area (VTA)."[1]

The devil's strategy to steal our joy is real and is the greatest spiritual battle to take control over this sophisticated reward system to destroy people's life. I discovered the reason the Creator carefully placed the reward system and the pleasure center in our brain to enjoy our temporary life because of the salvation we received on earth while preparing for the greatest joy in heaven, where our eternal reward is waiting for us. Without the reward system, people cannot enjoy physical and spiritual life. God will not ask humans to do something that He did not provide the pathway for the process of. The human's reward system employs the hippocampus, amygdala, ventral stratum, nucleus accumbens, PFC, dorsal striatum, substantia nigra, ventraltegmental area, dopaminergic projections, GABA projections, dopaminergic regions, and dopaminoceptive regions.[2]

Science demonstrated that our body and brain are created with pathways for life to be able to move, think, learn, solve problems, change behavior, and enjoy it. "Dopaminergic pathways in the brain influence (1) reward processes (i.e., wanting and liking, and the reinforcement of pleasure behaviors), (2) executive functions (i.e., goal-directed behaviors, cognitive flexibility, and problem solving), (3) associative learning (i.e., acquiring and modifying behaviors, skills, etc.), and (4) motor control (i.e., coordination and control of reflexes and voluntary movements)."[3]

We were created to feel healthy emotions through the pathways created in our brain and our body and to feel the pleasure through the reward mechanism. "These dopamine pathways and processes play a critical part in boosting motivation, focus, and cognitive flexibility, while also promoting a healthy emotional life, including sensations of reward and pleasure."[4]

Our reward system must be stimulated with healthy emotions to release healthy neurochemicals to function for the purpose that was created in human's brain. Science discovered that "when exposed to a rewarding stimulus, the brain responds by increasing release of the neurotransmitter dopamine and thus the structures associated with the reward system are found along the major dopamine pathways in the brain. The mesolimbic dopamine pathway is thought to play a primary role in the reward system."[5]

Behavior is reinforced by the reward pathway deep in our brain, helping us to repeat main actions as eating, drinking, relationships, and romance, to become a part of our life for life to continue on earth. The reward pathway communicates with other brain structures to retrieve information and memories and strengthen the brain circuits that control behavior and movement.[6]

Based on memories in other parts of the brain, you will feel good when you engage in a specific behavior from your experience in the past with the same behavior. Our senses of joy will cause the neurons to release the neurochemical dopamine and other neurochemicals, giving a jolt of pleasure regularly.

Reprogram Your Brain by Rejoicing

The reward pathway builds the memory through signals to the memory regions with details on how to get the joy of salvations and will make you go back to do it again. The reward system gets stronger as we live with the joy of salvation every day, living with eternity in mind that a great reward waits for us. Focusing on the eternal reward will activate the reward mechanism in our brain, and we will live with great joy continuously, as the apostle Paul stated. "Rejoice in the Lord always. Again I will say, rejoice! Let your gentleness be known to all men. The Lord *is* at hand" (Phil. 4:4 NKJV).

Jesus Christ will reward us for our obedience of His commandments. "And behold, I am coming quickly, and My reward *is* with Me, to give to every one according to his work. I am the Alpha and the Omega, *the* Beginning and *the* End, the First and the Last." Blessed *are* those who do His commandments that they may have the right to the tree of life, and may enter through the gates into the city" (Rev. 22:12–14 NKJV). The brain circuits are strengthened to experience the reward when we focus on that promise for eternal reward. Through signals to the motor center in the brain, and with more repetition, your actions will become your habits to rejoice every day. Our rewarding stimulus must be the joy of salvation that our sins are washed away and we have eternal life when we leave this planet. The brain releases jolts of dopamine to rejoice, giving us a pleasant sensation. Science demonstrated that "through little jolts of dopamine, the reward pathway motivates us to repeat behaviors that are necessary for survival."[7]

We know that earthly happiness cannot last, is temporary, and sometimes, if it based on material things only, destructive behavior and immorality lead to suicide when people do not see with earthly eyes God's purpose for the eternal reward. Self-inflicted anger is the enemy strategy in people's life. But the fruit of the Spirit, as love and joy, will trigger the nucleus accumbens, the special region in the brain that is the pleasure center. Through supernatural love and supernatural joy, we can break all other addictive cycles that high-jacked this extremely important brain structure and are trying to destroy neurons in the brain and someone's entire life and destiny. You can feel again energized and vibrant if you use your brain structure for supernatural love and joy that come directly from God, who created humans for His purpose and who is the source of love.

Reprogram your brain by rejoicing always. The reward system must be reprogrammed because Christ made reservation in heaven on your name, with your name written in the Book of Life. Our reservation there is possible only through Christ's salvation. Our joy is God, who saved us from our sin and its pain through Jesus Christ, our Redeemer, who was full of joy. "In that hour Jesus rejoiced in the Spirit and said, 'I thank You, Father, Lord of heaven and earth, that You have hidden these things from the wise and prudent and revealed them to babes. Even so, Father, for so it seemed good in Your sight'" (Luke 10:21 NKJV).

Keep the Reward System Active

He gave clear instructions about giving thanks for everything and in every situation and to rejoice always. Following those instructions will keep the reward system active. God wants real people to glorify Him in any situation. Giving God thanks is bringing Him glory and praises, and that positions you in His will. "Rejoice always, pray continually, give thanks in all circumstances; for this is God's will for you in Christ Jesus" (Thess. 5:18). "Always giving thanks to God the Father for everything, in the name of our Lord Jesus Christ" (Eph. 5:20 NIV). Thanksgiving connects you with the heaven, and you enter in God's atmosphere of peace.

When you are connected with heaven in your spirit, nothing can interrupt you. Your reward system is strengthened when you gather together with other people of faith and rejoice. You receive authority over the forces of darkness that steal your joy and peace. "Assuredly, I say to you, whatever you bind on earth will be bound in heaven, and whatever you loose on earth will be loosed in heaven. Again I say to you that if two of you agree on earth concerning anything that they ask, it will be done for them by My Father in heaven.

For where two or three are gathered together in My name, I am there in the midst of them" (Matt. 18:18–20 NKJV).

Our Creator carefully created our brain with a reward system, but Satan's snares, through our careless behavior, try to destroy what God created for us to rejoice. Worries, lies, pessimism, depression become more real in your life and steal your joy, your visions, weakening your reward system, and you cannot fulfill your call on earth and your destiny. You forget that your families, children, spouse, city, and nation are in God's hand. God has all the pieces of the puzzles in His hands. You must eliminate worries, anxiety, depression, lack of trust in God. God's Word tells us about Peter, who despised everything; he looked directly in Jesus's eyes and started to walk on water when other disciples did not get out of the boat and did not try to walk on water, being overwhelmed with fear.

When Peter looked at the circumstances, he started to drown, but Jesus had Peter's situation in His hand. Jesus is ready to rebuke the wind, the storm, if you trust Him, obey Him, waiting for Him calmly, full of peace and trust. Worries will cloud your vision and will hinder you to be the light of the world, to be the solution for the problems of those around you. You must know God, talk to Him, and open your heart to him, because He is love. Love counteracts emotions of anxiety and worries and reduces the cloud of high level of cortisol from your increased fear and anxiety, obstructing your vision. When you nurture love, oxytocin, serotonin, dopamine, and other healthy neurochemicals will be released in the body and will change the way you feel.

The Stone of Remembrance Activates the Reward System

Put the stone of remembrance as a testimony of joy of accomplishment. When we finished the construction of thirty beds of Tabor Crest I (Memory Care), our dearest friend Kay brought a big stone from Sandy River in Oregon, and we wrote "1 Samuel 7:12" on it and we literally placed that stone in our office, where we did our business daily to remind us about who God is in our life, that He is the one who helped us succeed to win many battles; He is the One who blessed us so much. But not only us; He also blessed our residents and their families in their time of sorrow and painful situation, our employees and their families, and all those involved in the care of the residents living in our facility.

When people came to our office and saw the "stone of remembrance" in our office, they wondered what that meant. We gladly explained with joy our story, how we came with empty hands, with no money, no English speaking, with different profession and different culture, in a foreign country and only trusting God and obeying His Word and His promises, which made us succeed. And He blessed us beyond our imagination. Our heart was full of joy to remember those accomplishments, and our reward mechanism was activated again and again. On the road of our life, when we were worried and discouraged and stressed, we looked back at the "stone of remembrance," remembering what God did for us in the past and trusted Him that He would do it again. And He did.

The joy in our spirit was refreshed, and we were able to accomplish even more. The reward system must be activated fresh every morning for motivation to overcome the world. We could not do anything without God's strength. Obey what God tells you to do and listen to the Holy Spirit and the Word of God, and joy will remain in your heart and soul and spirit. Remember, Job, even when his life was broken into pieces and he was deeply crushed in his spirit, stated, "For I know *that* my Redeemer lives, And He shall stand at last on the earth" (Job 19:25 NKJV). Job knew that His Protector is the Maker of the heavens and earth.

You can declare that your Redeemer lives and He keeps you motivated to live a joyful life. If your life, too, is broken into pieces, raise your voice and give God your pieces. He will take them to glue them, not with superglue to put them together and mend them; He will use fine adhesive, "the cross," and refine all the pieces and transform them in a nice, fine, brand-new portrait that will be displayed for many to see. We had to keep that in mind in our struggles, battles, and difficult situations and let God put all our broken pieces together to be able to keep our heart full of joy. God's restoration will be efficient. He will fill your cup to overflowing, and then you will be a blessing for your family, community, nation, and world. God has a special plan for you, like how He had one for us. But you need to let Jesus Christ come inside of you, to live in you, to be alive in you, to become your Lord and King.

Righteous Award

Waiting for the eternal reward will bring joy. The apostle Paul's reward system was activated by the power of the Holy Spirit when he was reflecting on the crown of righteousness award prepared for him by the Lord Jesus. "For I am already being poured out like a drink offering, and the time for my departure is near. I have fought the good fight, I have finished the race, I have kept the faith. Now there is in store for me the crown of righteousness, which the Lord, the righteous Judge, will award to me on that day—and not only to me, but also to all who have longed for his appearing" (2 Tim. 4:6–8).

Holy Spirit Activates the Reward System

Besides food to eat and water to drink from the ground, God gave us the Holy Spirit from His Trinity to bring spiritual food and drink to our soul, to enjoy good feelings and good emotions, joy and peace. "For the kingdom of God is not a matter of eating and drinking, but of righteousness, peace and joy in the Holy Spirit, because anyone who serves Christ in this way is pleasing to God and receives human approval" (Rom. 14:17–18 NIV). The Creator fills our mouth with laughter and puts the songs of joy in our hearts and on our tongues to create feelings of pleasure for our hearts to glorify God for His great work on this planet among His people. "Our mouths were filled with laughter, our tongues with songs of joy. Then it was said among the nations, 'The LORD has done great things for them.' The LORD has done great things for us, and we are filled with joy"

(Ps. 126:2–3). We must sing of joy that God has done great things for His creation. The Word of Christ dwells in us creating spiritual songs in our heart. "Let the word of Christ dwell in you richly in all wisdom, teaching and admonishing one another in psalms and hymns and spiritual songs, singing with grace in your hearts to the Lord" (Col. 3:16 NKJV).

God's Joy and Good Pleasure

God's joy and good pleasure is to give us the kingdom. "Do not fear, little flock, for it is your Father's good pleasure to give you the kingdom" (Luke 12:32 NKJV). It is God's great joy and good pleasure to give humankind His kingdom. That is Jesus's reward for His sacrifice to see every soul saved. "Yet it pleased the LORD to bruise Him; He has put *Him* to grief. When You make His soul an offering for sin, He shall see *His* seed, He shall prolong *His* days, And the pleasure of the LORD shall prosper in His hand. He shall see the labor of His soul, *and* be satisfied. By His knowledge My righteous Servant shall justify many, For He shall bear their iniquities. Therefore I will divide Him a portion with the great, And He shall divide the spoil with the strong, Because He poured out His soul unto death, And He was numbered with the transgressors, And He bore the sin of many, And made intercession for the transgressors" (Isa. 53:10–12 NKJV).

David, spreading his hands toward the heavens, stated, "Restore my joy, restore my soul." He felt that his emotions needed restoration. In his spirit, King David knew that he was programmed for joy, and in desperation, he prayed for a clean heart and restoration of his joy. "Create in me a clean heart, O God, And renew a steadfast spirit within me. Do not cast me away from Your presence, And do not take Your Holy Spirit from me. Restore to me the joy of Your salvation, And uphold me *by Your* generous Spirit" (Ps. 51:10–12 NKJV). Without a clean heart, a renewed spirt, and emotional restoration, there is no joy.

David needed nonpharmacological supernatural intervention from heaven for his psychological distress from his sin and his hurting emotions in his soul. Emotional wounds hurt the most. They produce pain in the body. David wrote psalms depicting the deep pain in his soul. He was expressing his negative emotional feelings. He needed God's love to touch him to be healed completely, to bring back joy in his soul and spirit. Through joy the reward mechanism is activated and produces neurochemicals that bring healing in the body. "You make known to me the path of life; you will fill me with joy in your presence, with eternal pleasures at your right hand" (Ps. 16:11 NIV). We were created with needs for restoration through God's supernatural intervention for our deep wounds from negative emotions to heal the soul, spirit, and body, by activating the reward system to rejoice again and be made whole as we were created from the beginning.

T. D. Jakes, in his book *Instinct: The Power to Unleash Your Inborn Drive*, stated that "the design is not greater than the Designer, so ultimately we acknowledge His handiwork in all that He has placed within us. Understanding how wonderfully and thoughtfully we were brought into existence, our best and most instinctive response is simply to live according to this abundance we've been given. It is our way of saying yes to what was in God's mind when we were formed. It is our way of letting our Creator knows we're ready for the next opportunity."[8]

The Reward System, Hijacked

The reward system is hijacked by addictions (food, sex, several drugs, pornography, gambling, etc.) that lead to increase levels of dopamine, the pleasure "neurotransmitter," leading further to psychosis. "Abnormally high dopaminergic transmission has been linked to psychosis and schizophrenia. Both the typical and the atypical antipsychotics work largely by inhibiting dopamine at the receptor level."[9]

Dr. Ananya Mandal explains that "dopamine is the chemical that mediates pleasure in the brain. It is released during pleasurable situations and stimulates one to seek out the pleasurable activity or occupation. This means food, sex, and several drugs of abuse are also stimulants of dopamine release in the brain, particularly in areas such as the nucleus accumbens and prefrontal cortex."[10]

In the society we live in now, with overwhelming worldly information, it is very difficult to focus on the truth that keeps our reward system activated by the things above. My friend Shaneen Clarke from London, in her book *Dare to be Great*, stated, "Glance over the titles displayed at a newsstand and you'll see dozens of magazines promoting health, beauty, sex, fashion and self-improvement. It's not hard to see why the average person finds it difficult to align their will with the Creator of the earth. Why? Because, we would rather sing, like Frank Sinatra, I did it my way." God's kingdom requires the opposite approach—doing things according to His will. I love these words penned by evangelist T. L. Osborn: "I am VALUABLE to God and to people because I am created in His class of being. I am VITAL because God's plan involves me. MY HERITAGE is to have God's best to enjoy His companionship and to use His wealth and power for the good of myself and others. I am CREATED for life, love, power, prosperity, success, and dignity. The SEEDS OF GREATNESS are in me. God never created me to be nobody, but a real somebody."[11]

Through our behavior we must keep our mind focused on the great purpose that we are created in God's image, to give Him glory, to keep our reward system activated by His presence, rejoicing in Him, and do not let the enemy take over the reward mechanism in our brain and to destroy it. We have divine origin to glorify Him with our entire being, enjoying the purpose for which we were created.

Programmed for Joy

▪ Connection with Our Creator Brings Joy

God did not create us only to love one another but also to bring joy to one another in our relationships. We must love God and others, and we must bring joy to God and others. At several women's conferences in USA and Europe, I noticed much joy on women's faces and in other attendees when words of encouragement and love did flow from my heart, and then I felt that their joy was flowing through my heart. We brought each other joy knowing that God is the source of our joy through Christ. When we worship together, and in our fellowship with each other, we feel the joy in God's presence. In the same way when we are filled with joy, we bring joy to our Creator and our Lord. "Shout joyfully to the LORD, all the earth. Serve the LORD with gladness; Come before Him with joyful singing" (Ps. 100:1–2). When we serve with gladness, joy possesses us and we possess joy. We are connected with God's heart when our heart sings for joy to our heavenly Father. "How lovely are Your dwelling places, O LORD of hosts! My soul longed and even yearned for the courts of the LORD; My heart and my flesh sing for joy to the living God" (Ps. 84:1–2).

Because the Holy Spirit is present, His love and joy are demonstrated when He passes the threshold in our brain and activates our pleasure center and reward system and releases the neurochemicals that are responsible for the emotions of joy and love, and we can feel God's good pleasure. Connection with our Creator brings joy in our heart. Jesus, as a man on this earth, rejoiced in the Spirit in His connection with His heavenly Father. "In that hour Jesus rejoiced in the

103

Spirit and said, 'I thank You, Father, Lord of heaven and earth, that You have hidden these things from *the* wise and prudent and revealed them to babes. Even so, Father, for so it seemed good in Your sight'" (Luke 10:21 NKJV). Jesus's joy is contagious, and He is pouring His joy in human hearts, which were programmed for joy from creation.

The Origin of Joy Is God

From first day of creation, humans were destined to enjoy God's presence and His creation. Before sin happened, man and woman were given dominion over the entire planet, to be fruitful and multiply and enjoy it. After the sin, true joy was hijacked, but God brought joy back into the world through His Son, Jesus. "Then the angel said to them, 'Do not be afraid, for behold, I bring you good tidings of great joy which will be to all people'" (Luke 2:10 NKJV). Joy must be discovered through the power of the Holy Spirit, who will show us who Jesus is for us and the joy that He brings through salvation. Divine joy is possible only through this supernatural prescription, with no expiration date. "Rejoice in the Lord always. Again I will say, rejoice! Let your gentleness be known to all men. The Lord is at hand. Be anxious for nothing, but in everything by prayer and supplication, with thanksgiving, let your requests be made known to God; and the peace of God, which surpasses all understanding, will guard your hearts and minds through Christ Jesus" (Phil. 4:4–7 NKJV).

We can only be gentle when we rejoice always in the absence of anxiety and worries of needs in this world. The supernatural joy that possesses you transcends the death and its dying process. We must discover that God is in the middle of our circumstances so we can still rejoice in our troubles by passing them. Only with spiritual eyes can we see Him for who He truly *is*. King David, in his terrible physiological distress, prayed to the God of heavens and earth, "Restore to me the joy of your salvation and grant me a willing spirit, to sustain me" (Ps. 51:12). The prescription to restore the human soul is to "pray without ceasing" with no expiration date, maximum potential, unlimited refills, with best prognosis for eternal joy.

Take God's prescriptions with a mega dose of joy. Saturate your environment with prayers and worship in His presence. The Prince of Peace arrives and, in His presence, restores hope, joy, and happiness in your soul. When you pray, your thoughts and mind are changed, hope arises, and you feel peace, joy, and happiness. Healing and restoration spontaneously take place in your soul during your praise-and-worship time due to His anointing that is flowing over you and through you. God releases His power in you during your time of prayer and worship to restore your joy. He is the source of joy. Apart from God, there is no true joy.

The oil of joy will be poured in your heart to restore your soul. He is Jehovah Rohi, God, the Good Shepherd, who anoints your head with the oil of joy. "The LORD *is* my shepherd; I shall not want. He makes me to lie down in green pastures; He leads me beside the still waters. He restores my soul; He leads me in the paths of righteousness For His name's sake. Yea, though I walk through the valley of the shadow of death, I will fear no evil; For You *are* with me; Your rod and Your staff, they comfort me. You prepare a table before me in the presence of my enemies; You anoint my head with oil; My cup runs over. Surely goodness and mercy shall follow me. All the days of my life; And I will dwell in the house of the LORD Forever" (Ps. 23:1–6).

The healing anointing power of the Holy Spirit leads you to the Word of God, the living water, to wash your negative thoughts from your mind that bring bitterness and heavy emotions of a broken heart from sin. Restoration of your soul happens instantaneously, and you fear no evil anymore because Jehovah Rohi is with you even if you walk in the shadow of death to anoint your head with oil of joy. I have seen people going through the shadow of death several times, and those who trusted Jehovah Rohi were rejoicing in the Lord for their salvation even on their deathbed because their soul has been restored and God's goodness and mercy followed them all the days of their life, and their desire was to dwell in the house of the Lord forever. Their eyes were gazing to see Jesus when their spirit departed, and their faces were shining due to the glory of the holy presence in that room where they ended their life.

Humans, created in God's image, must mirror God's character to fulfill the purpose they were created for in the beginning. Pride destroys God's purpose for people's life. Pride takes people captive and makes them lose the purpose they were created for. "But if you will not hear it, My soul will weep in secret for *your* pride; My eyes will weep bitterly And run down with tears, Because the LORD's flock has been taken captive" (Jer. 13:17 NKJV). Pride takes people away from their connection with the Creator and away from His presence. Without God's presence, there is no peace, no true joy, no happiness deep in the soul and spirit that will last forever. "But when his heart was lifted up, and his spirit was hardened in pride, he was deposed from his kingly throne, and they took his glory from him" (Dan. 5:20 NKJV).

You can enjoy life to the fullest only when you follow God's instructions to meditate on things that are praiseworthy. "Finally, brethren, whatever things are true, whatever things *are* noble, whatever things *are* just, whatever things *are* pure, whatever things *are* lovely, whatever things *are* of good report, if *there is* any virtue and if *there is* anything praiseworthy—meditate on these things" (Phil. 4:8 NKJV). Satan makes people offend the Holy Spirit through indecent attitude and angry words that become destructive, stealing joy and peace, leaving them with no love and no godly character. "But know this, that in the last days perilous times will come: For men will be of themselves, lovers of money, boasters, proud, blasphemers, disobedient to parents, unthankful, unholy, unloving, unforgiving, slanderers, without self-control, brutal, despisers of good, traitors, headstrong, haughty, lovers of pleasure rather than lovers of God, having a form of godliness but denying its power. And from such people turn away!" (2 Tim. 3:1–5 NKJV). Humanity without God's love and without Jesus Christ is lost.

◾ Joy Is Contagious

The world is searching for happiness and joy because we were programmed for joy at creation. Humans are hungry and thirsty for joy, but true joy is only in Christ. Many scriptures are addressing the true joy in our life with eternal impact on our physical and spiritual health. Jesus was able to endure the cross because of the eternal joy that saw in His Spirit that the Father would exalt Him above all names and He would sit at the right hand of the Father. "Therefore, since we are surrounded by such a great cloud of witnesses, let us throw off everything that hinders and the sin that so easily entangles. And let us run with perseverance the race marked out for us, fixing our eyes on Jesus, the pioneer and perfecter of faith. For the joy set before him he endured the cross, scorning its shame, and sat down at the right hand of the throne of God" (Heb. 12:1–2 NIV).

The joy for the eternal reward waiting for us will help us endure trials and gain more patience during difficult times in life, considering going through trials a great joy. In James 1:2–3 we are instructed, "Consider it pure joy, my brothers and sisters, whenever you face trials of many kinds, because you know that the testing of your faith produces perseverance" (NIV). God, the Creator of the entire universe, wants to fill your heart with joy that helps you to live a life full of hope through the power of the Holy Spirit, even when we are surrounded by the darkness of this world. "Now may the God of hope fill you with all joy and peace in believing, that you may abound in hope by the power of the Holy Spirit" (Rom. 15:13 NKJV).

The joy that God wants us to have and He is willing to give to each human being is the joy of the harvest. "You have enlarged the nation and increased their joy; they rejoice before you as people rejoice at the harvest, as warriors rejoice when dividing the plunder" (Isa. 9:3 NIV). The harvest that God prepared for us in eternity for the work that we have done brings joy in our soul while we are living on earth. Jesus answers prayers to make us happy and our joy to be full. "Until now you have not asked for anything in my name. Ask and you will receive, and your joy will be complete" (John 16:24 NIV). People who know who their God is are happy and content, counting on His goodness and faithfulness, that He will bless them here on earth and will reward them in heaven, which will bring a greater joy also.

He makes nations happy when they recognize the Creator as their God and Lord. "Blessed is the people of whom this is true;

blessed is the people whose God is the LORD!" (Ps. 144:15 NIV). God's joy and happiness bring global healing emotionally, spiritually, and physically. It is God's prescription for global health. It is the hope of the glory of God that brings joy for those who live in faith in Jesus Christ. "Those who sow in tears Shall reap in joy" (Ps. 126:5 NKJV). God's ultimate goal is to restore people's joy, which He programmed in our DNA from creation, to give people eternal joy. God's heart's desire is that we live a joyful life here on earth and in eternity, after we finish our earthly journey and our work. "His Lord said to him, 'Well *done,* good and faithful servant; you were faithful over a few things, I will make you ruler over many things. Enter into the joy of your Lord'" (Matt. 25:21 NKJV). We were not created for sorrow; we were created for everlasting joy. "And the ransomed of the LORD shall return, And come to Zion with singing, With everlasting joy on their heads. They shall obtain joy and gladness, And sorrow and sighing shall flee away" (Isa. 35:10 NKJV). Through joy we receive strength in our body, soul, and spirit. "Do not sorrow, for the joy of the LORD is your strength" (Neh. 8:10 NKJV).

Our Father in heaven created us for His eternal kingdom, that is joy, peace, and happiness, through the power of the Holy Spirit. "For the kingdom of God is not eating and drinking, but righteousness and peace and joy in the Holy Spirit" (Rom. 14:17 NKJV). True joy is the salvation of our soul. "Whom having not seen you love. Though now you do not see *Him,* yet believing, you rejoice with joy inexpressible and full of glory, receiving the end of your faith—the salvation of *your* souls" (1 Peter 1:8–9 NKJV). Our joy is full when Jesus Christ lives in us. "These things I have spoken to you, that My joy may remain in you, and *that* your joy may be full" (John 15:11 NKJV). That is the reason for the reward mechanism created in our brain, to live a life full of joy in the Lord.

Only in God's presence is there fullness of joy. We were created to live in God's presence forever and to be full of joy, but sin separated humans from its Creator's presence. God is holy and cannot tolerate sin. Sin brought destruction, diseases, pain, and death. By confessing our sin, and through repentance, we can receive salvation by faith in the death and resurrection of the Son of God, and in the blood of the Lamb of God, who was slain to redeem us from our sins. That will bring us back in God's presence, where there is fullness of joy. "You will show me the path of life; In Your presence *is* fullness of joy; At Your right hand *are* pleasures forevermore" (Ps. 16:11 NKJV). He knows our needs for love and joy. That is why He let His only Son die on the cross, to show His eternal love for humanity and to restore the joy of salvation. He wants to fill our hearts with love and joy so we may know Him. He loves us so much that He rejoices over us with singing.

God is our joy. In His presence we experience unspeakable joy. Love brings great joy. Joy is lovable. God promised to power His Spirit in us to accomplish His purpose to live again in His presence full of joy. God is our joy. "Then I will go to the altar of God, To God my exceeding joy; And on the harp I will praise You, O God, my God" (Ps. 43:4 NKJV).

Dr. Caroline Leaf, in her book *Who Switched Off My Brain? Controlling Toxic Thoughts and Emotions*, stated that "many studies show why laughter deserves to be known 'the best medicine.' It releases an instant flood of feel-good chemicals that boost the immune system and almost instantly reduce levels of stress hormones. For example, a really good belly laugh can make cortisol drop by 39% and adrenalin by 70% while the 'feel-good hormone,' endorphin, increases by 29%. It can even make growth hormones skyrocket by 87%! Other research shows how laughter boosts your immune system by increasing immunity levels and disease-fighting cells."[1]

Obedience Brings Joy

Obedience never brings disaster in the family, at work, in the community or the society. Obedience will always get you closer to your family, make you a better employee or a better boss at work, a better neighbor, and a better citizen in society. Walk in obedience. Obedience brings peace, joy, and happiness in any family. When in a family a godly wife submits to her husband, you please Jesus with your obedience. Same thing with the godly man obeying Christ to love his wife as He, Christ, loved the church and gave Himself for her, bringing joy to his wife and his children and those around him. When you compromise, you determine the loos of spiritual influence in your family and in society. When we lose influence, it's tough. There is no power in your word when you live a life of compromise. Many families are destroyed because one of the spouses compromises and does not obey God's voice.

Often, when you forget that request of obedience and disobey God's Word and lose your joy, peace, and happiness, leading to worries, anxiety, and depression, your physical and spiritual health is affected. True obedience brings true joy in our heart. We need to invest in our joy by obeying God's instructions and prescriptions for joy. Jesus sacrificed with joy His own life, obeying the Father to leave heaven's splendors and the glory He had from the Father to come on this planet in a very humbled way and die on the cross to save us, to bring us back in relationship with the Father, to forgive our sins and fill us with the Holy Spirit so we will not be orphans in the world. Without Jesus, this planet will be orphaned. Jesus said, "I will not leave you orphans; I will come to you" (John 14:18 NKJV).

Obedience fulfills God's plan in your life and brings satisfaction and fulfillment. God approaches you in your loneliness to speak to you. Moses was alone on the mountain, and God came to him in an unusual way to speak to him. God can meet you on "the mountain where are burning bushes" to get your attention. God will highlight situations for you so you can go to Him to listen to His advice.

Obeying God's Word was my first priority since I received Jesus in my heart at a very young age. During high school in a Communist country where you could not have religious material or a Bible, I did read the New Testament in secret places about five times. I memorized key verses from the Bible so I could repeat them frequently when attacked by the enemy, to increase my faith and hope. They gave me joy deep in my soul and strength. God's Word became part of my chemistry from a very young age. I loved the Word of God, which gave me so much joy, peace, and satisfactions, and I still love God's Word today with the same passion. It is my spiritual food, my "daily bread," which feeds my soul and my "living water," which has

quenched my thirst since I was very young (I started at about thir-
teen years old).

Unspeakable Joy in His Presence

The joy of the Lord connects you with heaven. Joy is contagious. Joy brings revival. I asked God in prayer to let me feel the Holy
Spirit's joy. He will come during my prayer and let me feel Him as
electricity passing through my body, an intense love, and my eyes fill
quickly with tears of joy that cannot be described, an overwhelming
joy, and everything in my heart melts.

The joy of the Lord is our strength. We get stronger when we
rejoice in the Lord. His joy gets deep in our heart and changes everything, making the neuropeptides responsible for our emotions flow
in the most efficient amount to displace bitterness, discouragement,
fear, depression, and anxiety, which lead us to grieve. Nehemiah said,
"Go and enjoy choice food and sweet drinks, and send some to those
who have nothing prepared. This day is holy to our Lord. Do not
grieve, for the joy of the LORD is your strength" (Neh. 8:10 NIV).

When you rejoice in the Lord, you become stronger in your
spirit, soul, and body. Joy makes dopamine, serotonin, oxytocin, and
other neurochemicals be released in your body, making you healthier
and stronger. Pray for the joy of the Lord to flood your heart. Joy is
the antidote for sadness and depression. Also, pray for vision in your
life to love. Love intercedes for those unlovable. Love is the antidote
for hate. Through love, oxytocin, serotonin, endorphins, and other
neurochemicals are released to elevate your feelings and be able to
rejoice and to get stronger. We cannot do anything without God.
When you are unthankful, you lose joy, peace, and happiness.

Lifting the name of the Lord higher, you enter in His presence
through praises and His presence. "For You have made him most
blessed forever; You have made him exceedingly glad with Your presence" (Ps. 21:6 NKJV). By His presence we know that God is drawing
us near to Him. David was praising God in the valley and gained
strength to kill the giant Goliath, God's enemy. Praising is the key to

be victorious when you face the giant, the enemy of your soul. The enemy brings thoughts of fear, worries, discouragement, uncertainty, rejection, and insecurity. We get entangled in our daily worries and lose our focus on spiritual joy and love and His presence. By sleeping spiritually, we are missing things from God. The devil comes disguised to distract us every moment to steal our true joy.

Joy in Prosperity

Before we enjoyed prosperity, we enjoyed giving to the poor, helping the needy, volunteering in community, extended hours, for about thirty years. Before we arrived in the USA, we did the same in Bucharest. Visitors were coming to Bucharest from poor villages that did not have money to stay in hotel, and we let them stay and eat in our house for free. Since childhood, I enjoyed helping others and sharing what I had. Prosperity brings joy when it's obtained in God's way, little by little. "Wealth *gained by* dishonesty will be diminished, But he who gathers by labor will increase" (Prov. 13:11 NKJV). Prosperity is a process, as God promised in His Word. The curse of poverty and insufficiency brings depression, oppression, and sadness in people's heart. Prosperity is a promise of God, who gave us authority and power to gain wealth. It starts in your heart. There is code in God's living Word to access prosperity.

You need to know the Word to know the code to enter in God's blessings. Obeying God's instructions by tithing, giving, serving others, sowing in good soil, investing in the kingdom of God is the code to access prosperity and to enter God's blessings. Take the Word of God as an instrument for your achievements. Use God's resources to fulfill God's will. We must work hard in order to prosper. We need to get revelation from the Word. Lack of knowledge as in any profession makes you wonder and accomplishes nothing. You experience joy in prosperity by walking in the will of God, where there is abundance, happiness, peace, and hope to overcome depression, lack, anxiety, worries, debts, and fear. When we obeyed, God flooded us with His blessings. His promises were fulfilled in our life. God is generous to make you the head and not the tail, above and not beneath, to bless the work of your hands (Deut. 28:1–14).

We enjoyed God's blessings since we applied God's principles in our business. We did work hard, but all the blessings came from God beyond our imagination. We never stopped helping others, blessing the needy, serving in community, helping the poor here and afar. We invested in the kingdom of God, and God opened the gates of heaven and poured out His blessings over us in unimaginable ways. Seek the kingdom of God first, and everything else will come, beyond what you can ask or imagine. Chase the kingdom, not the prosperity, then the prosperity will come, so you can have the needed resources to reach the lost in the nations. "Those who sow in tears shall reap in joy. He who continually goes forth weeping, Bearing seed for sowing, Shall doubtless come again with rejoicing, Bringing his sheaves *with him*" (Ps. 126:5–6 NKJV).

Curses will hinder the feelings of joy and happiness through an avalanche of worries and fears. The curses from sin and emotions from fear and anxiety passed from Adam and Eve to all generation through epigenetic mechanism. It is an influence that affects all parts of your life until you stop those curses. Adam and Eve had abundance in the garden but needed to work the garden, and God did His part, what Adam and Eve couldn't do. When you partner with God, He breaks the curses and transforms your wilderness in paradise.

He is the one who gives people ideas on how to work and implement their thoughts, using their hands for things to happen. When I started my business to take care of elderly in my own house, I felt like in dryland, with no water, because I did not speak English very well and could not move too far except looking for God's favor over my life to meet nice people who would understand my accent and would have patience with my English. I worked hard to prove myself as a hard worker, doing extra work for less money in order to get favor with people. God showed His glory in my wilderness and blessed what I was doing. It is God's idea to bless people with wisdom, inspiration, new ideas for invention, innovation to create beautiful, necessary things. We can see that the earth is filled with God's glory.

▪ Losing Joy Is Losing Health

Disobedience causes people to lose joy. God does not bless disobedience. They do not follow God's principles. Self-infliction happens because of disobedience. The devil is sowing curses so people can feel their emotions as bitterness from unforgiveness, sadness, irritation, anger, judgment, discontent, hate, etc., stealing and killing the feelings of joy, peace, happiness, contentment, and thanksgiving. Those negative feelings, with no hope and no goals to accomplish and no motivation, affect the amygdala's response and activation in the limbic system. "Recent research and theory has highlighted the dynamic nature of amygdala activation. Rather than simply being sensitive to a few limited stimulus categories, amygdala activation appears to be dependent on the goals of the perceiver. In this study, we extend this line of work by demonstrating that the means by which a person seeks to accomplish a goal also modulates the amygdala response."[2]

We must be intentional about our actions and set goals for good seeds (God's promises are the catalyst for hope and motivation for accomplishments to live an abundant life in Christ) for our brain for a positive activation of our limbic system in the brain. The seed we sow in our brain will bring a blessed harvest of pleasant emotional feelings of joy, peace, happiness, and all the characteristics of the fruit of the Holy Spirit, who come with supernatural power to touch our brain cortex, to make the good seeds bring such feelings. To be filled with true joy to activate the reward system, to increase dopamine level. In order to have joy, we need to sow seeds of joy. Joy is one of the characteristics of the fruit of the Spirit and is manifested as harvest after the Word is sown in your hearts and mind. "A cheerful heart is good medicine, but a crushed spirit dries up the bones" (Prov. 17:22. NIV).

When you follow this prescription every day of your life, you will promote a healthy body, soul, and spirit and prevent spiritual and physical diseases. Joy will give you strength in the body by releasing dopamine, which makes you feel good, move faster, accomplish tasks, and keep you healthy and happy. I cannot emphasize enough the instructions that Nehemiah gave to his people. "Do not sorrow, for the joy of the LORD is your strength" (Neh. 8:10 NKJV). Joy, peace, and happiness are emotions felt in our hearts as a result of the seed from the Word. God is the sower, and His Word is the seed for our thoughts and mind to activate the reward system to bring a rich harvest of emotions of love, joy, peace, gladness, pleasing to us and to others.

"When I am afraid, I put my trust in you" (Ps. 56:3 NIV). The problem becomes bigger when you focus on the problem. In order not to lose joy and health, you need to change your focus when you face temptation to disobey. "No temptation has overtaken you except what is common to mankind. And God is faithful; he will not let you be tempted beyond what you can bear. But when you are tempted, he will also provide a way out so that you can endure it" (1 Cor. 10:13 NIV).

False Joy Defects the Stop System

People, in their emptiness from being lonely and depressed, seek solutions in wrong places to satisfy their emotional needs and comfort for their soul. Often, people have a hunger inside of them, and instead of seeking the true source of joy, they turn in the wrong direction for drugs, alcohol, smoke, outside-marriage sex, and other unsafe behaviors.

George F. Koob, PhD, director of the National Institute on Alcohol Abuse and Alcoholism (National Institutes of Health) stated that the illicit drugs such as methamphetamine increase dopamine about 400 percent, an excessive activation of the pleasure system, abnormally activating the reward system, damaging its functions. Other examples are nicotine, marijuana, and alcohol, which activate all systems of addictions, making one feel high on drugs, leading to compulsive eating or overeating when anxious and depressed for the reward, motivation, craving, leading to bad addiction.[3]

God put a "stop system" in our brain for bad behavior, but those bad actions cause the "stop system" to be defected. In addictions, the "stop system" is impaired and the person is vulnerable and impulsive. The decision-making capacity is decreased in the frontal cortex, causing impaired executive functions, leading to an inability to communicate with other brain structures to keep the whole being in balance. Addiction withdrawal activates the brain's stress system. Compulsion increases for bad habits craving due to the abnormality of the reward system function, and those people feel the anticipation of the craving state and will pay back later with dopamine deficiencies, depletion of the reward mechanism. Every day, life needs about 20 percent of dopamine to help move in the morning. We are instructed in 2 Timothy 2:22 to "flee the evil desires of youth and pursue righteousness, faith, love and peace, along with those who call on the Lord out of a pure heart" (NIV). We have the willpower "to flee" the desires of evil even from a young age to protect our reward system mechanism from being damaged.

Our willpower is a built-in feature in our DNA to overcome evil desires and sins, which bring death. "But each one is tempted when he is drawn away by his own desires and enticed. Then, when desire has conceived, it gives birth to sin; and sin, when it is full-grown, brings forth death" (James 1:14–15 NKJV). Death is birthed in sin. Without the Word of God, the internal negative things are "impossible to change." Teenagers are vulnerable to anxiety and depression due to the emptiness inside of them and feel lonely even though they spend time on social media or frequently attend different parties. They may go through stressful situation as losing control, negative rumination, exaggeration, anticipating negative effects, lacking true joy.

The Joy to Bless Others

I always wanted to help others. It was something inside of me that prompted me to have a heart full of compassion and be a friend to the friendless around me. For example, years ago in Bucharest, in the Academy of Economic Science, I had a student friend with poliomyelitis. Her walking was very difficult, and she was extremely slow and always behind. I felt her loneliness deep in my heart and started to walk with her at her own difficult pace even though I had to slow down, feeling like I was falling far behind with all my tasks of the day. I felt in my heart the need to help her carry heavy books and things that she needed for the day to the bus station or subways. She carried a heavy purse and two heavy bags for the entire day at work and school; due to her walking problems, she could not go home and change her purse and bags. During that time, you could not have carry-on luggage on wheels. You had to carry everything with your hands, back, and shoulders, making it extremely difficult for a disabled person.

We became close friends, and I was visiting her at home and helped her there too with different things to the point that I painted her rooms, staying late even until 11:00 p.m. My reward was the joy that I got, and the blessings of helping her were overwhelming. That joy healed my soul, spirit, and body in my own struggles at a very young age.

There is power to heal in the joy that you get from the Spirit of God in your soul by helping others. God loves a cheerful giver and opens doors of opportunity that bring more joy. To my amazement, later on, after many years, when I applied for visa to come to the States, this friend of mine with disability introduced me to the person who was in charge with processing information and documentation for visas to the USA. At that time in Romania, it was a big deal to know someone in that department during the Communist regime. If you didn't know somebody, you were nobody. I was astonished with how God orchestrated everything from the beginning of our friendship long before I was even thinking about traveling abroad, when that was impossible in a Communist country. But besides the reward we get on this planet, a great reward awaits for us in heaven. "And behold, I am coming quickly, and My reward *is* with Me, to give to every one according to his work" (Rev. 22:12 NKJV).

Programmed for Love

The Origin of Agape Love

God's heart is the origin of agape love, a love that "suffers long *and* is kind; love does not envy; love does not parade itself, is not puffed up; does not behave rudely, does not seek its own, is not provoked, thinks no evil; does not rejoice in iniquity, but rejoices in the truth; bears all things, believes all things, hopes all things, endures all things. Love never fails" (Cor. 13:4–8 NKJV). He poured out His love in humanity so we can pour out in others. We can love others the way we are loved by God when His love flows through our heart. Our heart must be opened to the love of God at all times. God expresses His love through His people on this planet. He empowered His believers through the power of the Holy Spirit to love and bring joy to others. Men are created to be vessels of God, through whom His love must flow toward others. Through the power of the Holy Spirit, God empowers believers to let God's love flow toward humanity with His supernatural love. The divine love of God opens our spiritual eyes to see through God's eyes. God's love is measurable and has physical manifestations in human soul, spirit, and body.

God demonstrated His supernatural love through Jesus, His prophets, and His disciples. They also demonstrated their love.

Love is not a word only; it is an action, and it must be demonstrated through our attitude and deeds. People around you can feel your love in their heart. Their attitude and body language will change instantly at an act or deed of love. The brain will release oxytocin, serotonin, dopamine, and other neurochemicals and will bring healing and restoration to yourself and those around you. Love brings healing. The world we live in is desperate for emotional and physical healing and restoration. The world is desperate for love.

God poured out His love in humans' heart by the Holy Spirit. Love is real, because the Holy Spirit is real. Where there is no love, there is nothing. Can you imagine a world with no love? Rejection takes love's place. Rejection is from Satan. Only the Holy Spirit changes a person's character and helps to possess its fruit and to demonstrate the characteristics of the fruit of the Spirit. God's Spirit demonstrates in man the characteristics of the fruit of the Spirit that a holy person desires continuously to be led in truth by an exceeding joy in God. The psalmist prayed just for that. "Oh, send out Your light and Your truth! Let them lead me; Let them bring me to Your holy hill And to Your tabernacle. Then I will go to the altar of God, To God my exceeding joy; And on the harp I will praise You, O God, my God" (Ps. 43:3–4 NKJV).

Programmed for the Purpose to Love

God inscribed his love in our DNA of our heart since creation. God's purpose for His creation was eternal love. "And now abide faith, hope, love, these three; but the greatest of these *is* love" (1 Cor. 13:13 NKJV). He poured out His love in our heart and the joy of salvation to reprogram our reward system to seek His love, which brings eternal joy. You must fight to keep your mind and thoughts focused on the true and great love and its rewards in heaven. You must fix your eyes on Jesus Christ, who is our eternal love, which brings a great reward.

It is through our heart and its pathways, through the autonomic nervous system, and through the power of the Holy Spirit that we develop attachment to our Father in heaven, who bestows His everlasting love over us through His Son, Jesus Christ. "See how great a love the Father has bestowed on us, that we would be called children of God; and *such* we are. For this reason the world does not know us, because it did not know Him. Beloved, now we are children of God, and it has not appeared as yet what we will be. We know that when

He appears, we will be like Him, because we will see Him just as He is. And everyone who has this hope *fixed* on Him purifies himself, just as He is pure" (1 John 3:1–3 NASB). Fixing our eyes on Jesus will keep a balanced communication through electrical impulses and neurochemicals between the heart and the brain, through the sympathetic and parasympathetic pathways, and the hope in the great love of the Father will bring unspeakable joy and happiness. He created the heart and brain pathways so we can think with our brain and feel with our heart.

The law is not needed when you possess the characteristics of the fruit of the spirit and live full of God's love, walking in the Spirit. He put His love in people's heart. He built in every human's cell features and the capability to love with Eros love, a unique love that develops desire and longing for pleasure in a man and a woman; to love with Philos, to love one another, developing a common interest, friendship, healthy and godly relationship; to love with agape love, which God showed to the world through the most needed blood of Jesus. Agape love never fails. God's way of love is beyond our way. God's love is supernatural, just as the Holy Spirit is supernatural. Love is one of the characteristics of the fruit of the Spirit that will last in eternity. God is Spirit. God is love. Humans were created through love, by love, and for love.

Wired for Love

All circuits in the brain were created for emotions of love. Because God is love, love casts out fear. "There is no fear in love; but perfect love casts out fear, because fear involves torment. But he who fears has not been made perfect in love. We love Him because He first loved us" (1 John 4:18–20 NKJV). In love there is no fear. God is love, and He created humans in His image, with the brain wired to feel the emotions of the love of God and to love those around us. We were created in love for love. He created us so we can create. Everything is created on earth from invisible things based on God's divine inspiration of fruitfulness, and multiplication happens through God's control and direction, through emotions of love programmed in the human DNA. Everything on this planet is the fruit of God's inspiration and His power invested by the Creator in man to create as the Creator placed the prescription in man's seed (the human DNA) and thoughts to create, and He gave the order for multiplication.

When you know who God is in your life, the thoughts of fear in your brain will be replaced with thoughts of love and the emotions attached to it. Love casts out fear because fear damages the brain and the body. The Spirit of God, through His divine love, will restore your brain structures. Love can reprogram your brain to create new neurons through emotions of love. Coming from a Communist country, I often think how Communists insulted the God of love, the Most High God, stating there is no God and creating so much confusion in people's mind, as the Bible says that "the fool hath said in his heart, There is no God. They are corrupt, they have done abominable works, there is none that doeth good. The LORD looked down from heaven upon the children of men, to see if there were any that did understand, and seek God" (Ps. 14:1–2 KJV). If there is no God, there is no love. Where there is no love, there is nothing.

My heart and mind were bombarded with the Communists' insults regarding my faith in God, the Creator of the universe, but the Holy Spirit enveloped my spirit and instilled in my spirit unshakable faith that changed my thinking, and emotions of love flooded my soul in the face of my adversary. He made me a new creation and transformed my life completely. His love overwhelmed me. He rewired my brain and changed my brain's structure, changed my personality, my character, my attitude, my behavior. I behaved differently, showing great love toward those around me even though they mocked me constantly. After I was baptized with the Holy Spirit, I felt like "flying," and I did not feel the burden from the Communists anymore. I had the burden of Christ, which was very easy. He was carrying my heavy burden for me.

My colleagues at school and dormitory noticed the radical changes in me and asked me questions about what happened to me. I couldn't hold it even though I knew that the persecution happened.

My cup was overflowing from the anointing of the Holy Spirit. Rivers of living water started to flow. I got to share with them from my experience with God's love and power, which changed my life. They were amazed because they did see the change in me since the last time they did see me before our vacation. They wanted the same power with unspeakable joy and the peace that passes all understanding. They wanted to have the same experience that I shared with them about God's supernatural power.

When you know God, indeed you get rid of all bitterness, anger, madness, discouragement, deceit, lies, deception, shame, unforgiveness, worries, fear, anxiety, depression, emotional pain, rejection, loneliness, and insecurity. You can control those signs and symptoms by redirecting your thoughts. You can bring them out from your unconscious memory to destabilize them and replace them with God's promises in His Word. Hope will rise inside of you, and instantly you can feel the emotions of joy, love, peace, and forgiveness instead, like a supernatural therapy. That is because only Jesus is the center of your joy. When Jesus comes in your heart, He takes control of your emotions. The love of Jesus will overwhelm you and will lead you. He never stopped to show His love to others. God created us with mirror neurons to mirror God's character so we are able to feel people's emotions. His love activates your mirror neurons to feel people's emotional pain and to comfort them with the comfort we have been comforted with. He knows and sees our struggles and feels our emotional pain because He has compassion. He fights the battle for us.

New York Times best seller Lisa Bevere, in her book *Without Rival, Embrace Your Identity and an Age of Confusion and Comparison,* stated that "God uniquely created your DNA and knit your frame in secret so he could surprise the world. He authored how your heart expresses itself; he was the architect of your smile, and the melody of your voice; he made all your features with thoughts of only you in mind. He celebrated along with your parents your first smile and watched with affection your first steps."[1]

◾ Heart-Brain Pathways for Emotions

Heart-brain pathways are involved in our emotions and are affected by our thoughts. Dr. Emilia Arden, cardiologist, at a Christian medical conference, talked about the heart-brain pathway and stated that "a thought, image, sound can generate emotions, will generate chemical reaction, and will generate symptoms" in the heart and entire body.[2]

God made the heart-brain pathways possible through the sympathetic and parasympathetic system connecting the heart and brain (parasympathetic pathway: cardioinhibitory centers, vagal nucleus, medulla oblongata, parasympathetic preganglionic fibers, synapses in cardiac plexus, parasympathetic postganglionic fibers; sympathetic pathway: cardio acceleratory center, spinal cord, sympathetic preganglionic fiber, sympathetic ganglia, sympathetic postganglionic fiber, and cardiac nerve).[3]

"There are at least 40,000 neurons (nerve cells) in the heart—as many as are found in various parts of the brain. In effect, the brain in your heart acts like a checking station for all the emotions generated by the flow of chemicals created by thoughts. It is proving to be a real intelligent force behind the intuitive thoughts and feelings you experience. The heart also produces an important biochemical substance called an atrial peptide (specifically ANF). It is the balance hormone that regulates many of your brain's functions and stimulates behavior. New scientific evidence on the heart's neurological sensitivity indicates there are lines of communication between the brain and the heart that check the accuracy and integrity of your thought life."[4]

The heart-brain pathways were created by God for all humans to feel His love and the love from one another. God programmed our brain from creation to release oxytocin, a neuropeptide hormone, to feel the love with the heart and to solve psychological and physical problems. God gave humankind wisdom even from in their mother's womb to be able to connect with our heavenly Father, to be faithful in all our ways. "Yet you desired faithfulness even in the womb; you taught me wisdom in that secret place" (Ps. 51:6). God desires faithfulness that endows humans with capabilities to become optimistic and to overcome fear through this neuropeptide released by the pituitary gland in our bloodstream. It helps in building trust, healing broken relationship, helping people to love one another, to overcome anxiety and depression, and to manage stress, feeling empathy for others, and becoming more generous. Oxytocin is the hormone that makes us human. This "love molecule" brings people together and helps husband and wife as family to develop trust, intimacy, and attachment.

It helps with childbirth, mother-baby bonding, trust, and attachments also. But it is our responsibility to guard our heart from deceitful things and its wickedness. "The heart *is* deceitful above all *things,* And desperately wicked; Who can know it?" (Jer. 17:9 NKJV). In His love, God promised that He will never forget us like a mother who is attached to her child through this "love neuropeptide." In Isaiah 49:15, we read, "Can a mother forget the baby at her breast and have no compassion on the child she has borne? Though she may forget, I will not forget you!" (Isa. 49:15 NIV). The father-children bonding in love is even greater than the mother-baby bonding. God is a good Father, with great love for His creation.

Scientists discovered that "oxytocin is involved in fostering emotions such as trust and love. The hormone is produced only in the brain and is released into the bloodstream by the pituitary gland. Until now it was not known why these oxytocin-producing neurons are linked to the brainstem and spinal cord. Researchers at the Max Planck Institute for Medical Research in Heidelberg have now discovered a small population of neurons that coordinate the release of oxytocin into the blood and also stimulate cells in the spinal cord. Stimulation of these cells increases oxytocin levels in the body and also has a pain-relieving effect."[5] When you feel the love of God, emotional and physical pain will go away. The love of God is superior to every emotion and pain.

When we are connected to our Father in heaven and feel His love, the brain produces oxytocin, which restores the body, soul, and spirit, and tridimensional healing happens. People around us are in desperation for tridimensional restoration. I have seen in my profession people with multiple chronic conditions, including different psychological distress manifested by irritation, yelling, screaming, crying, restlessness, agitation, anger, violence, in a great need for love, joy, peace, and tridimensional restoration and emotional healing. During my education, I took mental health classes to provide care to a patient population with neurocognitive disorders and behavioral disturbance, and I discovered deep in my heart that these conditions will respond very well to medications for the physical body, love for emotions/soul, and prayers for the spirit.

After almost thirty years spent in providing care for people with multiple chronic conditions, including neurocognitive disorders such as dementia with behavioral disturbance, I arrived at the same conclusion that medications, love, and prayers are needed for the best results in managing challenging behavior and for comfort and tridimensional healing. Tridimensional healing needs nonpharmacological and pharmacological interventions (medication, love, and prayer), "the best of medicine and the best of Christ," as Dr. Crandall, cardiologist, stated in his book *Raising the Dead*, that "[his] medical practice is now based on providing [his] patients with 'the best of medicine and the best of Jesus.' This can bring astounding results, and I've seen miracle after miracle occur in the lives of my patients. We start as simply as possible, though, because aiding God's healing in a person's life is not about testing God to see whether God will amaze and delight us with supernatural fireworks. God created us in His image so that we could reason our way to many solutions—as modern medicine shows so well. God expects us to employ all the knowledge that has come through His gifts of reason and imagination to bring about the healing we know He desires. At the same time, not to understand the spiritual nature of people causes purely secular medicine to miss many opportunities for healing. I would even say that sometimes God grants me spiritual insight as an uncanny diagnostic tool. Although I'm sure some of my colleagues find the way I pray with patients and address their spiritual ills as well as their physical maladies peculiar, I think recognizing the spiritual dimension of people makes me a much better doctor."[6]

It is extremely important to not ignore the signals, the signs and symptoms, of physical and spiritual diseases. Ignorance leads to ruins and destructions. Ignoring ungodly emotions will grow and will cause trouble as bitterness and discouragement, which are poisonous to the body, by suppressing our love and joy, decreasing dopamine, oxytocin, serotonin, endorphin, and other neurochemicals and hormones, leading to depression and further depleting the body from the healthy neurochemicals very important for homeostasis and physical and spiritual health. "Pursue peace with all *people,* and holiness, without which no one will see the Lord: looking carefully lest anyone fall short of the grace of God; lest any root of bitterness springing up cause trouble, and by this many become defiled" (Heb. 12:14–15 NKJV).

It is similar as physically ignoring high blood pressure, high blood sugar, and high cholesterol level, increased weight, unhealthy diet, then the body gives us signals of deterioration in the circulatory system, developing arteriosclerosis, coronary artery diseases, and pretty soon experiencing more deterioration, leading to multiple chronic illnesses, leading to heart attack and stroke and premature death.

The Need for Love at Any Age

Because God is love, we can love. Sin separates us from God, from love. Love is our lifestyle in every environment we spend our time in. Every moment of our life, we are assigned by the Creator to fellowship in His love. God expresses His love through us when we love one another. That is our "commercial advertising for the Lord" in the world. This is how we advertise that Jesus loves the world, and the world will know that we are His disciples when we love with the love He loved us. God wants to advertise His love to the world through your love. We are to display His love to the world around us ("This is how they will know that you follow Me, when you love one another"). "By this all will know that you are My disciples, if you have love for one another" (John 13:35 NKJV). God demonstrated His love. "But God demonstrates His own love toward us, in that while we were still sinners, Christ died for us" (Rom. 5:8 NKJV). Jesus loves you so much. He is desperate for you, and you are overwhelmed with His love. If there is *no* love, there is nothing. No love, no God. We must be the same to Him.

Love is beyond our emotions, as faith is beyond your intellect. Faith will resolve all problems. Anxiety, worries, wrong thoughts, and fear are felt due to the neurochemical reactions, neurotransmitters, and hormonal changes that were programmed by God at creation to be released to fight and preserve life. The devil creates situations to get you in the position of increased emotions of fear and oversolicitation of the brain structures and the body to release unhealthy amount of neurochemicals in your body to poison your soul and spirit. God knows your problems maximize your joy. Emotions have feelings due to neurochemical reactions in the body.

In the entire world, no physical surgery can be done to remove negative thoughts and negative emotions.

The Word of God is the mirror for your Spirit. The Holy Spirit, the resurrection power of Jesus Christ, works in our soul and mind, to heal, to restore, to give wisdom and power to transform the mind, changing our thinking, and to save our soul and spirit. The Word of God has the power to transform life through faith. Faith activates the Word. God's Word has an aroma that brings life, success, and wisdom. Listen to the Word; hear the Word. Faith comes by hearing the Word of God. Hearing the Word of God increases your faith. Feed your soul and spirit on the Word of God daily as you feed your body daily with food. Your soul and spirit need spiritual food and spiritual nutrients daily as your body needs nutrients daily to live. You also need to drink from the living water to water your brain and your neurons with healthy thoughts from God's promises, which bring hope. Explore the Word daily, meditate day and night, and apply the Word to your every situation and each circumstance in life.

The First Love

The world's circumstances deprived its inhabitants of the true joy and happiness because the first love for Christ is lost, causing spiritual darkness and sickness in every community, city, at the national and global level. Modern technology leads to isolation—lonely time spent on the internet, TV, social media—and the lack of individual prayer, lack of true repentance, leads to spiritual negligence. People's thoughts are influenced by what the media presents and their agenda, making people lack true fellowship. Many people seek love in wrong places and are deceived, being deprived emotionally and physically of true love. The first love for Christ is lost, and the interest to help others is lost. There is no desire for saving the soul from eternal death. The best values from older generations are lost, and the quality of the fruit of the spirit is seen less and less.

People lost their first love for the Word of God and for His work. In Revelation 2:2–5, we read that to turn back to the first love is mandatory for those who received Christ as their Lord and Savior. "I know your works, your labor, your patience, and that you cannot bear those who are evil. And you have tested those who say they are apostles and are not, and have found them liars; and you have persevered and have patience, and have labored for My name's sake and have not become weary. Nevertheless I have *this* against you, that you have left your first love. Remember therefore from where you have fallen; repent and do the first works, or else I will come to you quickly and remove your lampstand from its place—unless you repent" (Rev. 2:2–5 NKJV). Repentance is imperative to return to the first love for Jesus in order to find true love, peace, joy, and happiness. They are essential for people to connect with one another to create a stable mental state, freedom in the spirit. That is obtained only through the Holy Spirit in relationship with Jesus's followers.

Science confirms that joy and happiness are associated with connections, creating a stable mental state, freedom, and self-control, stating that "attributes of joy describe a spontaneous, sudden and transient concept associated with connection, awareness, and freedom. Attributes of happiness describe a pursued, long-lasting, stable mental state associated with virtue and self-control."[7]

Everybody can remember the power and the purity of the first love physically and emotionally in life, filled with strong emotions of clean thoughts. That is a mirror and a reflection of our first pure love spiritually for our God and our Lord Jesus Christ that must burn deep inside every heart and mind because He first loved us with unconditional love limitlessly.

Leif Hetland, in his book *Transformed by Love*, stated that "God's love is an unrelenting force, an unyielding and unending river of pure goodness that does not grow tired and does not grow weak. It is not a placid lake that waits calmly only for those willing to seek out its shimmering shores. God's love moves throughout the Earth, seeking any and all methods of entry into every heart, open or shut. It is not a limited resource, doled out conservatively so that each may have their fair share. It is without limit and without end. He is really to pour it all out on anyone and everyone, and there is nothing that can stand against it."[8]

Hypothalamus: The Natural Pharmacy Manager

The Biggest Natural Pharmacy Manager Is in Your Body

The hypothalamus in our brain, besides regulating thirst, hunger, and sleep, sensing those needs of the body, regularly coordinates the biggest natural pharmacy in the body. The hypothalamus is known as the gland that supervises and directs the fabric of natural chemicals and where the production of chemical starts to your emotional responses, and neurochemicals (neuropeptides) are created by small sequences of amino acids, named peptides, responsible for the emotions in our body.

According to John Hagelin, physics professor and director of the Institute for Science, Technology, and Public Politics of the University of Maharishi, dedicated to the development of theories of unified quantum field, "there's chemistry for anger, for happiness, for suffering, envy..."[1]

You have your own chemical factory in your body that produces chemicals based on the quality of your thoughts and the memories activated by those thoughts. The emotions attached to your thoughts determine the chemistry and neuropeptides in our brain structures that flow through the bloodstream, determining the feelings in your body. Nobody has access to your thoughts but you. The most sophisticated technology cannot see your thoughts. But it can see the electrical impulses and signals representing your thoughts, decodified by the brain. Emotions interact with your thoughts. Your emotions

131

trigger the release of the neuropeptides in our bloodstream, affecting every cell's structure in your body and your feelings. Your thoughts trigger more emotions, positively or negatively.

Dr. Candance Pert, holder of patents about modified peptides and professor at the University of Medicine in Georgetown, explains it this way: "Each cell is a little home of consciousness. When a neuropeptide enters a cell this equals a discharge of biochemical which may modify the nucleus of the cell."[2]

"Our brain creates these neuropeptides and our cells get used to 'receive' each one of the emotions: anger, anguish, happiness, envy, generosity, pessimism, optimism… Once we get used to them, thought habits are created. Through the millions of synaptic endings, our brain is constantly recreating itself; one thought or emotion creates a new connection, which is reinforced whenever we think or feel 'something' repeatedly. The more those thoughts and emotions are repeated or reinforced, the stronger the connections in the brain will become positively or negatively."[3]

Damaging thoughts of fear, bitterness, unforgiveness, anger, unhappiness, rejection, uncertainty, and resentment are inserted in our cells through neuropeptides created by our brain due to our negative thoughts caused by lack of faith and disbelief, even at unconscious level, changing our personality. Our thoughts dictate our emotions and chemistry and who we are as a person. People are seeking wrong solutions, running drugs, alcohol, dangerous sex, pornography, gambling, internet frauds, etc., to replace fearful thoughts, leading to self-destruction and losing the purpose in life that they were created for.

The Word of God speaks about this wrong attitude that leads to evil practice, stating, "But if you harbor bitter envy and selfish ambition in your hearts, do not boast about it or deny the truth. Such 'wisdom' does not come down from heaven but is earthly, unspiritual, and demonic. For where you have envy and selfish ambition, there you find disorder and every evil practice" (James 3:14–16).

Through emotions of love, joy, peace, and happiness, as the characteristics of the fruit of the Spirit, we can replace those damaging thoughts and restore our brain cells, creating healthy, strong connections in the brain for great, positive attitude through great faith and good practice for the restoration to take place. Science demonstrated that "in state of meditation, our brain is constantly restoring itself, even in old age. For that reason, it can unlearn and relearn new ways of living the emotions."[4]

Instructions from the Lord builds hope in our soul and mind even at unconscious levels during the night. The psalmist stated, "I will praise the LORD, who counsels me; even at night my heart instructs me" (Ps. 16:7). We have God's prescription written approximately 3,400 years ago about meditation at the Word of God, which is life for us, creating a new mind and restored brain cells to give us success and be prosperous. With a renewed mind and restored soul, we make the best decisions through clear thoughts, possible through a transformed mind when we meditate day and night with God's promises. "Keep this Book of the Law always on your lips; meditate on it day and night, so that you may be careful to do everything written in it. Then you will be prosperous and successful" (Josh. 1:8 NIV).

Our deep perception of life is changed when we meditate at God's instruction for life and we receive wisdom from above that is full of a good fruit, as is written in James 3:17–18. "But the wisdom that comes from heaven is first of all pure; then peace-loving, considerate, submissive, full of mercy and good fruit, impartial and sincere. Peacemakers who sow in peace reap a harvest of righteousness" (NIV). The reward system is activated in our brain, and the characteristics of the fruit of the Spirit are manifested, reaping their harvest.

Thirsty Center in Hypothalamus

The biological sensation of thirst is created by the hypothalamus when it receives signals of high plasma concentration from osmoreceptors. "An osmoreceptor is a sensory receptor that detects changes in osmotic pressure and is primarily found in the hypothalamus of most homeothermic organisms. Osmoreceptors detect changes in plasma osmolarity (that is, the concentration of solutes dissolved in the blood). When the osmolarity of blood changes (it is more or less dilute), water diffusion into and out of the osmoreceptor cells changes. That is, the cells expand when the blood plasma is more dilute and contract with a higher concentration. When the osmoreceptors detect high plasma osmolarity (often a sign of a low blood volume), they send signals to the hypothalamus, which creates the biological sensation of thirst. Osmoreceptors also stimulate vasopressin (ADH) secretion, which starts the events that will reduce plasma osmolarity to normal levels."[5] (The hypothalamus is located in the brain close to the thalamus, infundibulum, anterior pituitary, and posterior pituitary.)[6]

Spiritually, the same way, you feel the spiritual thirst in your soul when an emotional feeling of emptiness from spiritual pressure rises from "dryness" and spiritual imbalance caused by lack of joy and peace. Pressure from worries, anxiety, sadness, and frustration builds up in your soul and spirit, increasing inside of you as the "osmolarity" is out of balance. Your spiritual thirst can be quenched by the Word of God, the "Living Water," to restore your soul and to prevent spiritual dehydration. We were created with spiritual "osmoreceptors" to detect the pressure from spiritual thirst. We are spiritual beings living in a physical body with spiritual needs as hunger and thirst for the Bread of Life and the Living Water.

Never leave the thirsty center unsatisfied and the reward mechanism with worldly pleasures to override your spiritual desires. There is a competition between the flesh and the spirit. But there is willpower in your mind and soul to make a choice that will have consequences in this life and eternity. Choosing to live a spiritual life, you must be filled with the Spirit of the Living God. Searching with all your heart is the key to find God. "And you will seek Me and find *Me,* when you search for Me with all your heart" (Jer. 29:13 NKJV).

Living Water for the Thirsty Centers in Your Soul

"On the last day, that great *day* of the feast, Jesus stood and cried out, saying, "If anyone thirsts, let him come to Me and drink. He who believes in

> Me, as the Scripture has said, out of his heart will
> flow rivers of living water" (John 7:37–38 NKJV).

The Living Water will heal spiritual dehydration. The entire world is spiritually dehydrated and experiences a spiritual infection through all the fleshly and worldly desire. Spiritual dehydration affects negatively the spirit, soul, and body. Only the Living Water can fix the world's needs for hydration. The Living Water will flow to bring life, restoration of spiritual dehydration, and to prevent spiritual infections. Spiritual hydration brings cleansing and restoration. "On the last day, that great *day* of the feast, Jesus stood and cried out, saying, 'If anyone thirsts, let him come to Me and drink. He who believes in Me, as the Scripture has said, out of his heart will flow rivers of living water'" (John 7:37–38 NKJV). The Living Water restores the soul, spirit, and body.

People around us wherever we go are thirsty and "dehydrated spiritually," sluggish, and unable to make well-informed spiritual decisions. Their cognition is affected by this lack of "Living Water," missing the "spiritual electrolyte" balance to function normal spiritually, causing spiritual diseases. The Bible tells us that people need the Living Water, for those who are thirsty to come and drink. "Come, all you who are thirsty, come to the waters; and you who have no money, come, buy and eat! Come, buy wine and milk without money and without cost" (Isa. 55:1 NIV). The Word of God can satisfy our spiritual needs at no cost. God invites us to come the way we are to be satisfied if we obey His call. He will come inside of us and guide our mind and thoughts and fill our soul, which will be restored with joy and peace. He knows how we are created, and He knows the pressure that we feel inside of us from the spiritual dehydration.

Thirsty Soul for the Lord

When you are thirsty for the Living Water, seek God and look for Him and see His power and His glory. "O God, You *are* my God; Early will I seek You; My soul thirsts for You; My flesh longs for You

In a dry and thirsty land Where there is no water. So I have looked for You in the sanctuary, To see Your power and Your glory. Because Your lovingkindness *is* better than life, My lips shall praise You. Thus I will bless You while I live; I will lift up my hands in Your name" (Ps. 63:1–4 NKJV).

Build a "wall" of protection in your mind to keep your spiritual pressure in balance. That will give you the ability to be willing to make the right choices and decisions. The enemy breaks the spiritual wall in your mind with seducing desires and worldly things that build the pressure in your spiritual life. Rebuild the wall like Nehemiah for his old city with great perseverance. The spiritual wall has the same struggles with the enemy as to build a physical wall. Nehemiah's example in building the wall of the city to protect the city from the enemy is a great illustration of the spiritual fight for thirsty soul. "Those from among you Shall build the old waste places; You shall raise up the foundations of many generations; And you shall be called the Repairer of the Breach, The Restorer of Streets to Dwell In" (Isa. 58:12 NKJV).

I had to protect my mind during the Communist regime against their doctrine days in and days out since my childhood. From the first grade, I was labeled as *repentant*, a derogatory word used by the Communists to mock Christians. I did build the wall of protection against the enemy with the Word of God through the power of the Holy Spirit to not give in and not give up. The enemy tried countless times to destroy the wall in my mind, but through the willpower God gave me, I made the decision to stay strong and resist the devil. God's Spirit helps you build the wall barriers against the enemy of your soul that makes you disobey spiritual things.

During the Communist regime, it was not only that they dishonored God by denying His existence but also disobeyed all His principles and His standards. They were mocking and laughing with inappropriate actions against God and His followers. But they reaped the consequences of their behavior, as written in Hagai, which says, "Now therefore, thus says the LORD of hosts: 'Consider your ways! You have sown much, and bring in little; You eat, but do not have enough; You drink, but you are not filled with drink; You clothe yourselves, but no one is warm; And he who earns wages, Earns wages *to put* into a bag with holes'" (Hag. 1:5–6 NKJV).

Life passes by very fast, and at the end there is no pleasure in them. "Remember now your Creator in the days of your youth, Before the difficult days come, And the years draw near when you say,; I have no pleasure in them'" (Eccles. 12:1 NKJV). God is a strong tower and a refuge for those who fear Him and obey. His Word confirms that. "In the fear of the LORD *there is* strong confidence, And His children will have a place of refuge" (Prov. 14:26 NKJV).

"But ye shall receive power, after that the Holy Ghost is come upon you: and ye shall be witnesses unto me both in Jerusalem, and in all Judaea, and in Samaria, and unto the uttermost part of the earth" (Acts 1:8 KJV). Our focus must be on God's promise that He wants to give us power to live a true Christian life to be His witnesses. When you are filled with the Holy Spirit, you have the power to become a new creation, a new person, who God wants you to be in this short time on earth. The power of the Holy Spirit activates the God-given purpose and His language in your DNA to become a new creation with God's spiritual DNA, the person He created you to be in the beginning. The evidence of the baptism of the Holy Spirit is the physical manifestation of His power that flows through your physical body, transforming your mind, changing your thoughts, your personality, attitude, and behavior. From His touch you know for sure in your spirit that you have been in His presence.

God puts a radical spiritual thirst and hunger in your heart for the power of the Holy Spirit in order for you to seek Him with all your heart and for Him to fulfill His plan in your life. Fresh move of the Holy Spirit brings breakthrough of rationalism to serve Him through faith. The Holy Spirit enters through the brain cortex in your soul, uniting with your spirit and transforming your soul, causing rivers of the Living Water to spring out from your inner being, changing your life, renewing your mind, soul, and spirit.

Thirsty of Eternity

God's purpose for creating human beings on this planet is eternity, where our everlasting home is. Aging is a gift from God to remind us that our home is not on this planet. How we live our life on earth determines how we spend eternity. Focusing on thoughts of eternity, our reward system produces emotions of joy in our mind and heart even in times of distress. God is our reward if we spend time building the kingdom of God one life at a time while on this planet. Eternity must be the goal of every person on earth to do the work that we were created for by God. Eternal investment is the best investment on this planet when we care for others. Through our deeds, we can change the destiny of needy people, orphans, and widows, through finance, words of encouragement, emotional support, food, medication, and therapy. Our goal must be to walk in the footsteps of Jesus and to have Jesus's character. "For we are God's handiwork, created in Christ Jesus to do good works, which God prepared in advance for us to do" (Eph. 2:10 NIV).

Our work was ordained by God to be imitator of Christ for the kingdom's purpose. For that reason, He equipped us with mirror neurons to be able to imitate Him and have compassion and feel the pain of those around us to do good deeds for them and to rejoice with those who rejoice all the days of our life that were ordained for us to live on the earth for eternity's purpose. "Your eyes saw my unformed body; all the days ordained for me were written in your book before one of them came to be" (Ps. 139:16 NIV).

Anger Is Dangerous

Anger Causes Physical and Spiritual Diseases

Anger is an emotional response to sadness from loss, to fear of rejection, to thoughts of discouragement from bad news, and others. Frequent outbursts of angry episodes bring diseases. Anger not only affects your soul and spirit but also leads to depression, which causes physical pain. Anger creates a cascade of reactions by activating the brain structures in the limbic system, as the amygdala activates the hypothalamus, which releases corticotropin-releasing hormone, signaling the pituitary gland, which releases adrenocorticotropic hormone to activate the adrenal glands to release cortisol (the stress hormone), adrenaline, and noradrenaline. High levels of cortisol affect negatively the serotonin level, leading to depression, taking the joy away and impairing your judgement and capacity to make the right decisions. The stress hormone affects all systems in the body by increasing heart rate, increasing blood pressure, increasing blood sugar, increasing incidents of cancer, increasing migraine and headache, reducing the immune system's capacity to fight infections, reducing bone density, and more. When those symptoms become chronic, the blood vessels will be damaged, leading to heart attack and stroke.

The stress hormones affect your brain and your body. High levels of cortisol decrease serotonin (a neurotransmitter that makes you happy), which takes your joy away and can make you easily feel anger and pain. That also makes you aggressive and depressed. The stress hormone affects the immune system by decreasing thyroid function, decreasing the natural killer cells, increasing virus-infected cells, and increasing incidents of cancer. High levels of cortisol kill neurons in the hippocampus and weakens short-term memory.[1]

The Word of God teaches us that our peaceful thoughts and right actions can keep those neurochemicals under control to prevent damages to our body, soul, and spirit. King David's revelation, through the power of the Holy Spirit, is right about his physical signs and symptoms when it's too long in psychological distress from his disobedience and of his sin, stating, "Bones wasted away through my groaning all day long" (Ps. 32:3 NIV).

Getting angry can become a sin that causes emotions that bring diseases physically and spiritually that can be preventable otherwise. You can keep anger under control. In health care, we try hard to use medication to stabilize angry patients with behavioral disturbance who put in danger others' life and their own. But we read in Proverb 29:11 that "fools give full vent to their rage, but the wise bring calm in the end" (NIV). You can get angry for the right reason and not sin. Get the anger that provokes you to start a mission to do beautiful and good to change the world so God will be glorified, as things for kids that die from preventable diseases.

The Bible gives us instructions to not get angry. "My dear brothers and sisters, take note of this: Everyone should be quick to listen, slow to speak and slow to become angry" (James 1:19 NIV). Dr. Emilia Arden, DO, cardiologist, stated in one of her lectures that strong emotions of anger can lead to sudden death, according to a study done by Lampert R. in *Circulation*, October 1, 2002, about heart and brain interaction.[2] During the heart-brain interaction, strong negative emotions such as anger can trigger polymorphic ventricular arrhythmia and sudden death. Emerging evidence shows that the central nervous system, which processes our emotions, plays a role in heart health.[3]

The apostle was led by the Holy Spirit to write such a true prescription for humankind to avoid outbursts of angry episodes, knowing that angry people have behavioral disturbance hard to be managed by those around them, further causing physical and spiritual damages. "Do not be angry" is God's prescription for a healthy body, soul, and spirit to be able to use our brain structures to think clearly and be able to make good decisions for daily life. The temporal and frontal lobes are essential for memory and abstract reasoning to know who we are and how to think about our identity and how to behave in difficult situations and in crises. Do not let anger damage your brain and your body.

Anger Causes Inflammations That Affect the Body

Anger turns on the inflammation genes, and the inflammatory process starts by increasing interleukin-6 (IL-6) (a pro-inflammatory protein) and other cytokines, as a response to acute stress. Researchers pay more attention to inflammatory processes that lead to cardiovascular diseases and other degenerative diseases as we age. "The pro-inflammatory cytokine, interleukin-6 (IL-6), has been proven particularly good at predicting CVD morbidity and mortality in healthy and unhealthy individuals."[4] "Elevated circulating IL-6 levels are similarly related to the development of frailty, disability, and common diseases of aging, such as inflammatory autoimmune diseases, type 2 diabetes mellitus, and some cancers."[5]

"Those who tend to ruminate, or perseverate, on past events that trigger anger (i.e., angry rumination) have particularly poor physiological recovery following stress. For example, angry rumination is associated with prolonged endothelin-1 increases, which in turn may mediate endothelial dysfunction and atherosclerotic plaque formations. IL-6 and endothelin-1 are significantly related, and in fact, endothelin-1-treated cells in culture have increased IL-6 mRNA and protein. It is likely then that a possible pathway through which anger induces increased circulating IL-6 levels (as seen here) is through increased endothelin-1 and that angry rumination may very well lead to even greater increases in IL-6 mRNA and protein."[6]

That is the reason God gave His creation instructions. "Be angry, and do not sin: do not let the sun go down on your wrath, nor give place to the devil" (Eph. 4:25–27 NKJV). In contrast, instead, love, peace, and joy eliminate emotions of anger and rumination, speeding up the psychological and physiological recovery by turning off the inflammation genes and the inflammatory process. Knowledge of the Lord gives you peace when your thoughts line up with God's thoughts. You can find God's thoughts in His promises in His Word. God's Word is God's mind for humanity. In Jesus all of God's promises are ours. You initiate a Christian life when you receive Jesus Christ in your heart and confess with your mouth that He is your own Lord and Savior. When you receive Jesus Christ in your heart, the Holy Spirit starts the changes of your thoughts, renewing your mind and transforming your life, replacing angry thoughts with the joy of salvation.

But you need to cooperate with the Holy Spirit to be born again, to become a new creation in Christ. Then, through baptism in water, you can be born again by the power of the Holy Spirit. It is God's mystery to transform our spiritual DNA through the power of His Spirit working in us with physical manifestation of a new creation living a new life with new personality, with Christ's DNA and a new character. Then you are a full representation of Christ. Christ lives in you now. You become a joint heir with Christ seated in heavenly places. With this flesh that generates angry thoughts, we cannot inherit everlasting life. We must be born of the spirit, and when this body dies, the spirit is free. To be identified with Christ, we must be baptized in the water and in the Spirit. Then His victory becomes our victory, and His resurrection becomes ours, living in peace and happiness.

You are forgiven before the foundation of the world when Jesus, the Lamb of God, was slain in the Father's heart. Your name was written in the book of the Lamb; your sins were forgiven and accepted through the Father's unconditional love. The price is paid; you are not in bondage of sin anymore. Through Jesus's blood shed on the cross, finishing the work of salvation, your sins are completely removed. He brought you liberty. There are no records of your sins, no condemnation; all things are passed away.

The devil convinces you that you are lost, that you cannot pray. Repentance has power to say no to sin. Repentance shows your love for Him. He promised to forgive all your sins. Invite Him now to come into your heart, and His promises are yours. When you say yes to Jesus and ask Him to come into your heart by faith, an instant miracle happens with your emotions. Take a moment and do it now. Just say, "Lord Jesus, come into my heart and be my Lord and Savior." He is there in your heart at work right now. Follow His voice. Read His Word daily to find His will for your life and pray throughout the day for Him to help you in every situation, to live as a new creation in Christ. He wants you to grow to become like Him through the power of the Holy Spirit.

PART III

Holy Spirit Is at Work

■ Holy Spirit Is Still Hovering

The Holy Spirit is still hovering on the face of the earth today, speaking to people's heart in unimaginable ways. A British business-man wrote me a letter because God moved his heart through the power of the Holy Spirit in London. He wrote, "I am compelled to write to you in the middle of the night." This was stated in his e-mail. He continued, "As I read your book, it is like fire in my hands, and on this second reading, the book has come alive. It is an incredible book and highly anointed… I remember our day out in Portland and often think of sitting with Stelica on the chairs after lunch and talking (I so enjoyed that memorable day), and like the fire that scorched the woods that time, your book scorches me."[1]

I cannot describe the joy that flooded my soul and my heart when I did read this email that next morning when routinely I was checking my e-mails, stating, "Your book is like fire in my hands." I knew that was the Holy Spirit hovering over London that touched Martin's heart as a "fire" so intense that he was writing that e-mail during nighttime, when people were sleeping. Apparently, he could not sleep that night. When my eyes were caught by that sentence, "I am compelled to write to you in the middle of the night," emotions of joy and thoughts were activated from my unconscious mind about the powerful story in the Bible when King Xerxes's sleep was disturbed by the Spirit of God and he was up throughout the night, reading the Chronicles, as is written in the book of Esther. "That night the king could not sleep; so he ordered the book of the chronicles, the record of his reign, to be brought in and read to him. It was found recorded there that Mordecai had exposed Bigthana and Teresh, two of the king's officers who guarded the doorway, who had conspired to assassinate King Xerxes" (Esther 6:1–2).

King Xerxes forgot about Mordecai's loyalty to himself and to his kingdom, but the Holy Spirit did not forget and prompted King Xerxes to read the book of Chronicles when it was, in fact, even an inappropriate time with an urgent question. "'What honor and recognition has Mordecai received for this?' the king asked. 'Nothing has been done for him,' his attendants answered. The king said, 'Who is in the court?'" (Esther 6:3–4a). King Xerxes felt the urgency in his heart to take actions right away. The Holy Spirit was pressing the king to not procrastinate because God's plan was bigger than the king's plan to save a nation from destruction. In the book of Esther we read, "Now Haman had just entered the outer court of the palace to speak to the king about impaling Mordecai on the pole he had set up for him. His attendants answered, 'Haman is standing in the court.' 'Bring him in,' the king ordered. When Haman entered, the king asked him, 'What should be done for the man the king delights to honor?'" (Esther 6:4b–6a).

The enemy of God's people was taken by surprise and, full of himself and confident in his evil desires, in a hurry answered the king's question, not knowing that the sentence for his evil plans to annihilate the Jewish nation was on his own lips. The writer of the book of Esther continues to tell us, "Now Haman thought to himself, 'Who is there that the king would rather honor than me?' So he answered the king, 'For the man the king delights to honor, have them bring a royal robe the king has worn and a horse the king has ridden, one with a royal crest placed on its head. Then let the robe and horse be entrusted to one of the king's most noble princes. Let them robe the man the king delights to honor, and lead him on the horse through the city streets, proclaiming before him, "This is what is done for the man the king delights to honor!"'"(Esther 6:6b–9). King Xerxes did not even wait a second to meditate on the advice received and gave direct order to God's people's enemy to honor the man who saved his life. "'Go at once,' the king commanded Haman. 'Get the robe and the horse and do just as you have suggested for

Mordecai the Jew, who sits at the king's gate. Do not neglect anything you have recommended.' So Haman got the robe and the horse. He robed Mordecai, and led him on horseback through the city streets, proclaiming before him, 'This is what is done for the man the king delights to honor!'" (Esther 6:10–11).

Led by the Holy Spirit of God, King Xerxes's let his eyes fall on a name that saved the life of the king from the plot of assassination and that did not get any reward for his kind and brave action of informing the king about an enemy's plan to take the king's life. Saving the king's life was translated later into saving the nation of Israel, which was purposed by the Creator of the universe to bring the Messiah on planet Earth to save the entire humanity from eternal death. The nation of Israel was created with a purpose for eternity. Each one of us has a purpose on this planet also.

The story goes on to tell us of the miraculous interventions of God's hand that started from that night when the king struggled with insomnia and could not sleep because Esther and all the Jews in the entire region of the Persian Empire fasted for three days and three nights and were crying out to God for the entire nation, whose life was on the genocidal plan of Haman (the king's evil counselor).

God turned the entire evil plan upside down, starting with the king's sleepless night, when the king remembered how his life was saved by Mordecai. The king was prompted by the Spirit of God that night to honor Mordecai for saving his life. Mordecai was honored the second day by the one who planned to kill him and all Jewish people, including Queen Esther. Read the entire book of Esther to see the miracles God was working through prayers and fasting to fulfill a nation's purpose on earth.

Esther made the choice to obey, to listen, to humble, to respect, to stay in faith to become the queen from being a Jewish orphan girl. The road was tough, but her unselfish attitude to pray and fast for three days and three nights attracted heaven's favors, and God moved the king's heart in her favor. Pursuing righteousness, you will have love, peace, success, prosperity, honor, and favors with heavens and with the Lord. Acts of kindness touch a stony heart. "For *so* you will heap coals of fire on his head, And the LORD will reward you" (Prov. 25:22 NKJV).

The Holy Spirit Is Real

Our friend Martin could not sleep in London when he was prompted to write that e-mail because the Holy Spirit that was hovering over the earth was at work in his heart. On our phone conversation later, he stated that his spiritual eyes were opened and his body started to vibrate, touched by a "divine hand," when he did read in *Beyond Science (Find Your Peace Book, a New Version of Beyond Science)* that "The Holy Spirit is real."[2]

During that time, I was praying in the USA for divine connections for my first book, *Beyond Science*, to be promoted at a larger scale, to be translated in other languages and be distributed in the entire world, to touch people's life and to promote physical and spiritual health and prevent physical and spiritual diseases. Martin from London did not know what I was praying for in Portland, but Martin, led by the Spirit of God, sent e-mails and messages that night to the CEO of Charisma Media / Charisma House Book Group in Florida, a world-renowned and great publisher with connections in the entire world, to publish my book. The Holy Spirit is real, hovering on the surface of the earth and at work in people's heart. Nothing can stop God from fulfilling His purpose and plan to reach out for the lost and to destroy the plan of the enemy. We were created with purpose.

Only the Holy Spirit, who is real, can touch someone's heart on the other side of the world, to be moved by His power and compelled to write e-mails and connect people for God's purpose throughout the night. In the book of Esther, only the Holy Spirit knew the plan of the enemy to destroy the king's life and to destroy the entire nation of Israel from the planet Earth, to prevent the Messiah from coming to save the world. In one night, God turned the Jewish people's situation upside down. It started with God's miraculous intervention in the king's thought at that night to reward someone who was faithful to the king (after a nation was fasting and praying).

The Holy Spirit is real for you too and present in your troubles to meet your need where you are. He is present in your physical and emotional pain and distress. Your suffering has a purpose, even though you may not see it. God is at work in your life, searching out everything through His Spirit. "But God has revealed *them* to us through His Spirit. For the Spirit searches all things, yes, the deep things of God" (1 Cor. 2:10 NKJV). The Holy Spirit, who searches the deep things of God, knows the plan of the enemy to destroy your life, and He intervenes at the right time with great power to give you victory the way you do not even imagine so He can get the glory for which you were created, the ultimate purpose of His creation.

We are created for a purpose, praising and worshipping in the Holy Spirit. God is calling us to pursue wisdom and to seek the right relationship with Him, to spend time in the Word, prayer, and worship and to know who God is. Our victories are in the praises to our God, who is love. Jesus's sacrifice for the human beings and His redemption displayed on the cross at Calvary shows us His love for humanity and tells us everything about who God is. The devil tries to cloud people's mind with increased levels of cortisol, the stress hormone, from excessive worries, bitterness, unforgiveness, rejection, uncertainty, disbelief, bringing fear and anxiety and spiritually dry people, churches, songs, preachers, sermons, etc. Deep in my heart, I like to feel the anointing to pray, to read the Word of God, and to worship, to pursue the heart of God filled with love and righteousness, to live for Him. Because "whoever pursues righteousness and love finds life, prosperity and honor" (Prov. 21:21 NIV).

The Holy Spirit Changes the Atmosphere in Your Brain

The atmosphere in your brain changes when you start to worship and praise God. Your faith is increased because you focus on His love for you, His promises, His power, His goodness. All the other negative thoughts are replaced with thoughts of hope and happiness. Hope comes alive where faith exists. Your confidence in God brings joy, hope, and faith. The atmosphere changes where faith is increased. In that moment, you start to fight the war in your mind from evil desires. There is storm inside of you many times. Open the eyes of your soul to see clearly your enemy.

We must create an atmosphere for praises in our souls and spirit, and that will flow out like rivers of "living water," washing away our fears and disbeliefs. God responds to our praises, making our mind, brain, and heart God's dwelling place. Where God dwells, there is no place for discouragements and fear. His love is overwhelming, casting out fear, replacing it with faith that "moves mountains." Praises bring victory. Taking actions physically by raising your hands and shouting to the Lord will create a shift in your mind and thoughts. There are many forms of worship in the Bible: raising words of praises, speaking up praises, shouting, lifting up hands, spreading hands, playing instruments, clapping hands, standing in His presence, bowing down, kneeling with face down to the floor, dancing for the Lord, staying still, whispering, etc.

If you are in dry places in your business, finances, marriage, health, family, and society, take time to spend in God's presence and just praise Him. The walls will fall down when you take time to connect with your heavenly Father to worship Him and praise Him from the bottom of your heart with all your strength and all your emotions, focusing on His goodness and faithfulness every moment. Spending time in prayer and focusing on God's promises will release the promises in your life through praise and worship in your prayers. The power is in your praises in prayers. Walk in obedience, with your brain saturated with praises and thanksgiving for the Word of God, and His promises for your life will bring restoration and healing.

In *Find Your Peace: Supernatural Solutions Beyond Science for Fear, Anxiety, and Depression* (page 138–139), I did write how I start my day with prayer and worship: "I start with the Lord's Prayer and acknowledge who God is for me. I tell Him in my prayer, 'Father God, You are Jehovah-Elohim, the Creator of heaven and earth. You made us in Your image and I carry your breath in my lungs every single moment. You are Jehovah-Tsidkenu, God my righteousness, through the power of Jesus Christ your only Son, who shed His blood on the cross when He died for my sins. I acknowledge that all my sins are forgiven and I am not stressed anymore by the weight of my past sins. You are Jehovah Mekoddishkem, the God who sanctifies me and gives me power over temptations and sins every single moment. By the authority of Christ's sacrifice on the cross I have the authority over all evil thoughts today, and over any bad habits and attitudes. You are Jehovah-Shalom, the God who gives me peace that passes all understanding in a world of uncertainty, worry, and fear. My thoughts are submitted to Jesus. I declare that I am covered with the blood of Jesus by faith, and I have authority over all the wicked spirits. You are Jehovah-Shammah, the God who is present, self-existent. You are always there when I need You. You are from eternity to eternity the everlasting Father, the Great "I AM." In Your presence is peace, joy and happiness. In Your presence all demonic spirits faint. What You speak will be created. Nothing is impossible for You. You have solutions for all my problems today. You are Jehovah-Rapha, God my Healer, who heals all my diseases. I declare that by your Son, Jesus's stripes I am healed completely. Jesus's body was broken so there will be no diseases, no pain, no brokenness, no bruises, no infirmity, no disability, no abnormality in my body. Each cell in my body will function perfectly according to Your divine programming. Father God, I declare that in my body there are no abnormal genetic mutations or uncontrolled cell divisions. I declare divine health and complete healing in Jesus's mighty name. I proclaim that You are Jehovah-Jireh, God my Provider, who provides all my needs. You have blessed and You continue to bless me and my family so much more than I could ask or think. You enlarged my territories in every area, Your divine hands are upon me to protect me from evil, and nothing will harm me. You bless me at home and in society, when I go out and when I come in. Everything I put my hands to, You will cause to prosper. You give me favor with all whom I speak with and come in contact with today. You are Jehovah-Nissi, the God who is my victory and my protection from my enemy. You send your angel ahead of me, and your angels surround me and fight for me. All the demonic strategies are in vain. I declare that You, Lord, fight for me. Your plans and Your will are done in my life to fulfill my dreams, visions and destiny, and to help me reach my full potential. I declare that no weapon formed against me shall prosper, and any language against me is condemned, according to Isaiah 54:17. My heavenly Father, You are Jehovah-Rohi, God my Shepherd, my guide. I shall not want. You cover my head with oil and my cup is overflowing. You give me inspiration, revelation, clear thoughts, and discernment, and I do not make any decision without You. You give me wisdom from heaven and the Holy Spirit takes control over my life, my emotions, my feelings, my thoughts, my entire being. You fill me with the Holy Spirit, take possession of all my being, and I surrender to you. You are Jehovah El Roi, the God who sees me when I stand up and when I sit down. You know all my deep thoughts. Nothing is hidden from you. My heavenly Father, You are Jehovah El Elyon, the Most High God, and in the shadow of Your wing I find divine protection. I rest because you put my enemies under my feet.'"[3]

I did describe how I usually start my day in prayer, reminding myself who God is for me every moment and His promises for every situation. Each time I spend time in prayer, worshipping and praising God, I feel His presence and my attitude changes. I am full of joy and energy all day long. The Living Water is flowing, and I feel refresh working on my assignments. People will notice my changed attitude. By praising and worshipping, it is not only that I glorify God the Father through His precious Son, Jesus Christ, through the power of His Holy Spirit; I realize that the right prescriptions for chemicals are released by my brain's structures as dopamine, serotonin, oxytocin, and endorphin and produce the fruit of the Spirit in me with physical manifestations in my behavior and attitude as programmed in our DNA by our Creator from creation. We just need to dial in to connect with our heavenly Father and align our attitude and actions with His instructions. The attitude of my heart is changed completely toward my work for the day, toward my husband, my family, my friends, my coworkers, my city, my nation, and the entire world.

For years I made a habit to read God's promises every morning and then thanking God and praising Him for all His benefits in my life and for everything He gave me and for everything He is doing in my life.

A breakthrough happened each time I started to praise the Lord, the Creator of the universe. Changes happen in my heart, mind, and body when I praise Him with everything that is within me, every cell and every organ, as is written in Psalm 103:1. "Bless the LORD, O my soul; And all that is within me, *bless* His holy name!" (NKJV). The programmed prescription in every cell and every system is released, and my weaknesses, fatigue, emotional pain, and worries disappear suddenly. I feel the power, energy, and electricity flowing through every cell's mitochondria in my body. Through praises I enter in my spirit in God's spiritual realm, passing the threshold of this physical world. Blessings start to flow beyond we can ask, think, or imagine as physical manifestation of His provisions and promises.

The Holy Spirit's Culture Starts Here

The Holy Spirit's purpose is to glorify God. The Holy Spirit changes hearts to do everything with pure love, with the fear of the Lord that brings glory to God. As a teenager, after I was touched by the power of God and infilled with the Holy Spirit, my heart was radically changed, and in my mind and my spirit, I did see with my spiritual eyes Lord Jesus, as my Shepherd, leading me with a scepter in His hand, going before me, and I was clinging to Him and my heart was beating for Him only. I could not take my eyes off Him. It was a powerful scene I will never forget. Something inside of me happened that changed me forever. Suddenly, I was consciously aware of my thoughts, words, and actions to not grieve the Holy Spirit. His small voice was speaking to my conscious mind what kind of thoughts to think, to carefully select the words and what kind of words to speak, how to interact with people and how to react to people's challenging, when it was appropriate to smile so I will not give people false impressions about their dirty jokes and inappropriate conversation. The Holy Spirit taught me how to resist the devil. "Therefore submit to God. Resist the devil and he will flee from you" (James 4:7 NKJV).

I heard testimonies from many people living in different parts of the world at different periods in history who were touched by God through the power of the Holy Spirit having the same experience, the same purpose, the same thoughts, the same speech, the same feeling, the same life in the Spirit, because they were infilled with the same power of God, His Holy Spirit, because they were God's people.

They, like me, experienced the same Holy Spirit's culture to glorify the Father through His Son, Jesus Christ. The power of the Holy Spirit crosses every culture, denomination, ethnic group, language, nation, territory, time, space, and place to bring conviction of the power of the blood of Jesus Christ, which washes every sin away to bring us back in His glorious presence. A supernatural "crossing over" happens in the spiritual realm to feel the power of the Holy Spirit.

According to J. Ryan Lister, in his book *The Presence of God*, "God works to create a people and a place for His Presence. That means that all of Scripture is about the Lord's redemptive mission centered on bringing the redeemed to a greater world covered by the Presence of God."[4]

God's purpose for every human being that He made in His own eternal image is to create "a new heaven and a new earth" with a culture where the presence of God will be with His children. He will fulfill His plan and the purpose for what we were created from the beginning of creation, to dwell with His people and to cover them with His glorious presence. The book of Revelation talks about that. "Then I saw 'a new heaven and a new earth,' for the first heaven and the first earth had passed away, and there was no longer any sea. I saw the Holy City, the new Jerusalem, coming down out of heaven from God, prepared as a bride beautifully dressed for her husband. And I heard a loud voice from the throne saying, 'Look! God's dwelling place is now among the people, and he will dwell with them. They will be his people, and God himself will be with them and be their God. 'He will wipe every tear from their eyes. There will be no more death or mourning or crying or pain, for the old order of things has passed away.' He who was seated on the throne said, 'I am making everything new!' Then he said, 'Write this down, for these words are trustworthy and true.' He said to me: 'It is done. I am the Alpha and the Omega, the Beginning and the End. To the thirsty I will give water without cost from the spring of the water of life. Those who are victorious will inherit all this, and I will be their God and they will be my children'" (Rev. 21:1–7 NIV).

The Holy Spirit's Purpose

The Holy Spirit Accomplishes God's Purpose

Holy Spirit was present at creation and *is* present today, working in people's mind and bodies to accomplish God's purpose on this planet. Only the Holy Spirit can work at our conscious mind to bring conviction about our sinful nature and cause the alteration at the DNA level to take place so we can become a new creation with new spiritual DNA, living in righteousness of God. That Christlike lifestyle will further alter our physical DNA, changing our character and personality. "Now He who establishes us with you in Christ and has anointed us *is* God, who also has sealed us and given us the Spirit in our hearts as a guarantee" (2 Cor. 1:21–22 NKJV).

Jesus told His disciples that He must ascend to heaven in order to send the Holy Spirit to infill His disciples to give them power and authority to change the world around them and to bring salvation and healing to the body, soul, and spirit. "Nevertheless I tell you the truth. It is to your advantage that I go away; for if I do not go away, the Helper will not come to you; but if I depart, I will send Him to you. And when He has come, He will convict the world of sin, and of righteousness, and of judgment: of sin, because they do not believe in Me; of righteousness, because I go to My Father and you see Me no more; of judgment, because the ruler of this world is judged" (John 16:7–11 NKJV). The Holy Spirit is at work in the world today.

In order to be regenerated and renewed in our spirit, we need the Holy Spirit from above to do that work in us. In Titus it is written that "not by works of righteousness which we have done, but according to His mercy He saved us, through the washing of regeneration and renewing of the Holy Spirit" (Titus 3:5 NKJV).

Our body, soul, and spirit belong to God. Our body is God's temple and our heart is God's dwelling place, and we must bring glory to Him and fulfill the purpose we were created for through the power of the Holy Spirit. It is written, "Or do you not know that your body is the temple of the Holy Spirit *who is* in you, whom you have from God, and you are not your own? For you were bought at a price; therefore glorify God in your body and in your spirit, which are God's" (Cor. 6:19–20). We must recognize that we belong to the Creator, body, soul, and spirit.

Through our secular attitude and fleshly desire, we alter the DNA in the wrong direction, leading to physical and spiritual diseases and destruction. The Holy Spirit of God is grieved when we suffer with all kinds of physical and spiritual diseases as a result of our disobedient life. We have clear instruction in the Word of God to not grieve the Holy Spirit. "And do not grieve the Holy Spirit of God, by whom you were sealed for the day of redemption. Let all bitterness, wrath, anger, clamor, and evil speaking be put away from you, with all malice. And be kind to one another, tenderhearted, forgiving one another, even as God in Christ forgave you" (Eph. 4:30 NKJV). "And do not be drunk with wine, in which is dissipation; but be filled with the Spirit" (Eph. 5:18 NKJV). The Holy Spirit is grieved when we harbor thoughts and emotions of anger, wrath, and malice in our heart and mind, because each of them destroys the spirit, soul, and body through spiritual and physical diseases.

The Holy Spirit Can Rebirth an Individual Soul and Spirit

Once sin entered the world, all of God's creation suffered physical and spiritual death. But the soul and the spirit received through God's breath and through Jesus Christ's sacrifice remained eternal. "For the wages of sin *is* death, but the gift of God *is* eternal life in Christ Jesus our Lord" (Rom. 6:23 NKJV). God gave humanity the possibility and the opportunity to get born again even at an old age to receive eternal life and be back in God's kingdom to live forever. "There was a man of the Pharisees named Nicodemus, a ruler of the Jews. This man came to Jesus by night and said to Him, 'Rabbi, we know that You are a teacher come from God; for no one can do these signs that You do unless God is with him.' Jesus answered and said to him, 'Most assuredly, I say to you, unless one is born again, he cannot see the kingdom of God.' Nicodemus said to Him, 'How can a man be born when he is old? Can he enter a second time into his mother's womb and be born?' Jesus answered, 'Most assuredly, I say to you, unless one is born of water and the Spirit, he cannot enter the kingdom of God. That which is born of the flesh is flesh, and that which is born of the Spirit is spirit. Do not marvel that I said to you, "You must be born again." The wind blows where it wishes, and you hear the sound of it, but cannot tell where it comes from and where it goes. So is everyone who is born of the Spirit'" (John 3:1–8 NKJV).

According to Jesus Christ, the Savior of the world, to be born again is mandatory in order to enter the kingdom of God and is God's provision through the power of the Holy Spirit that enters in our mind, soul, and spirit through the threshold of our physical body (brain). To be born again, to restart a new life, and to be regenerated in your soul and spirit is the process of a transformed mind and a life changed to become a new creation, with Christ living in you for a glorious life filled with hope. "To them God willed to make known what are the riches of the glory of this mystery among the Gentiles: which is Christ in you, the hope of glory" (Col. 1:27 NKJV).

The Purpose of the Holy Spirit to Live Forever

The purpose of the Holy Spirit from creation was breathed in the human body (God's image) and was to live forever with eternal soul and spirit. The sin committed by the first man, Adam, through disobedience grieved the Holy Spirit, and man was left with his sinful nature and condemned to eternal death. But Jesus Christ redeemed us from our sins and stated that He will pray to the Father to send the Holy Spirit to live in us forever, as is written in John 14:16. "And I will pray the Father, and He will give you another Helper, that He may abide with you forever" (NKJV). We are sealed with the Holy Spirit and must live and walk in God's Spirit. The Holy Spirit manifests Himself in you, guiding you, directing and teaching you, leading and edifying, helping you to live according to God's will and purpose. It is the Holy Spirit that is praying for you and interceding through you, helping us in our weakness. "Likewise the Spirit also helps in our weaknesses. For we do not know what we should pray for as we ought, but the Spirit Himself makes intercession for us with groaning which cannot be uttered. Now He who searches the hearts knows what the mind of the Spirit *is,* because He makes intercession for the saints according to *the will of* God" (Rom. 8:26–27 NKJV).

The Holy Spirit Has Unlimited Influence

We were created with purpose to be loved and to love without conditions, to bring pleasure to God, to worship Him and rejoice in His presence. Humans' worship brings Him glory, and He shows His glory. He likes to be present in our life when we worship because of His love for us. He wants every human being to experience unspeakable joy in His presence through worship in spirit and truth. He wants us to experience His presence here on earth and then in eternity. We need to get used to the joy of His presence here on earth. He wants to redeem us from the sin that separates us from God and to give us His unspeakable joy and to bring us in His presence forever. The Holy Spirit has unlimited influence on humanity since creation. Separation from God's intimate relationship by sin motivated God to work a plan for salvation through the Messiah to come on this planet to restore our relationship with our Father. We were destined to win.

Kris Vallotton, in his book *Destined to Win: How to Embrace Your God-Given Identity and Realize Your Kingdom Purpose,* stated that "the force to absolutely positively transform everything in your life (to bless your relationship, fix your finances, heal your body, give peace to your soul, and fully actualize every aspect of your life) is in the Presence of God Himself. The Holy Spirit is within you, and His Presence can profoundly bless you!."[1]

Fulfill Your Destiny Starting Here

Meditating on God's purpose for our future develops a morning routine to start your day with great joy. Optimize your health by developing healthy routine in the morning; be consistent with your devotion in the Word of God, feeding your soul with His promises that bring hope for the mind to make better decisions that will have a positive influence on everybody around you.

As we live our life on this planet to accomplish our goals and our destiny, we must stay healthy and pay attention to our lifestyle. Being physically active and exercising regularly will have great benefits in our temporary life. Exercise prevents diseases by decreasing the stress hormone, decreasing inflammation. It produces brain-derived neurotrophic factor (BDNF); increases blood flow to the brain; increases endorphin, "the happy hormone," which helps you to feel better; stimulates and promotes neurogenesis process, creating new neurons, new neuropathways, and connections; increases cognition, the mental ability to interact with the world around you and people, to make good decisions to be successful in the world. Exercise also increases executive function in the frontal lobe, named by many "the CEO" of the brain. "The frontal lobe is the part of the brain that controls important cognitive skills in humans, such as emotional expression, problem solving, memory, language, judgment, and sexual behaviors. It is, in essence, the 'control panel' of our personality and our ability to communicate."[2]

Exercise is the key sources in our life for health, success, managing skills, learning, memorizing, adapting to circumstances. It is recommended to choose the type of exercise that you enjoy and to be consistent to increase the executive function in the prefrontal cortex. Minimum recommended is 150 minutes of moderate exercise per week. The more you exercise, the more benefits you get for your health. Even more benefits will be added if you are physically active, serving the Lord with joy, helping others with great love; you will have great benefits physically, decreasing blood pressure, reducing sugar level, and lowering cholesterol level. We are instructed by God's Word that love must be sincere. Hate what is evil; cling to what is good. Be devoted to one another in brotherly love. Honor one another above yourselves. Never be lacking in zeal, but keep your spiritual fervor, serving the Lord. Be joyful in hope, patient in affliction, and faithful in prayer. Share with God's people who are in need. Practice hospitality" (Rom. 12:9–13 NIV).

Dr. Don Colbert, in his book *Reversing Diabetes*, talks about the "many benefits that come with regular activity:

- It decreases the risk of heart disease, stroke, and the development of hypertension.
- It helped prevent type 2 diabetes.
- It helps protect you from developing certain type of cancer.
- It helps prevent osteoporosis and aids in maintaining healthy joints.
- It slows down the overall aging process.
- It improves your mood and reduces the symptoms of anxiety and depression.
- It increases energy and mental alertness.
- It improves digestion.
- It gives you more restful sleep.
- It helps prevent colds and flu.
- It alleviates pain.
- And the favorite reason among overweight and obese people...it promotes weight loss and decreases appetite."[3]

To illustrate, one summer, we had to take a road trip to Europe. The streets in the center of the cities in Europe are very narrow, and you cannot drive a car on those roads and there are no parking lots available to park the car. We were walking long distances about eight to ten miles daily in every city we visited that summer. Upon our return home, our labs were due and my husband and I proceeded with our doctors' visit. We were astonished by the improved results.

My HgA1C (glycated hemoglobin, used to test the level of blood sugar for a period of two to three months) went down from 6.4 percent to 5.8 percent; bad cholesterol and triglycerides decreased and good cholesterol increased also. No hypertension. We lost about eight to ten pounds. We felt great. Indeed, increased physical activities like walking regularly about five to ten miles per day, a healthy diet, stress management, and a healthy lifestyle will cause great health benefits. I cannot emphasize enough how important it is to talk to your doctor about health promotion and disease preventions for your own life.

Created for Breakthrough

▪ Breakthrough for a Rich Spiritual Life

Through praying, fasting, and worship, you empty your soul and spirit of fleshly things that are felt like a heavy burden that is hard to carry, clouding your mind, making you unable to think clearly. The breakthrough happens to make your heart and mind available to God to fill your hearts with the quality of the fruit of the Spirit. "But the fruit of the Spirit is love, joy, peace, longsuffering, kindness, goodness, faithfulness, gentleness, self-control. Against such there is no law. And those *who are* Christ's have crucified the flesh with its passions and desires" (Gal. 5:22–24 NKJV). Through breakthrough and the quality of the fruit of the Spirit in your life, you become a public display of a transformed life for people to see God's love so people will desire to experience the same touch from heaven and His transformational power in their desperate life. Bill Johnson, in his book *The Supernatural Power of a Transformed Mind: Access to a Life of Miracles*, emphasized, "Let's not waste our miracles. Let's not watch God do something awesome, then give a little golf clap, a little 'amen' and walk away unchanged. Let's recognize that we are equipped for each storm. We have been trained by past miracles to see present solutions."[1]

During my education as a young girl in high school in Bucharest, students were watching my attitude in difficult circumstances and were surprised that my reactions were different from theirs. They were cursing, swearing, and using bad words, dirty language, and ugly attitude. I remember after the earthquake, one of the Communist girls who constantly mocked my faith in God was in the same class with me and heard that I was talking to God in prayers and had seen the joy I had and my love for people around me. She realized that there was something different in me and asked me if she could come to the church that I attended at that time in Bucharest. This girl was an outrageous atheist, hating God before this earthquake. I could hardly stand her attitude toward me and my faith and her negative and hostile belief system. She had a way to intimidate me with her stinging words, despising my faith in God.

The fear of the Lord gripped her heart during the earthquake, and she wanted to pray and worship at the same church with me. I invited her to church reluctantly, knowing who she was and with no hope that she would attend. I was surprised when I did see her in church that week. She confessed later that she felt miserable inside when she lived an immoral and perverse life following the Communists' teaching for purposeless life. She stated that she was trembling when she saw me praying on my knees in church. She knelt, too, and gave her life to Jesus Christ, and her life was transformed completely by the power of the Holy Spirit, who made her a new creation in Christ, a completely different person to this day.

The work of the enemy was destroyed in her life, and she started to experience a new, joyful, transformed life in Christ. She had a prophetic destiny in her DNA that she needed to fulfill. There is a prophetic destiny in your DNA. Jesus's purpose on earth was to destroy Satan's work and to seek and save people like my friend in Bucharest. The Holy Spirit is at work on this planet. He activated my friend's desire in her heart in her spiritual DNA to seek God, and she found Him on her knees in that church in Bucharest, a busy city with over two million people at that time. God had a purpose for my friend and for a miraculous breakthrough, and the power of the Holy Spirit accomplished it in her life.

According to Dr. Guillermo Maldonado, the author of the book *Breakthrough Prayer: Where God Always Hears and Answers*, "In reality, most of us need breakthrough in various area of our lives-for example, in our personal life, our family, our business, our education, our health, and even in our emotions. Breakthroughs must include deliverance, because demonic bonds are preventing us from moving forward in supernatural power, from knowing more about God, from leaving behind a sinful life, or from persevering in prayer." He goes on and describes this: "To break is defined as 'to separate into parts with suddenness or violence.' Similarly, breakthrough prayer generates an abrupt, violent, and sudden rupture of what is hindering us, pushing us beyond that limitation and into freedom. Breakthrough prayer must be engaged in persistently and consistently until we sense that something has broken in the spiritual realm, and until what we are asking for manifests. With a breakthrough, what we need is brought from the spiritual world to the natural world, so that we can see it in a visible or tangible demonstration of God's power or provision."[2]

Do not be discouraged, because your miraculous breakthrough for a rich spiritual and joyful life is on the way when you persevere in prayer. He wants to give you abundant life here on earth and eternal life.

Restoring Your Soul by Reprogramming Your Brain

In the world we live in today, the human soul longs to be restored. Only the Word of God can restore a soul by healing emotional pain through love, joy, and peace that last this life and in eternity. "Then the seventy returned with joy, saying, 'Lord, even the demons are subject to us in Your name.' And He said to them, 'I saw Satan fall like lightning from heaven. Behold, I give you the authority to trample on serpents and scorpions, and over all the power of the enemy, and nothing shall by any means hurt you. Nevertheless do not rejoice in this, that the spirits are subject to you, but rather rejoice because your names are written in heaven'" (Luke 10:17–20 NKJV). The joy we experience in this life is temporary. The joy that lasts eternally matters the most.

The true joy that we must possess and will last forever is the joy that our name is written in heaven. We must live with that truth in mind. The joy of salvation overrides the emotions caused by circumstances. King David, in his emotional distress, asked the Lord in prayer, "Restore to me the joy of Your salvation, And uphold me by Your generous Spirit" (Ps. 51:12 NKJV). The joy of salvation is the true joy that comes from God. We all come from God and go back to Him because our origin is from Him and we were created in His spiritual image for eternity. Salvation belongs to Christ. "And crying out with a loud voice, saying, 'Salvation belongs to our God who sits on the throne, and to the Lamb!'" (Rev. 7:10 NKJV).

To illustrate, one of my patients with multiple chronic diseases had multiple visits to the emergency room. Because of his poor prognosis, he was sent home on hospice program with end-of-life support. He came two weeks later at the clinic by himself without oxygen supplement, with great joy, to show me that he trusted God and He helped him to improve and he would not die. While speaking, he started to shake a little bit as he pulled an old book from beneath his charts and paperwork. I thought he was having seizures again or a panic attack when I did see the slight tremor in his hands and heard it in his voice. He raised his "old book" up, and with a tremor in his voice, he stated with great joy, "I believe in the Word of God." He was holding the holy Bible and, with strong faith and great affirmation, said, "I believe in God and Jesus Christ, His Son. I am not alone. I trust in Him. I am alive because of Him, and I will not die." Until that day, I had never seen him so excited. He grew up in a Communist country, too, and never expressed his values and beliefs. In fact, I thought he was an atheist, from all the biases in my mind. He said, "I pray and I feel better." He was full of true joy in the doctor's office during that visit. His soul had been restored.

We must reprogram the brain by rejoicing without ceasing. We become sad and lose our joy when we lose the focus on our free salvation and that we are saved by grace. We do not have to work for our salvation; it was done by Christ when He died on the cross at Calvary more than two thousand years ago. The Lamb of God paid with His holy blood for all our sins. In John 1:29, John announced, "The next day John saw Jesus coming toward him, and said, 'Behold! The Lamb of God who takes away the sin of the world!'" (John 1:29 NKJV). Our joy must be full by meditating and knowing the truth that we have a permanent place reserved for us in heaven, with our name written down in the reservation of the Book of Life. Christ made our reservation according to Hebrew 12:18–24. Our reservation is in the New Jerusalem in heaven. "But you have come to Mount Zion and to the city of the living God, the heavenly Jerusalem, to an innumerable company of angels, to the general assembly and church of the firstborn who are registered in heaven, to God the Judge of all, to the spirits of just men made perfect, to Jesus the Mediator of the new covenant, and to the blood of sprinkling that speaks better things than that of Abel" (Heb. 12:22–24 NKJV). Salvation belongs to Christ. The reservation for you is made by the Lamb of God through His sacrifice. He wrote your name in the Book of Life. He is the restorer of your soul through the character of righteousness.

John G. Lake, in his book *Your Power in the Holy Spirit*, stated, "Jesus was bringing forth and establishing in the world a new character, a character that would endure forever, a soul quality that would never fail, a faith that knew no possibility of defeat. In establishing such a character, Jesus saw that the character could be established only in depth of a man's being, in the very spirit of his being. Then, when once the soul was grounded in the path of righteousness, all the activities of the nature would be along righteous line and in harmony with the laws of God. God has a call in His own Spirit. If we study our spirit, we will understand the nature of God. The call of the Spirit of God is the call of righteousness, the call of truth, the call of love, the call of power, the call of faith."[3]

Holy Spirit Power

The Holy Spirit Is Present to Guide

It is the Holy Spirit that directs our steps, not ourselves, as is written in the book of Jeremiah. "O Lord, I know the way of man *is* not in himself; *It is* not in man who walks to direct his own steps" (Jer. 10:23 NKJV). The Holy Spirit is present on this planet, but humanity grieves the Holy Spirit through sin. "Let all bitterness, wrath, anger, clamor, and evil speaking be put away from you, with all malice. And be kind to one another, tenderhearted, forgiving one another, even as God in Christ forgave you" (Eph. 4:31 NKJV).

Repentance of sin is God's desire for humanity. "For godly sorrow produces repentance *leading* to salvation, not to be regretted; but the sorrow of the world produces death" (2 Cor. 7:10 NKJV). Sin can make us slaves and keeps us in bondage and causes sorrow and emotions of pain when we have those sins stored in our memories, leading to diseases and premature death when we do not recognize the power of the Holy Spirit that is present and guiding us.

The Holy Spirit brings conviction of sin so we can confess our sin, getting rid of the emotions and pain of sin. The Holy Spirit can be grieved and experience emotion of pain from our sins. Confession is the key to bring those memories of sin from the unconscious mind in our conscious mind to be destabilized and replaced with the joy of the Lord, which gives us strength daily. God promised that He is faithful to forgive our sins if we confess them. "If we confess our sins, He is faithful and just to forgive us *our* sins and to cleanse us from all unrighteousness" (1 John 1:9 NKJV). God is faithful. Why don't we take advantage to confess our sin and prevent destruction of our body, soul, and spirit? You can overcome the power of sin that destroys your life through the power of the Holy Spirit that lives in you. "You are of God, little children, and have overcome them, because He who is in you is greater than he who is in the world" (1 John 4:4 NKJV). The Holy Spirit is the Lord Himself, present in you to guide your steps and not walk in sin anymore.

Michael Koulianos, in his book *Holy Spirit: The One Who Makes Jesus Real,* stated that "so many people want power, yet they've never gone to the Lord of power and discover Him. Let's remember that the presence of the Lord is the Lord Himself. So when the Lord breathed on His disciples, they received His indwelling presence. This was enough for them to go to Heaven and fellowship with Him every day at any moment. Today, if you know Jesus, you carry the presence of the Lord. He has promised to never leave us or forsake us, even until the end of the age (see Heb. 13:5)."[1]

The Holy Spirit's Mission from Creation

The Holy Spirit's mission in the universe is to create, to renew, to refresh, and to maintain the entire universe, including our physical and spiritual being, through the power of His Word. We are alive because of the Spirit of God, which gives us breath. Job stated in chapter 27 verse 3, "As long as I have life within me, the breath of God in my nostrils" (Job 27:3 NIV). "When the day of Pentecost came, they were all together in one place. Suddenly a sound like the blowing of a violent wind came from heaven and filled the whole house where they were sitting. They saw what seemed to be tongues of fire that separated and came to rest on each of them. All of them were filled with the Holy Spirit and began to speak in other tongues as the Spirit enabled them" (Acts 2:1–4 NIV).

I like to imagine that the "blowing of a violent wind" is the power that comes from heaven from the Father, the Holy Spirit that blows through the billions of dendrites, becoming action potential and electrical impulses flowing through every cell in our body, affecting the gene expression in the human DNA, producing a new creation in Christ, causing neurotransmitters to be released in the brain and the body so people experience the supernatural transformation of the mind and pleasant emotions of joy, love, peace, happiness, which bring hope, renewing our mind and our thoughts, which transform lives. This experience leads to trust in God and belief in Jesus, who restores in us the joy of salvation forever. This is a heavenly experience that you never forget. The Bible is full of examples of the physical manifestations of the power of the Holy Spirit in people's lives.

You Shall Receive Power

I like Dr. Crandall's testimony about his spiritual life when he was so thirsty for the presence of God and was praying to be filled with the Holy Spirit and was touched by Him in an unusual way in the operating room. He stated that he prayed many times even in his car, driving to work, to receive the power of the Holy Spirit as he was reading in the Bible, "You shall receive power." He stated that as a cardiologist and the director of the largest heart transplant center in the world, he had authority to perform invasive procedures to take the diseased heart out from patients' bodies and to perform heart transplants, but spiritually, he had no authority because he was not filled with the Holy Spirit, as is promised in the Word of God.

The power of the Holy Spirit came over him and filled his body, soul, and spirit, and he started to speak in a heavenly language, his hands lifted up, and to pray in the Holy Spirit, the power of the Holy Spirit came over Dr. Crandall in the operating room mightily, and he stated that his hands were automatically lifted in the air above his head and his mouth started to speak with no control while his mind was alert.

Dr. Chauncey Crandall described that moment in his book *Raising the Dead: A Doctor Encounters the Miraculous* when a dying woman came in the operating room with a massive heart attack. "I was standing over this woman, working catheters through her groin to the heart, inserting stents, trying to get her blood pressure up. We started IVs and hit her with atropine, epinephrine, and the clot-dissolving drugs called thrombolytics. We were trying to abort the heart attack by going in and helping the artery open itself up. But as we worked on her, death entered the operating room and her heart flat-lined. All of a sudden my hands went up in the air, uncontrollably. There I was with my arms raised, dressed in my scrub suit, with my mask on. I had no control over my arms. And I started speaking this unknown language. This river of a language I didn't understand started pouring out of my mouth. I thought, I can think, I can see, I can hear, but I have no control over what is coming out of my mouth. And I still had no control over my hands, which were hover-ing in the air over her body. This was embarrassing and I tried to put my hands down, but I couldn't. I continued mumbling an uncon-trollable river of language that I'm as far from understanding now as I was then. I could only wonder, What is going on? I looked at the nurses, and they were sure looking at me. They were waiting for me to give them further instructions, but all I could do was pray in a lan-guage I did not understand. I noticed that the words I was speaking came from deep down inside, rolling out, coming out of my belly. My brain did not have anything to do with it. Again, I could think. I could see. I could hear. But I couldn't control what I was saying and I couldn't bring my arms down. This went on for what seemed for-ever, although probably no longer than three to five minutes. All this time the heart monitor was sounding the piercing note that declares a patient has flatlined. Then a heartbeat came back. Then another heartbeat, and then the first perfect one. After about a dozen perfect heartbeats, I was able to put my arms down and speak normally."[2]

Praying for the sick in the hospital, clinic, or mission field, Dr. Crandall stated that Jesus is the name above all names. There is power and authority in the name of Jesus to heal the sick and to restore physical and spiritual health of those who are suffering and dying.[3] "Wherefore God also hath highly exalted him, and given him a name which is above every name: That at the name of Jesus every knee should bow, of things in heaven, and things in earth, and things under the earth; And that every tongue should confess that Jesus Christ is Lord, to the glory of God the Father" (Phil. 2:2–11 KJV). Have confidence in the authority of the name of Jesus Christ and the atoning power of the blood of Jesus that gives you power to destroy the work of the enemy and to overcome evil.

Michael Koulianos, in his book *The Jesus Book: Fall Recklessly in love with Jesus*, stated, "Jesus is not asking you to believe that He is God through your imagination or by blind hope. The greatest event in history was the moment He destroyed the power of death by walking out of that tomb two thousand years ago. Because of this miracle, we no longer have to fear death. Christ conquered this old enemy which so many fear. I have walked into that tomb in Jerusalem-and it is certainly empty! If His body were still in a grave on Earth, don't you think that it would have been found? He was the most famous person to have ever lived. Even holidays and our calendar hinge on His life. Good morals find their roots in His teaching. The greatest nations of the world are those who govern according His ways and instructions." Michael goes on saying that "the reason no one has ever discovered the remains of the Son of God is because He's not in the grave. He is in Heaven, waiting to come and receive His Bride, which are those who love Him. Jesus lives!"[4]

The Power of Praying in the Spirit

> "And they were all filled with the Holy Spirit and began to speak with other tongues, as the Spirit gave them utterance" (Acts 2:4 NKJV).

I was baptized in the Holy Spirit when I was a teenager back in Romania. The moment I was touched by the power of the Holy Spirit, my mouth started to speak fluently a new language. My mind was alert, but I had no control over my mouth and language. Since then, during my fervent prayers, the Holy Spirit will take control over my tongue and will intercede for different things that I do not know how to pray. In my early twenties, I was working in a big company with about three thousand employees, and I was the only believer in the baptism of the Holy Spirit. In my break time, I went close to a heating unit to warm up, and I started to whisper a prayer for the people around me. I vividly remember when the power of the Holy Spirit surged through my spirit and I started to pray in heavenly languages and sing praises to God.

The atmosphere changed among nonbelievers. They were more joyful and started to smile, helping one another, being more kind, and speaking words of encouragement to one another. I knew that change happened because the Holy Spirit was interceding for them when I was praying in the Spirit. There is power in the gift of speaking in the spiritual languages because our faith increases supernaturally when we pray in the Spirit. "But you, beloved, building yourselves up on your most holy faith, praying in the Holy Spirit" (Jude 1:20 NKJV).

You can know the wisdom of God and His will for every moment of your life when you speak in heavenly tongues. Jack Hayford, in his book *The Beauty of Spiritual Language: Unveiling the Mystery of Speaking in Tongues*, stated that the reason that speaking in spiritual language is so important is "that [it] is so obviously a miracle manifestation personal to the believer. It is proof that the Living God is ready to come and work in the life of every believer in a miraculous way, which can have special meaning to the believer and can also be shared with others through the gift of interpretation. When the gift of spiritual language comes, there is every reason to believe that other miracles will also become a part of this life to which Jesus invites us."[2]

Faith, insight, and wisdom will be increased, and miracles of healing and deliverance will happen through the power of the Holy Spirit. Because the Holy Spirit is praying through you, when you speak in spiritual language, it's praying the answers to your prayer. This is because only the Spirit knows the mind of God. Do you see the connection that the Holy Spirit is making between God's spiritual realm and our physical world? Science shows that worshipping and speaking in tongues change the activity in our brain structures.[3]

Researchers at the University of Pennsylvania School of Medicine have discovered decreased activity in the frontal lobes, an area of the brain associated with being in control of oneself. This pioneering study, involving functional imaging of the brain while subjects were speaking in tongues, is in the November issue of *Psychiatry*

Research: Neuroimaging, the official publication of the International Society for Neuroimaging in Psychiatry.[4] The decreased activity in the frontal lobe demonstrates what is written in the Word of God that the mind is fruitless when we pray in the Spirit. "For if I pray in a tongue, my spirit prays, but my understanding is unfruitful" (1 Cor. 14:14 NKJV)

The Holy Spirit knows what a cell in your body needs to be touched at the microscopic level. The Holy Spirit connects your spirit with God's anointing power. He helps us in our weakness. He makes intercessions when we speak in heavenly language as the Spirit leads us. "In the same way, the Spirit helps us in our weakness. We do not know what we ought to pray for, but the Spirit himself intercedes for us through wordless groans" (Rom. 8:26 NIV). Scientists demonstrated that when we speak in heavenly languages, the activity in the frontal lobe decreases. "Now, in a first of its kind study, scientists are shining the light on this mysterious practice—attempting to explain what actually happens physiologically to the brain of someone while speaking in tongues."

John G. Lake, in his book *Your Power in the Holy Spirit,* stated that "God is trying to get your mind occupied with Himself. God has come into you, and now He is drawing you into Himself."[5]

John G. Lake, in the same book, *Your Power in the Holy Spirit,* adds, "Many times I have talked with others in the Spirit by the Spirit, through the medium of tongues, and comprehended everything that was said to me, but I did not know it with my rational mind. It was not the sound of their words. It was that indefinable something that made it intelligent to my spirit. Spirit speaks to spirit, just as a man speaks to man. Your spirit speaks to God. God is Spirit. He answers back. Bless God! And I believe with all my heart that is what Paul had in mind when he talked about the 'unknown' tongues. (See 1 Corinthians 14.) The unknown tongue is that medium of internal revelation of God to you, the common language of the spirit of man, by which God communicates with your spirit."[6]

The Lamb of God

The Supremacy of the Name of Jesus

God is on a mission to redeem humanity. He walked in history to be the sacrifice Himself to shed His holy blood that His creation can overcome the devil through the power of the blood of the Lamb. "And they overcame him by the blood of the Lamb and by the word of their testimony; and they loved not their lives unto the death" (Rev. 12:11 KJV). Since creation, God knew that the devil wants to torment people with fear and shame from sin. Sin made Adam and Eve hide because their disobedience and sin against God's instructions made them shameful and afraid. Sin brings bad consequences in this life and for eternity. Only perfect love casts out fear. And God the Father, in His perfect love, sent Jesus Christ, His Only Son, to shed His blood on the cross to pay the price in full for our sins, to deliver the humanity from the shame of sin and from the fear and power of darkness. The blood of Jesus has the authority to wash your sins away and deliver us from all its bad consequences.

By faith in Jesus Christ's sacrifice and the power of His resurrection, the strategies of the devil are exposed. Resist the enemy to overcome through the power of the blood of Jesus. The power of His resurrection is at work in us so we can understand God's plan for salvation from eternal shame, fear, and death. God's plan for the followers of Jesus is to live in heaven, where Jesus went to prepare a place for us to be with Him forever. He transferred us from the kingdom of darkness to the kingdom of God's dearest Son, Jesus Christ, our King, to live forever. Keep your eyes on Jesus.

Without the Holy Spirit, you cannot understand things happening in heaven and the supremacy of Jesus Christ. Develop a tight relationship with the Holy Spirit. The Holy Spirit came with power, breathing spiritual life in those who ask of Him. The Holy Spirit came as violent wind, blowing, breathing, and giving life. He does the same today, blowing over the cortex in your brain through billions of dendrites, becoming electrical impulses, influencing your emotions and your feelings. He is flowing over you and through you, and you are immersed in God's presence. Then, living water springs from inside of you to quench the spiritual thirst of those around you. Jesus announced that faith in Him will cause rivers of living water to flow from our heart. "He who believes in Me, as the Scripture has said, out of his heart will flow rivers of living water" (John 7:38 NKJV). God's Word, the Living Water, can heal any emotional pain and disease through the power of the blood of Jesus.

Emotional Healing Through the Blood of Jesus

God is the Father of mercy, comforting you in your discomfort and troubles. "Blessed be the God and Father of our Lord Jesus Christ, the Father of mercies and God of all comfort, who comforts us in all our tribulation that we may be able to comfort those who are in any trouble, with the comfort with which we ourselves are comforted by God" (2 Cor. 1:3–11 NKJV). When you feel overwhelmed by stress from difficult situations and bad circumstances, discouraged, without hope, cry out to God in prayers. The power is in your prayers. When you pray, God hears your cry, and He supernaturally answers your prayers. You also rewire your brain for healthy connections with healthy thoughts, and you get healthier and stronger because "He gives strength to the weary and increases the power of the weak" (Isa. 40:29 NIV).

After I got married, as most parents desire a healthy family with healthy children, I got pregnant and everything was going well with my pregnancy. I did all the tests and ultrasound and followed all the advice from health-care providers by the book. But when I was very close to the due date, the baby stopped moving. I was alarmed by that and went for an extra ultrasound, and we were informed that the baby's heart had stopped beating and I would have a stillborn baby. I was admitted to the hospital for the natural birth of a stillborn baby. During the Communist regime, you cannot express your faith in any institution, including the hospital. You could not have your husband support you, or anybody from your family. You had to fight alone. My soul, my mind, my heart, and every cell inside of me were crying to God for help. Now my life was in danger, too, because I had been carrying a dead baby inside of my body for several days. My husband and I were afraid of me dying also. I had no medical knowledge then. I had only Jesus Christ, my Savior, on my side. I trusted Him with my whole heart. Family and Christian friends who knew the situations prayed also. That was our first baby. We did grieve intensely.

I remember that when I was at home to recover in my postdelivery period while my husband was working, I was very depressed, crying for long hours. But the Holy Spirit prompted me (besides the Bible that I was reading every day, especially the psalms and encouraging verses with God's promises) to read a book that secretly I got from a friend of mine. With the Bible next to me, I started to read this book *The Robe* (the book was translated in Romanian language and distributed secretly underground during the Communist regime in Romania at that time), where the Roman soldier who crucified Jesus suffered from a major depression from what he saw at Calvary and from his own thoughts, that he crucified the Lamb of God. He was healed instantly, miraculously from his terrible catatonic behavior when he touched Jesus's robe still stained with Jesus's own blood from the crucifixion.

The author Lloyd C. Douglas described that miracle with much detail in the book *The Robe: The Story of the Soldier Who Tossed for Christ's Robe and Won*, that when the soldier was reaching the bag for a weapon to kill himself because he could not endure anymore being oppressed and humiliated by those tormenting thoughts, he touched the robe that was placed purposefully by his slave in the same bag to save his life. The author stated, "For a long moment Marcellus stood transfixed, his fingers buried in the dreaded, hateful garment.

Then, sitting down on the edge of the couch, he slowly drew the robe toward him. He stared at it uncomprehendingly; held it up to the light; rubbed it softly against his bare arm. He couldn't analyze his peculiar sensations, but something very strange had happened to him. His agitation was stilled. Rising as if from a dream, he laid the robe over his arm and went out into the peristyle. He sat down and draped it across the broad arms of his chair. Smoothing it gently with his hand, he felt a curious elation; an indefinable sense of relief. A great load had been lifted. He wasn't afraid anymore! Hot tears gathered in his eyes and overflowed. After a while he rose and carried the robe back to Demetrius's room, replacing it where he had found it. Unaccustomed to his new sense of wellbeing, he was puzzled about what to do next. He went into the studio and laughed as he looked at Demetrius's poor little statuette. The house wasn't quite large enough to hold him; so, donning his toga, he went out into the garden. It was there that his slave found him."[1]

I believe that story is true. I cried even more because I was touched by God's invisible hand that day. Tears were flowing from my eyes on my face and wet the pages of that book when I was reading about the power of the blood of Jesus that healed the Roman Marcellus, who won Christ's robe as a prize through gambling. The book says that he was determined to find the truth about Jesus's robe in his possession, which was carrying literally Jesus's blood on it. The book says that during his time of analyzing the situation, that he took part of Christ's crucifixion, he was miraculously healed from his oppression and severe psychosis.

The restoration of my soul started when I started to understand the truth about the power of the blood and the cross of Jesus Christ at a deeper level. I felt an unspeakable joy that was greater than my oppressive thoughts and the peace of God, which passes all understanding. My painful emotions of depression were replaced with hope, knowing that the blood of Jesus did not lose its power to cleanse us all from our sins and to restore our physical and emotional health. I was healed instantly by faith in the power of the cross and the blood of Jesus Christ, understanding that truth by reading the book *The Robe*, knowing that there is power in the blood and the cross of Jesus Christ. That gave me an impulse and more motivation to read more the Bible, to memorize verses to sustain further my healed soul, spirit, and body.

If you are going right now through a tough time and feel very depressed and your soul and spirit are crushed by the heaviness of pressure of a loss and painful situation and you need a fresh touch from heaven, read the Bible, the Living Word of God, and also the book *The Robe*. I was healed completely while meditating on the love of God and His sacrifice to give His only Son to die on the cross at Calvary for my sins and to heal all my diseases. Depression disappeared supernaturally. I did not need antidepressants, and I did not need psychological counseling. They are good interventions, too, but for me, Jesus Christ, the Lamb of God, was my only counselor.

For you may be different, you may need antidepressant for situational depression and a psychologist to advise you and counseling for your unique situation. I recommend that you use both of them and not underestimate the power of the blood of Jesus Christ to heal your crushed spirit, restore the joy in your soul, and mend your broken heart. I am glad that in the most difficult time in my life, God provided the book *The Robe* (when it was unlawful to read Christian literature or Christian books during the Communist regime), which led me again to the cross of Jesus Christ, who died for me not only to wash my sins away but also to heal my broken heart. I loved that book so much. I fell in love with Jesus one more time. He became my true friend forever. I felt that Christ was living in me. "To them God willed to make known what are the riches of the glory of this mystery among the Gentiles: which is Christ in you, the hope of glory" (Col. 1:27 NKJV). His blood has the power to cleanse you from all your sins (small or big) and give you hope that brings healing to your body, soul, and spirit. Nobody can take that hope away from you. "He heals the brokenhearted and binds up their wounds" (Ps. 147:3 NIV).

His Word is true. He healed my broken heart and bound up my wound. I was able to get up in the morning and function again with joy in my heart that God had healed me. He is the same yesterday, today, and forever. God's promises are true, and His Word is alive, and the hope we receive is real, bringing us alive again. Spiritually, my soul and spirit were dehydrated from the brokenness and thoughts of discouragement and depression. I was crushed in my spirit, discouraged, confused, and unable to make decisions for my daily life, but the Lord restored the joy of salvation of my soul and spirit. He was close to me and was at my side every moment, as He promised. "The LORD is close to the brokenhearted and saves those who are crushed in spirit" (Ps. 34:18 NIV).

Put a covering of the blood of Jesus over yourself, your children, and your family. We are at a spiritual war. Speak against the enemy and stand up and fight, pleading the blood of Jesus over you, your family, your friends, your neighbors, city, country, and the world that God loves so much. "For God so loved the world that He gave His only begotten Son, that whoever believes in Him should not perish but have everlasting life" (John 3:16 NKJV). Stand your ground in Jesus's name. All authority belongs to Jesus Christ. Fight with authority that Christ placed inside of us. Stay under the authority of the blood of Jesus. Understand who the enemy is. It is not the people that is your enemy; it is the devil's agenda working through people who do not recognize the enemy's strategy and are not aware of the devil's plan and methods of attack. They do not have the discerning spirit because they are not on the spirit wave channel to catch the voice of the Spirit. The devil is pushing his agenda because he has little time left and is looking to deceive many. Live according to the Word. Use God's Word to fight the enemy. Pray with authority in faith, using God's promises. Our battle is not against flesh and blood but against evil spirits. You cannot battle with flesh solutions but with spiritual solutions, which are the blood of the Lamb and His living Word. Open your spiritual eyes to see that the Lord fights for you.

Wisdom and Revelation in Jesus's Name

The Holy Spirit blows in our mind, giving wisdom and revelation, teaching us how to discern the will of God in every move we make, in every thought we have, and in every word we speak, influencing the world around us. "But the Advocate, the Holy Spirit, whom the Father will send in my name, will teach you all things and will remind you of everything I have said to you" (John 14:26 NIV). He will remind you of all things if you spend time to learn the Word of God, to memorize scriptures, to be consolidated by the hippocampus area, involved in memory consolidation, and deposit them in your other brain structures and cortex. The Holy Spirit will activate them and bring them in your conscious mind when you pray and meditate on His promises and when you need them, and they will strengthen your thoughts of hope and faith when you go through the storms of life and different trials and need them the most.

I did experience that during the Communist system, when everyone around me was mocking my faith in Christ and when the enemy was roaring to destroy my spiritual life. The Holy Spirit inspired me, reminded me of God's promises, guided me, gave me wisdom and discernment to make the right decisions to stay strong in the most difficult situations, and brought so much joy and peace that I could not comprehend. But that happened because I memorized and stored in my memory storage God's promises in His living Word, that the battle is the Lord's and He will never leave me or forsake me. The Holy Spirit brought those powerful verses in my conscious mind, and the fear of persecution dissipated.

God's Image Restored Through Jesus

■ Christ Restores Your Image

Each of us has our own image about ourselves from what we think about us and what others tell us what they think about us. But each one of us was created in God's image. God placed His image in every human DNA at creation. We mirror with our Creator. He imprinted His image and His language in each human DNA. He built in our human being and programmed our DNA to be the imitator of Jesus and become like Jesus. He placed in the human brain mirror neurons to mirror and imitate Christ. Human image has been deformed by sin. Your image is restored through Jesus's death and resurrection. Your identity in Christ is well documented in God's Word and revealed by the power of the Holy Spirit. You are a child of God, wonderfully made, whole in Christ, a saint, an ambassador of Christ, God's masterpiece, forgiven, washed clean, free, a temple of the Holy Spirit, co-heir with Christ, new creation, righteous, adopted in God's family, holding a secured future, never alone, set apart, a sweet aroma, and more.[1]

We have mirror neurons placed in our brain to be able to learn from one another. But we must use those mirror neurons to learn good things, to develop good behavior. The fruit of kindness and goodness can be achieved through compassion and love poured in us by Christ. God placed mirror neurons to have compassion for people and to love them unconditionally, to cry with those who cry, to feel their pain.[2]

◾ The Purpose of Mirror Neurons to Imitate Christ

Christians think alike, act alike, and talk alike because they renew their mind through the power of the Spirit of God and the washing of His Word and have the mind of Christ. We must be genetically like Christ because Christ lives in us. One friend of mine who did not know Jesus Christ many years ago was spending more time around Christians due to her increased needs for help due to her illness. Many Christians surrounded her with love and helped her in her time of need, and she observed their behavior, language, attitude, good deeds, love for people, serving tirelessly. She stated one time about Christians around her that "these people speak the same thing, tell the same experiences, act the same, behave the same, love the same, care the same, pray the same." She was laughing, stating that "they are made of the same mother." These people she was observing and talking about all were born-again Christians, followers and imitators of Christ, who had Christ's DNA.

God created the human brain with mirror neurons to have the mind of Christ and to imitate Christ to become like Him. "In your relationships with one another, has the same mindset as Christ Jesus" (Phil. 2:5 NIV). When you imitate Christ, you reprogram your brain to think like Christ and start to live like Christ. Your mind is connected to a different source of power and energy for different thoughts that they create neuropeptide, switching on genes to express themselves through epigenetic mechanism, creating new, strong connections in the brain, renewing your mind.

Science discovered that the brain's structure (involved in memory consolidation as hippocampus) gets enlarged when they are challenged by cognitive demands. An example is driving a taxi in London. Science demonstrated that "taxi drivers had plumper memory centers than their peers. It seemed that the longer someone had been driving a taxi, the larger his hippocampus, as though the brain expanded to accommodate the cognitive demands of navigating London's streets."[3]

To imitate Christ, we must navigate the Word of God with perseverance, putting demand on our cognitive brain to memorize

His Word to be able to become like Christ. "Therefore be imitators of God as dear children" (Eph. 5:1 NKJV). Going in opposite direction, living with negative thoughts will bring negative changes in your brain's cells and your entire body. "When we have feelings of anger, sadness, guilt, excitement, happiness or nervousness, each separate emotion releases its own flurry of neuropeptides. Those peptides surge through the body and connect with those receptors which change the structure of each cell as a whole."[4]

The devil distorted your image and makes you experience low self-esteem. The devil wants you to feel discouraged, inappropriate, unworthy, rejected, abandoned, broken, and oppressed. The devil brings fear to make you anxious, depressed, with negative thoughts and negative effects on your brain structures to release neurochemicals in unhealthy amount, to cause unpleasant emotions with negative physical signs and symptoms and further affect your body, soul, and spirit. But the power of the Holy Spirit reveals that you are a friend of God; you are not rejected. In Christ you are justified, forgiven, chosen, inseparable from God's love, with abundant life, redeemed, belonging to Jesus Christ and His kingdom with no end. That brings hope that lets you experience emotions of joy, peace, happiness, and healthy thoughts, growing new healthy neurons, healing your inside emotional pain.

Led by the Holy Spirit

The Holy Spirit Gives Instructions

To illustrate how the Holy Spirit is at work in our lives, I can share our experience in our business when we were extremely busy (thirty-bed memory care facility, providing care twenty-four hours a day, seven days a week). The Holy Spirit inspired and prompted us to build another memory care facility with thirty-bed capacity. We felt that we needed to reach our full potential and to fulfill our destiny. We proceeded with the project and prayed for acceleration. God gave us victory after victory when the devil started to create barriers and to stop us from moving forward. Many people showed up for different phases in the project, but the Holy Spirit helped us contract with the right people and at the right time, to finish the project on time and to accomplish His will. God brought loyal associates and moved on very fast despite all the adversities.

When we were close to retirement, God sent the best investors to buy both facilities and take over the business right when we finished the project beyond our imagination. We did not even list or advertise for sale. The broker came four times to ask if we wanted to sell even before the construction of the second facility with thirty more beds was done. The prophecy was fulfilled as the Bible says in Amos 9:13, "'The days are coming,' declares the LORD, 'when the reaper will be overtaken by the plowman and the planter by the one treading grapes. New wine will drip from the mountains and flow from all the hills'" (Amos 9:13 NIV). It was God's hand moving through this broker to insist that we sell even when we were still in construction, before we finished the project. We were overtaken by surprise, and blessings started to flow in abundance in a new way. We knew that was God's hand moving through these amazing investors and made us free to travel in the world to speak at different conferences, to have interviews with radio programs and TV and dedicate time doing more mission work in the health field. The Holy Spirit will show you the best associates in business; He knows every solution to your problems.

The Holy Spirit Prevents Depression When You Are Burnt Out

People get easily depressed when they are burnt out due to their increased responsibilities at work, the culture changing, new rules and regulations, changes in organization, new practice, new environment, people with different personalities, new technology, new skills, abilities, personnel, etc. Everything is changing at a very fast speed, causing more demands and challenges to be burn out and in great distress. My example, I arrived in the US with nothing about thirty years ago. I did not speak English, I had no money (one hundred dollars in my pocket borrowed from my sister), and I had different profession but no social support. In that situation, it was very easy to get depressed and discouraged. Thoughts were racing in my brain. What was I going to do? Nobody could see my thoughts or the battles inside of me. But the Holy Spirit knew. He guided me step by step and helped me to focus on positive things, believing God's promises for my life and for my future.

I was grateful that I was in the greatest country in the world. I looked at every circumstances with optimism; I detached myself from negative thoughts.

I had passion for work, for prayer, and for the Word of God. I did not lose my focus even when all circumstances were against my desires and my dreams. I looked for a job right away. But I did not speak English to apply for the right profession. I learned to say over and over, "I like to work." So I applied for a job as a caregiver in a nursing home, and by God's grace, they allowed me to work as a "bed-maker," to be around disabled people, and I was able to assist them as much as I knew how. My passion had always been to help others, especially the disabled, even from a young age in my country of origin, when I did not know anything about caregiving. The Holy Spirit was right there with me, increasing my passion and compassion, and by God's grace, I was able to work two jobs from the beginning to keep my thoughts busy, focusing on work.

As a caregiver in training to become a nursing aide, I had to have a white uniform and a stethoscope. At that time, instead of looking at my problems, I started to use my gift of being optimist and I allowed the positive thoughts to grow. I said to myself, "Now, you look like a doctor instead of an economist." I did not know that the Holy Spirit dropped that idea in my head long ago, before I actually became a doctor. At that time in my spirit, I felt happy, leaping of joy on the hallways of that nursing home, that I had a job and I was able to help those old folks with so many conditions and many physical needs and behavior problems. I started to pray for them, leaving my problems aside. My problems were minor now compared with those of people with disabilities, who spent the rest of their lives in a wheelchair or in a hospital bed. Through my attitude, I did build a strong resilience, and I was rejoicing in the Holy Spirit, that He was with me and gave me strength when I was weak and discouraged.

The Holy Spirit Helps You Build a Strong Resilience

Meditating on the Word of God and His promises, you can build a strong resilience by using optimism, seeing God's purpose and meaning in your life. You develop skills to solve problems to overcome obstacles. Your mind and thoughts are directed by the Holy Spirit. I had to communicate inside of me and to fellowship with the Holy Spirit to be strong and fulfill my destiny from day 1, when I arrived in the USA, as is written in 2 Corinthians 13:14. "The grace of the Lord Jesus Christ, and the love of God, and the fellowship of the Holy Spirit, be with you all" (NASB). Fellowship with Holy Spirit can empower you to reach out unthinkable things through strong resilience.

Many times when I was discouraged, I was meditating on God's mercy and grace during my young age in a Communist country. The Holy Spirit reminded me about the prophecies, about my future, that I would be blessed beyond imagination, more than I could ask or think. I was encouraged many times when I attended prayer meetings back in Romania through simple Christians who had the gift of prophecy. They spoke from the Holy Spirit. They did not know that one day I would go to the greatest nation in the world and God would open so many doors of opportunity for me and my family, beyond any imagination there in a Communist country. Because we are created in God's image and carry His Spirit, the Spirit desires things from above, to refresh, renew, restore, revive our emotions of love and joy, accomplishing His plans in our lives. We are moved by the impulses of the Holy Spirit when He manifests Himself in our physical world. "The mature children of God are those who are moved by the impulses of the Holy Spirit" (Rom. 8:14 TPT).

The Spirit revives us and restores our dreams, giving us hope and peace for life. "The mind governed by the flesh is death, but the mind governed by the Spirit is life and peace" (Rom. 8:6 NIV). The flesh desires to live according to its desire. Renew your mind according to the Holy Spirit. Let the Holy Spirit renew the part of your mind that is not renewed. We are transferred from the kingdom of darkness to the kingdom of light. We recognize the work of the King of light and Spirit of life. We are here with a purpose, to be the light in a dark world, to represent the King.

The Holy Spirit Heals Emotional Wounds

Kris Vallotton, in his book *Destined to Win: How to Embrace Your God-Given Identity and Realize Your Kingdom Purpose*, talks about "tridimensional wholeness," giving the example of tridimensional healing in Acts chapter 3, stating about "Peter and John going to the temple at 3:00 p.m. to pray. There was a man there who had been born lame, and he was begging for money. Peter basically said, 'We don't have money because we are ministers, but what we do have we will gladly give to you. In the name of Jesus, walk!' Then Peter grabbed the guy by the hand and lifted him up. Suddenly the guy jumped up and started walking, leaping, and praising God. In other words, he was healed physically (walking), he was healed emotionally (leaping: a physical manifestation of excitement or joy), and he was healed spiritually (praising God)! It's a beautiful demonstration of tridimensional nature of God because God heals the whole man (Acts 3:1–8)."[1]

To have our emotional wounds healed, we do need tridimensional touch from heaven. At conferences during praying time in the Spirit, many people will testify that they were touched by the power of the Holy Spirit in a profound way, being healed emotionally from wounds created in their hearts for a long time, and fear, anxiety, depression, and thoughts of desperation disappeared. The burden and weight of sins disappeared. They were full of joy and hope. The written Word is confirmed each time, as is written in Isaiah 1:18, "'Come now, and let us reason together,' says the LORD, 'Though your sins are as scarlet, they will be as white as snow; though they are red like crimson, and they will be like wool'" (NASB). Once the sins are forgiven, the burden from sin disappears and the emotional healing of our deep wounds in the soul takes place. "And these signs will follow those who believe: In My name they will cast out demons; they will speak with new tongues; they will take up serpents; and if they drink anything deadly, it will by no means hurt them; they will lay hands on the sick, and they will recover" (Mark 16:17–18 NKJV).

The Holy Spirit Does Immeasurable Things

The same Spirit that raised Jesus from the dead lives in us to do immeasurable things for His glory. "Now to him who is able to do immeasurably more than all we ask or imagine, according to his power that is at work within us, to him be glory in the church and in Christ Jesus throughout all generations, for ever and ever! Amen"

197

(Eph. 3:20 NIV). Nature waits and discovers the sons who live in the Holy Spirit; the sons walk in the light, and there is no darkness or bondage. "The creation itself, also, will be delivered from the bondage of corruption, into the glorious liberty of the children of God" (Rom. 8:21 NKJV). The Holy Spirit works in us with power for the glory of the Father through the Son. God acts in heaven, but His Word was sent to earth to work through the power of the Holy Spirit. "He sent out his Word and healed them; he rescued them from the grave" (Ps. 107:20 NIV).

You will receive supernatural power when the Holy Spirit comes; holy fire will touch your heart and mind, and you will be filled with boldness to speak God's Word and save the lost. "After they prayed, the place where they were meeting was shaken. And they were all filled with the Holy Spirit and spoke the word of God boldly" (Acts 4:31 NIV). My husband and I attended a medical Christian conference a few years ago where Dr. Crandall was the main speaker, and he prayed for about three hundred doctors and other medical professionals for boldness and a holy fire to come into our hearts. And God answered that prayer. Boldness came over us all. Dr. Crandall gave his testimony on how boldness came over him when the Holy Spirit came over him. We all are changed from glory to glory when the Holy Spirit comes over us and in us. The Holy Spirit wants to use you to demonstrate His supernatural power.

The supernatural power of the Holy Spirit must enter in your physical body to manifest Himself through you for the world to see the signs of the kingdom and the immeasurable things that the Holy Spirit is doing. More than four decades ago, the power of the Holy Spirit came to me unexpectedly. I was praying, but I did not know what to experience. The Holy Spirit from the spiritual realm entered in my physical body like a "wind" passing the threshold of the physical cortex in my brain, becoming electrical impulses, traveling through my neurons (the nervous cells body, axons, dendrites) like a jolt of electricity and holy fire, and there was an intense physical heat that I sensed in my whole body. My tongue started to speak, without control, the highest praises to God Almighty in a heavenly language. When praises were aroused in my spirit, I suddenly entered

God's spiritual realm, rejoicing in His presence. It was in the middle of the night, passing from New Year's Eve of 1973 to the first day of New Year 1974, but time was nothing when I started to experience His presence.

I was immersed in the Spirit of the almighty God; my body was shaking, feeling His glory in that room, and my soul was filled with unspeakable joy. The wind of the Holy Spirit blew over me, passing the threshold of the physical brain's cortex, and the electrical impulses started to rush through my body, releasing neurotransmitters that made my body show physical manifestation with signs as a pleasant feeling of very fine shaking and vibration to rejoice, to feel an intense heat, unspeakable joy, and overwhelming heavenly love. They were such beautiful feelings that I did not want them to stop from the inside of me. The "rivers of living waters" started to spring and to flow. I was immersed in the Holy Spirit. That happens when the Holy Spirit invades our physical body, soul, and spirit and transforms our life.

Nicodemus came to Jesus at night to ask about being born again, and Jesus told Him, "Very truly I tell you, no one can enter the kingdom of God unless they are born of water and the Spirit… You must be born again. The wind blows wherever it pleases. You hear its sound, but you cannot tell where it comes from or where it is going. So it is with everyone born of the Spirit" (John 3:5–8). Indeed, "the wind" was blowing; we did not know what to expect, where it was coming from over us and through us to change our thinking, our mind, to become new creation, to get born again with new spiritual DNA. The Holy Spirit comes to dwell in us so can witness for Jesus, because Christ lives in us. "I have been crucified with Christ and I no longer live, but Christ lives in me. The life I now live in the body, I live by faith in the Son of God, who loved me and gave himself for me" (Gal. 2:20 NIV).

Oneness with Christ is a supernatural phenomenon done by the power of the Spirit, and nothing can touch you. "But whoever is united with the Lord is one with him in spirit" (1 Cor. 6:17). Do not block His power through your doubts and unbelief. Your purpose on this planet and your destiny is to represent Him everywhere you go and to be a sign. The Holy Spirit helps you represent God everywhere you are called to represent Him. He wants to bring restoration, deliverance, and healing to a broken world around you.

The Holy Spirit Gives Authority

"Truly I tell you, whatever you bind on earth will be bound in heaven, and whatever you loose on earth will be loosed in heaven" (Matt. 18:18 NIV). In the name of Jesus Christ, through the power of the Holy Spirit, you have authority to bind and to release on earth and will be bound and released in heaven. God is looking for faithful servants to follow His call to use the authority through the blood of Jesus and the power of the cross, His death, and His resurrection. All the power was given to Him when He rose from the dead and gave to His disciples His authority to continue His work on this planet until He returns.

The Power of Prayer

A New Level of Prayer

When God touched my life and, through Jesus, washed my sins away, He sent the Holy Spirit, who changed my way of praying and my actions. I hardly waited to pray on my knees to fellowship with the Father, to feel His presence and His supernatural touch. I knew that in His presence I would be filled with unspeakable joy. I experienced the fruit of the Spirit when I spent time in prayer, and God poured out His Spirit over me. I remember, when I was in my first love as a born-again believer, one night I arrived home late from a late night of prayer and fell on my knees to pray more. It was two o'clock in the morning, and I knelt again in prayer, and the Holy Spirit was praying through me. My hands went up uncontrolled, and my face was gazing toward heaven, my mouth filled with words of praise and thanksgiving, praying in a heavenly language.

In a Communist country, we did not have the teaching about lifting up of hands and praising God to give Him thanks. We were only wailing in our prayers because of the oppression. But the Holy Spirit took control of my mind, my heart, my tongue, and my hands. My heart was rejoicing in the Lord, filled with the Holy Spirit. The Holy Spirit will teach you how to pray. God is asking you to grow to a new level of prayer. You first must remain in Him and let His Word remain in you. When you remain in Him, whatever you ask, you will receive. "If you abide in Me, and My words abide in you, you will ask what you desire, and it shall be done for you" (John 15:7 NKJV). We must come with fasting in desperation for God to move in us. In desperation we pray differently for ourselves, for our family, for our city, and for our nation.

201

Daniel came with humility and prayed with fervency and intensity and got God's attention. He made confession for himself and for the entire nation, "Great God Almighty, we sinned and committed iniquity." Shadrach, Meshach, and Abednego confessed the sins of the government and their people as their own sins. Confessing the sins of people to God as our own sins does not mean that we take the sins of the government or other people on our shoulders. We need to confess the government's sins and repent on their behalves intentionally. Ezra fasted with a broken heart for the sins of the Israelites and confessed their sins to God in prayer. "At the evening sacrifice I arose from my fasting; and having torn my garment and my robe, I fell on my knees and spread out my hands to the LORD my God. And I said: 'O my God, I am too ashamed and humiliated to lift up my face to You, my God; for our iniquities have risen higher than *our* heads, and our guilt has grown up to the heavens'" (Ezra 9:5–6).

I vividly remember how we prayed for the people's sins in the government of the Communist country who denied God, back in Romania, during the Communist regime. At a very young age, I attended prayer meetings with believers who spent hours late in the night on their knees in secret places, hiding from Communists, making intercession for the country. God heard his children's cries and looked down with mercy, and the time came suddenly when the Communist regime failed unexpectedly and evangelists flooded Romania from Europe and America to bring the good news of the gospel even on a stadium after seventy years of denying the existence of the sovereign and almighty God. Another great example is Daniel, who sought God's mercy in prayer. He knew God's heart for his people. Daniel took personal interest in others. We must take personal interest in others. We need to know the needs in close relationship. Daniel knew the needs of his nation. He knew God's heart's desire to set people free. Daniel knew the future of his nation.

Perseverance in Prayer Shapes the World

It is God's desire to get us to a higher level. Perseverance in prayer is very important. It is a spiritual battle. We must humble in front of God and stay in the battle until we win. We stayed in the battle during the Communist regime every single day until Communism collapsed. He heard our prayers from the first day when I started to pray. We were desperate in front of God. I learned to pray at a different level. We must pray with expectation that God answers prayers. The twenty-four elders are bowing down in worship in heaven. The prayers of the saints are before God. "Now when He had taken the scroll, the four living creatures and the twenty-four elders fell down before the Lamb, each having a harp, and golden bowls full of incense, which are the prayers of the saints" (Rev. 5:8 NKJV).

When we persevere in prayers, God answers. We know the power of prayer when we get results from the prayer. God called us to pray and to stand in the gap for our family, nation, the next generation and for restoration. We need to humble ourselves in fasting, praying; as Daniel did, God will intervene on our behalf and show His power. When you fight in prayer, declare the Word of God with authority given by Jesus against disobedience, discouragement, unforgiveness, disbelief, disengagement, anger, corruption, perversion, pornography, abortion, crimes, divorce, drugs, laziness, and sin. God created man with free choice, but sin is like a disease. God gave the antidote for sin—that is, repentance and salvation through the blood of Jesus. We must be people quick to repent.

From creation, Adam gave his authority to Satan. Satan took authority over the earth and started to destroy it. Everything bad is the result of sin. Jesus took back the authority from Satan through the power of the cross and His holy blood shed on the cross, and through His death and resurrection, all authority was given back to Jesus and He gave it back to His children. That was God's plan for redemption for mankind from creation. Author Derek Prince, in his book *Shaping History Through Prayer and Fasting*, stated, "God's purpose in man's redemption reflects His original purpose in man's creation. God's redeeming grace lifts man from his position of slavery and restores him to his position of dominion."[1] In the same book, Derek Prince also talks about a level of prayer in his life, that for him "the power of prayer to shape history is no mere abstract theological formula. I have seen it demonstrated in my own experience in many occasion."[2]

Use the authority given by Jesus to rise against every demonic strategy and generational curses through prayer. Jesus Christ, who is seated at the right hand of the Father, in glory, reaches down to earth through the power of the Holy Spirit to bind the wounds of the broken people in the lowest points. He knows your brokenness and the curses on your life and wants to set you free.

When you pray, you enter God's presence and the curse of hate, depression, and suicidal ideation—which is a curse that is passed to three to four generations, causing physical diseases—is broken in Jesus's name. Jesus took the authority from Satan and gave it to us, you and me. All authority belongs to Jesus, and He gave it to us. When we sin, we lose authority. Due to sin, people feel miserable and we compromise God's power given to us. But we are a new creation and have authority in Jesus's name. Jesus lives in us, and He is the one who lives in you, greater than the one who lives in the world.

Praying before the problems is the best approach to solve them with no worries and no struggles. A few years ago, I made a commitment to pray one hour every day before work for a few years. During my prayer times were moments saturated with power and energy that I cannot describe, and the Holy Spirit was interceding in English or Romanian and in heavenly languages for several minutes for many unknown problems at that time. I knew that was the Holy Spirit, because I did not have control over my prayer. Something like a fountain was inside of me, and like "rivers of the living waters," it was flowing through my mouth. Little did I know then that the Holy Spirit was interceding at that time for our business and for the future problems that we did not know would exist. We were in the process of building a new memory care facility with thirty units. The devil knew that great blessings would come from that project both for us as owners and for the disabled old people who needed care with dignity to the end of their lives. The devil started the battle with all kinds of issues.

To enumerate just a few, the banks could not qualify us for the construction loan because the general contractor did not cooperate with the bank in their terms and conditions. He started the construction with no permit from the city and no finances in place. Our contract stated clearly for the general contractor, "Do not commence construction without permit from the city and without finances in place." It was from the bank, but he started anyway. We got an order to stop construction from the city with fines and penalties that we had to pay every single month for more than one year because the general contractor did not respect the terms and conditions mentioned in the contract and started construction with no construction permit.

During this time, while we waited for the city to issue permit for more than a year, the erosion of the slope started because it was left too long in the rain. In the Northwest, it rains a lot. Above this property was a church newly built. The pastor from the church, who was in desperation of the situation, started to complain to the city for taking too long to proceed with the construction, threatening us that they would call the attorney to sue us for leaving the slope too long exposed to the rain, causing terrain erosion and affecting the church's property. From every side we encountered injustice from the general contractor, no cooperation from the city to issue the permit in time, and to make matters worse, the church pastor was threatening to sue us. This is just a very short version of the situation we were in after I started to pray one hour every day. It was like every demon from hell came out, trying to stop our blessings and causing financial damages and increasing our stress level to the roof. I recognized the spiritual warfare right away. I started a different level of prayer. (I wrote that model of prayer in *Find Your Peace*.)

There was delay in the project because of the work of the enemy trying to hinder and raising all kinds of barriers. I started to pray for acceleration to be able to meet the deadlines with the bank for finances. God honored our prayers. He sent a new general contractor to our door who asked us to give him the job without knowing what we were struggling with. He got everything in order, cooperated with the bank, who qualified him in a matter of weeks, and we got the construction loan right away, got the permit from the city in short time, and finished the project in time. Pastor Larry Huch and Tiz were visiting from Texas and, per our best friend Kay's arrangements, stopped by at this facility and prayed for the entire morning and broke all the curses of that project. We got the inspection done in the same day and obtained the license to operate the business with no problems. All the beds were filled miraculously in a few months. Then a great investor knocked on the door to buy the business, and we were really blessed beyond what we could ask or think. To God is *all* the glory. Even with our own power, wisdom, skills, and expertise, we could not have made that happen without the prayers in the Holy Spirit at a different level.

I am giving my testimony (not with much details, though) there to increase your faith, that when you pray in the Holy Spirit, you do not waste your time. The Holy Spirit knows the things of God; He knows the solutions to your problems and the answers to your prayers. Start praying in good time before problems arrive. Pray when all is fine, because you do not know when the enemy strikes. Deposit prayers of any kind in your account in heaven. Then in due time, you can be more than a conqueror. Keep the enemy under your feet through different levels of prayers.

Dr. Scott Hannen, in his book *Stop the Pain: The Six to Fix: A Complete Six-Step Approach to Detect and Correct the Cause of Chronic Pain and Suffering*, emphasizes that "according to scientists, prayer and meditation are not mere practices for someone of faith, but are viable option to assist in improving the quality of life, Prayer and meditation have been found to produce a clinical significant reduction in resting as well as ambulatory blood pressure, to reduce heart rate, to result in cardiorespiratory synchronization, to alter levels of melatonin and serotonin, to boost the immune response, to decrease the levels of reactive oxygen species (oxidation), to reduce stress and promote positive mood states, to reduce anxiety and pain and enhance self-esteem. Most everyone should be able to find 15 minutes for prayer and meditation each day to help their body reduce its levels of stress, inflammation, and oxidation."

The Source of Motivation

God Is the Resource for Pleasure Forever

You must fight the battle with God's army. Use the resources God gave you. Fight with wisdom and kindness, with dedication in your families, willing to change the destiny of your spouses, children, siblings, parents, etc. We read in Proverbs 31 that the wise woman gets her strength and her resources directly from God and involves Him in making decisions.

"She speaks with wisdom, and faithful instruction is on her tongue. She watches over the affairs of her household and does not eat the bread of idleness. Her children arise and call her blessed; her husband also, and he praises her: 'Many women do noble things, but you surpass them all.' Charm is deceptive, and beauty is fleeting; but a woman who fears the LORD is to be praised. Honor her for all that her hands have done, and let her works bring her praise at the city gate" (Prov. 31:26–31 NIV). The Holy Spirit gives you wisdom, discernment, revelation, understanding, and knowledge. Involve God in your daily decisions. You must grow because you have a role in everything.

The power of the Holy Spirit works in you. The Holy Spirit is the chief of the universe. The Holy Spirit must transform your life and change you completely. He is the source of wisdom in every decision you make. People make bad decisions when they are looking for joy and pleasure in the wrong places. The joy and pleasures they will find in those wrong places are only a Band-Aid to a very deep and infected wound. I did wound care for several patients for many years, and I know how serious those deep wounds look like and how serious and aggressive the wound care must be to prevent septicemia and premature death from those wounds if treated irresponsibly and superficially. According to the prophet Jeremiah, "They dress the wound of my people as though it were not serious. 'Peace, peace,' they say, when there is no peace" (Jer. 6:14 NIV). People live with deep wounds in their soul in fear, with no peace when they do not trust God and do not let the Holy Spirit to guide their life even though in appearance they look at peace.

People make decisions in life and forget that in God's presence is the fullness of joy and pleasures forever. "You will show me the path of life; In Your presence *is* fullness of joy; At Your right hand *are* pleasures forevermore" (Ps. 16:11 NKJV). Only God can restore the true joy that brings healing physically and spiritually. There is unspeakable joy when you are restored from the wage of sin, which is death. "For I will turn their mourning to joy, Will comfort them, And make them rejoice rather than sorrow" (Jer. 31:13b NKJV). God wants to bring you back in relationship with Him to restore your joy. Sin separates us from God because of His holiness.

God does not like separation from humanity. God likes to fill our hearts and minds with joyful thoughts so we can experience pleasant emotions in Him when we involve Him in our decisions. We were created for His eternal pleasure. The pleasure center in our brains has been highjacked by the temporary pleasures in the world when we do not involve God in our decisions. Discussing about Christ as the true source of joy, Beth Moore, in one of her Bible study books, *Living Beyond Yourself,* stated, "Once again we discover that the fruit of the Spirit originates in the heart and personality of God: 'I have told you this so that my joy may be in you and that your joy may be completed' (John 15:11). Chara just like agape belongs to Christ. He is the Possessor and Giver of true joy. Fleeting moments of 'happiness' maybe experienced through other channels but inner joy flows only from Christ."[1]

You can experience spiritual happiness when you rejoice in Him. "I have been crucified with Christ; it is no longer I who live, but Christ lives in me; and the *life* which I now live in the flesh I live by faith in the Son of God, who loved me and gave Himself for me"

(Gal. 2:20 NKJV). We remain in Christ when His Word lives in us, and by faith we live in the Son of God. The joy in Christ is experienced by many believers. People who lose joy are sad and become depressed, fearful, and anxious. As primary care provider (a general practitioner doctor of nursing practice), from time to time I see people suffering from sadness and depression in catatonic phase because of a sudden drop in dopamine level due to their sadness. The lack of joy and their deep sadness, causing the sudden drop in dopamine, will debilitate those people. Their speech is gone, their movements are affected, and their eyes are staring purposeless. They cannot communicate their emotions. They disconnect themselves from people around, giving up eating and drinking. Motivation is gone. My heart is breaking when I see those patients in those devastated situation. Yet they do have physical diseases present in their body. Only severe sadness and lack of joy will cause those debilitating symptoms.

Their condition, created by sadness, brings slow deterioration if they do not eat or drink, leading to physical condition and further decline in their physical health. It is easy to get exhausted without energy when we are burnt out and we lack joy. Signs and symptoms of depression can be felt when you let sadness disconnect you from the source of joy and love. That is the time to get closer to God and hear His whispering voice to you. When alone in your secret place, incline your heart's ear to Him to hear His voice. The Father loves you with an eternal life through His beloved Son, Jesus.

Jesus gave His life for us. Jesus's presence changes everything, brings the joy of salvation, and restores souls. Our provisions are in Jesus's sacrifice, and when you can, be overwhelmed with great joy in His presence. Jesus's presence represents heaven on earth. Joy flows from Him through His presence. His joy gives strength, peace, and happiness. His presence activates your reward system so you can enjoy His presence. When your reward system is activated by Jesus's presence, the right formula of neurochemicals is released in your body, changing your vital signs, normalizing and optimizing them for an abundant life that Jesus came to bring on earth. "I have come that they may have life, and that they may have *it* more abundantly" (John 10:10 NKJV).

◾ Find Strength in God's Spirit

Faith as a mustard seed is a pure faith to know God. David knew God. He cried to the Lord in His distress until he had no more tears. "So David and his men wept aloud until they had no strength left to weep" (1 Sam. 30:4 NIV). "But David found strength in the LORD his God" (1 Sam. 30:6 NIV). Our physical resources are limited, but the Holy Spirit can renew our strength every morning through pure faith. He has unlimited resources. When your physical resources are used up, the Holy Spirit takes over to give us the strength to overcome impossible situations. You will flow with confident hope through the power of the Holy Spirit. Only the Holy Spirit infiltrates that hope that brings confidence in God's ability to get you out of any circumstances, and you become more than conqueror in Jesus Christ, the finisher of your pure faith, to be full of joy and peace, trusting in God's mighty power in the darkest moments of your life. "May the God of hope fill you with all joy and peace as you trust in him, so that you may overflow with hope by the power of the Holy Spirit" (Rom. 15:13 NIV).

The Holy Spirit is at work and never stops working. Benny Hinn, in his book *Good Morning Holy Spirit*, stated, "And the Holy Spirit showed me more. He was the one who gave Moses the power to be the deliverer of the children of Israel. He was the power in the life of Joshua. He was the force behind the wind that divided the Red Sea. He was the mighty power that smashed the walls of Jericho. He was the energy behind David's rock when Goliath fell. The Holy Spirit. He was the force in the life of Samuel, in Elijah-and in Christ the Lord."[2]

Higher Standards

Higher Standards Established from Creation

We are the bride of our Lord Jesus. We must live like a bride without spot and wrinkles. Those are the highest standards, and Jesus wants His bride, the church, and every believer to live with no spots and no wrinkles. People lower the standards and try to live after the standards of the world because of the brokenness they experience and the pain they feel from all the discouragements, disappointments, and bitterness of the soul. The devil tries to take your eyes from God's eyes, not to see how big God is, but to focus on how big the problem is, and lower the standards by which we live in this life.

Wounds in your souls are painful when you lower the standards established from creation for human beings. Science demonstrated that "wounds of the soul," which are emotions of sadness, lack of hope, discouragement, and depression, hurt. The Lord gave you power to meditate and believe in His healing Word. You have authority through the blood of Jesus to get up and walk in His name. You can resist the devil, who brings discouragement, sadness, oppression, depression, and release the power of God. You must go step by step; with Jesus, you can do anything.

In difficult situations, I had to meditate on God's promises for me and my family and proclaim His powerful Word to reprogram my brain, that "I can do all things through Christ who strengthens me" (Phil. 4:13 NKJV). When you trust in the Lord and His powerful Word and proclaim it, know that He will fight for you and will bring you peace that passes all understanding. People in the world do not understand that kind of peace that will protect your mind, your brain, your heart, and your health, your soul, spirit, and body, from physical and spiritual diseases.

We must know the Word of God, which established healthy standards for life. We need to know who we are. If we do not know who we are, we cannot use our rights as citizens of heaven. As a US citizen, I cannot benefit from my rights as a citizen if I do not know them well. God is able to fulfill His promises; He is an all-powerful, almighty God. He is a grandiose God, majestic, immense, ferocious. He is indescribable. There is a supernatural power that can touch your life if you are thirsty and hungry for Him. When you obey the Word of God and live according to God's principle, biblical standards, and His will, and when you love His precepts and make His Word become part of who you are, He will live inside of you and you worship in Spirit and truth, God's highest standards.

Make a priority to live according to God's standards and instructions and follow His directions, and the King of Kings and the Lord of Lords will live inside of you. Forget what is behind and run to Jesus toward the prize. "Brethren, I do not count myself to have apprehended; but one thing *I do,* forgetting those things which are behind and reaching forward to those things which are ahead, I press toward the goal for the prize of the upward call of God in Christ Jesus" (Phil. 3:13–14 NKJV). That will give you motivation to persist to be touched by the powerful hand of the almighty God, who is above everything. He loves you, and He is rejoicing over you with singing when you trust Him, obey His Word, worship Him in spirit and truth, and praise Him. He will come and dwell in you, and you will be a different person when the Spirit of the living God lives in you.

God has a glorious destiny for you, but your vision is affected by worries in the world. Things of the world can bring blindness. Sin blinds people and causes psychological distress. The power of darkness was broken through the power of the cross and the resurrection of Jesus Christ. Even though you do not receive an answer to your prayers and your unsolved problems, you still can believe because God's name is Overcomer. Bring all your discouragement, depression, unforgiveness, sadness, fear that paralyzes you, and suicidal ideation to the cross, where the exchange is happening.

Dr. Crandall spoke to a medical healing conference with about three hundred medical professionals about physical and "spiritual heart transplant." He presented the beautiful exchange that Jesus will give you His heart to receive unspeakable joy and the peace that surpasses all understanding. Bring all your worries in prayers right now, one by one, and wait patiently for God's hand to work in your life. Through prayer you have access to the throne of mercy and bring the solutions to all the problems that overwhelm you with worries and fear and all unhealthy emotions. Then you can pray for those who cause unhealthy emotions in your life. When you pray for others, you become the solution to their problems also. Use the strategies in prayer, fast, memorize God's promises, listen to others' testimonies, reflect on your own testimonies that have the power to increase your faith. Knowing the Word of God and His promises is a must. God's promises are prophecies for your future.

Brenda Kunneman, in *The Daily Decree*, stated that "the foundational point of reference to our Christianity is found in the Bible. The written Word of God is what determines truth and boundaries. It builds our level of faith. It admonishes and corrects. Without the Word of God hidden in our hearts, we have no point of reference to determine the way and will of God. As you decree today, declare that the Word of God is rich within you. Doing so will develop in you a hunger for the Scriptures and it will become the resource that will cause you to be a well-balanced, discerning believer. It will give you a thirst to make time in the Bible a priority. The Word of God will saturate you with life, healing, faith, and hope. Become hungry for His living Word every day!"[1]

Sweet Aroma in God's Standards

God's standards are written for us to bring sweet aroma. I had to hold on and follow God's instructions because they were His standards for my life. I had to fight using the Word of God and the sword of the Spirit. Embodiment of the Holy Spirit will fill you with the fruit of righteousness and help you grow in the knowledge of God and His Word to apply it in your daily life and use it as an offensive weapon to fight the devil that comes against God's standards. "Therefore submit to God. Resist the devil and he will flee from you" (James 4:7 NKJV). To be able to be a sweet aroma, you must resist the devil's temptations. When I was a student in Bucharest, I was invited many times to parties with nonbelievers. I knew what they were doing at those late parties: trying drugs, drinking alcohol, engaging in ungodly behaviors. I had to say no many times and turn my back to those invitations and temptations as a young girl. I knew that God's Word had the highest standards.

It was difficult to share my Christian beliefs with others during the Communist regime, but the sweet aroma was smelled by many when I made a stand to follow God's standards. The fragrance was spread in the atmosphere. Jesus's disciples, in their spirit, were able to sense and catch the smell of the sweet aroma of Christ. As I had Christ in my heart, the fragrance of His gentleness, compassion, love, joy, and peace revealed Jesus's aroma to those around me and revealed the power of the Holy Spirit that brings convictions to those who smell it.

Standards to Meet God Face-to-Face

In praise and worship, you meet God face-to-face. God gave us a spirit of love, peace, and sound mind. When you worship in your heart, you acknowledge who is Lord in your life. Worship God in bad time and in good time. Praise and worship is a choice you must make: "But if serving the LORD seems undesirable to you, then choose for yourselves this day whom you will serve, whether the gods your ancestors served beyond the Euphrates, or the gods of the Amorites, in whose land you are living. But as for me and my household, we will serve the LORD" (Josh. 24:15 NIV). Learn to trust God in worse situation and choose to serve Him only. Joshua met God in praising Him in his obedience and worship. He developed a relationship with the Father as he met Him face-to-face. He did choose to serve the Lord with his entire house. After you have a close relationship with the Father in heaven, you choose to serve Him only as you met Him face-to-face, worshipping in Spirit and truth.

Bill Johnson, in his book *Face to Face with God: Get Ready for a Life-Changing Encounter with God*, stated that our prayer must be, "Lord, I desire to behold You more fully. Remove the veil of unbelief from my heart. Let your light shine on my heart so I may know Your glory in the face of Christ. I desire to know the One in Whose image I was made. Help me to cease attempting to find my identity in my performance. Help me find my true self revealed in Your countenance."[2]

Spiritual Food

Food for the Brain

God's Word can form new people by nourishing the soul and spirit with God's truth. Communists falsely declared that their doctrine will form a "new man." I heard that phrase for decades since childhood in Romania but never saw that happen under Communism. Man struggled under the curse of Communist doctrine denying the Creator's existence. It demonstrated that they could not form new persons. Only the Word of God can influence our thinking and change our mind through the power of the Holy Spirit and transform a life completely. We know from the Bible that the prophet Samuel told King Saul that he would be changed into a new man and a different person when the Holy Spirit would come powerfully upon him. "The Spirit of the LORD will come powerfully upon you, and you will prophesy with them; and you will be changed into a different person" (1 Sam. 10:6 NIV). When the Holy Spirit comes, He will change the loneliness, discouragement, isolation, disobedience, doubts, and disbeliefs. The Holy Spirit can change any situation. Too many people are lonely and isolated due to their sins and disobeying God's Word, going through difficult situations. The brain needs to feed on different food to form new people.

Naturally, we recommend people, for example, to take multivitamins to strengthen the immune system, follow a healthy diet, eat healthy food, such as fresh vegetables and fruits, be active and exercise regularly, keep blood pressure at 120/80 mmHg and blood sugar between 70 and 99 mg/dl, and total cholesterol under 200 mg/dl, bad cholesterol under 100 mg/dl. Also, follow health-care professionals' clinical advice for health promotion and diseases prevention, see your doctor regularly for checkups, screening, and follow-up visits, etc. All of them are good medical advices that everyone should seek to follow to prevent physical diseases in our body. But there are invisible foods that feed the brain 24-7 through the Spirit of God, which can change completely our spiritual personality and improve one's quality of life physically and spiritually.

Studies (Cleveland Clinic) show that "your brain determines every aspect of your life and without your brain, there is no self and no awareness of the world. Your brain is a three pound universe that processes 70,000 thoughts each day using 100 billion neurons that connect at more than 500 trillion points through synapses that travel 300 miles/hour. The signals that travel through these interconnected neurons form the basis of memories, thoughts and feelings. Throughout your life your experiences create patterns of activity that explain how our brains code our thoughts, memories, skills and sense of self."[1]

Healthy thoughts are real food for a healthy brain and healthy body. Invisible thoughts in the unconscious brain can influence our physical body and our daily life according to the quality of thoughts that we allow to cross our mind. Healthy thinking will cause the hippocampus to communicate with our limbic system and prefrontal cortex (with the prefrontal lobe having executive functional ability) and other brain structures to process healthy, positive emotions to build a strong resilience when facing difficult circumstances and hard situations. Science shows that "increased resiliency has been shown to slow aging and improved overall health and quality of life. Research in the neurobiology of stress resilience, particularly throughout the aging process, is a nascent, yet, burgeoning field."[2]

Mindfulness in the Bible to Live in Peace

Mindfulness is used in cognitive therapy. People realize that the human brain is assaulted with disruptive thoughts that steal their peace, creating psychological distress and imbalance in their mind.

Professional people try to develop strategies to bring back peace of mind through different methods as mindfulness. "The ideology behind mindfulness is to achieve stillness and balance of the mind. Man's efforts to calm the mind and rid the life of stressors—through mindfulness or other New Age techniques—are an attempt to manufacture peace."[3]

The new age technique is not biblical. The Word of God, the Bible, teaches us that only Jesus is the Prince of Peace (Jehovah Shalom), who gives us peace that passes all understanding. "And the peace of God, which transcends all understanding, will guard your hearts and your minds in Christ Jesus" (Phil. 4:7 NIV). This biblical truth is God's prescription for peace that was written about two thousand years ago for every humankind if it is followed with faith, trusting God's faithfulness. "Peace I leave with you; my peace I give you. I do not give to you as the world gives. Do not let your hearts be troubled and do not be afraid" (John 14:27 NIV).

Mindfulness and meditation have been prescribed by God in His Word more than three thousand years ago. "Keep this Book of the Law always on your lips; meditate on it day and night, so that you may be careful to do everything written in it. Then you will be prosperous and successful" (Josh. 1:8 NIV). It appears that meditation and mindfulness have been taken from the Bible and used to assist people to cope with high levels of stress to control their thoughts and emotions associated or attached to their thoughts. But only the Holy Spirit can monitor people's thoughts and emotions and make people experience and feel peace as a fruit of the Spirit. Through prayer, studying the Word to get more hope from insights, and revelation to increase faith and God's power and worshipping in spirit and truth. Being attentive and having the mind of Christ, obeying God's directions and instruction to renew their mind and transform their life and every thought to be obedient to Christ.

Meditation on God's promises and His power to control our thoughts affects the brain area that is involved in controlling attention span and makes it to grow. Meditation and mindfulness can affect the genes involved in inflammation to improve your health. Science demonstrated that "after eight hours of mindfulness practice, the meditators showed a range of genetic and molecular differences, including altered levels of gene-regulating machinery and reduced levels of pro-inflammatory genes, which in turn correlated with faster physical recovery from a stressful situation."[4]

I mentioned earlier that inflammation is "the mother of all diseases." Science revealed that "all disease starts with cellular inflammation," Nemec says. "Whether you have cancer, heart disease, diabetes, digestive disorders, autoimmune disease, or Alzheimer's, it all starts with inflammation at the cellular level, which leads to either early cell death translating into specific organ or gland disease, or into cancer stem cell stimulation, which fuels cancer cell growth and metastasis."[5]

Meditation on God's instructions in the Bible helps you process the emotion as anxiety, mood disorder differently and makes you able to control them, reducing stress levels and thus inflammatory process. It can be started in childhood. Through meditation on God's Word and His promises, you develop more awareness of what is going on in that moment in your life. You develop thoughts and feelings that improve your well-being physically and psychologically. You can observe those thoughts and feelings through meditation. Meditation and prayer help you manage stress better and with your sickness, by improving your immune system, preventing infections, lowering blood pressure, and helping you handle the painful situation and chronic conditions and mood disorder. "Some research suggests that meditation may help people manage symptoms of conditions such as:

- Anxiety
- Asthma
- Cancer
- Chronic pain
- Depression
- Heart disease
- High blood pressure
- Irritable bowel syndrome
- Sleep problems
- Tension headaches."[6]

Meditation increases positivity, which strengthens the prefrontal cortex. We are able to mold the brain's structures involved in rationalizing things, modulating emotions processed in our limbic system and the fear center. Delighting in God's Word and His instructions and meditating on them day and night will bring great peace and blessings. "Blessed is the man Who walks not in the counsel of the ungodly, Nor stands in the path of sinners, Nor sits in the seat of the scornful; But his delight is in the law of the Lord, And in His law he meditates day and night" (Ps. 1:1–2 NKJV). You are blessed when you do not associate with the ungodly and the sinners, which will lead to stressful situation, but when you delight in the Lord, the Holy Spirit helps you to meditate on God's Word and makes you feel His love and joy from the hope in God's promises, molding and strengthening your brain's structures.

Power to Control Emotions

You are created with willpower to control your emotions and to overcome stressful situations. Science demonstrated just that, stating, "The results of the study generally confirmed the prediction that individuals who are high in regulatory control were relatively unlikely to experience high levels of negative emotional arousal in response to stressors, but this relation held only for moderate- to high-intensity stressors. Moreover, under conditions of moderate to high stress, highly regulated individuals were likely to cope constructively with the stressor."[7]

Our positive or negative thoughts in general are tied to emotions that affect all cells in all systems with all organs, tissues, and cells functioning in the body according to the quality of thoughts because all systems and all organs are connected to the brain through the autonomic nervous system (ANS), composed of the sympathetic nervous system and the parasympathetic nervous system.

The sympathetic nervous system dilates the pupils of the eyes, stimulates weakly salivation in the mouth, relaxes bronchi in the lungs, accelerates heartbeats in the heart, inhibits activities in the stomach, duodenum, and intestines, stimulates glucose release by the liver, stimulates secretion of adrenaline and noradrenaline by the adrenal glands, and relaxes bladder. By contrary, the parasympathetic nervous system contracts pupils, stimulates strongly salivation, constricts bronchi, slows heartbeats, stimulates activities in the stomach, pancreas, duodenum, and intestine, and stimulates gallbladder, contracts bladder, etc.[8]

In times of crisis and discouragement, you need positive thoughts to increase your faith and decrease negative thoughts to lessen your fear, to reduce anxiety, and to keep the ANS in balance. Meditate on God's promises and speak them with your mouth out loud to increase your faith. Faith increases by hearing those promises. God's perfect love casts out fear. When you memorize God's promises about His eternal love for you and repeat them, they will become part of your life thoughts with stronger faith attached that brings hope with emotions of joy, happiness, love, and kindness that bring the peace of God in your mind and your heart. Your mind must be saturated with thoughts of being healed when sickness tries to enter your heart and your body and you get overwhelmed with fear of those diseases that get worse. You make the choice to receive your promise by picturing it in your mind's eye and declaring it with the words of your mouth as "By His stripes I am healed." Your faith becomes stronger. You begin to experience the unspeakable joy and peace that is beyond all understanding.

Your thoughts of blessings during crises are God's desires for your life. He is waiting for you to ask in prayer what you need Him to do for you. Thoughts of prosperity of your soul and health of every organ, system, tissue in your body are God's prescription in His Word for us all. "Beloved, I pray that you may prosper in all things and be in health, just as your soul prospers" (3 John 1:2 NKJV). When finances are lacking, ask God to open doors of opportunities for better jobs, business, strong relationships, and right connection. He has unlimited resources and ways to bless you. When all human resources are out, then God will intervene. God intervenes in maximum crises when people will abandon you and you are lonely.

When you are out of resources, God brings deliverance. "But today I am freeing you from the chains on your wrists. Come with me to Babylon, if you like, and I will look after you; but if you do not want to, then don't come. Look, the whole country lies before you; go wherever you please" (Jer. 40:4 NIV). In crises, Jeremiah was forgotten, but he was delivered and blessed with abundance when people were dying in famine. You get freedom of those crises, and chains are broken. He lifts you up and He blesses you with an abundance of provision. When you obey God in crises, He will make you prosper; even if all businesses around you fall, your business will prosper because of your obedience to His Word.

Many times in our business, we had seen God's provisions miraculously even when other businesses around us were struggling with their finances, having vacancies in their facilities when the economy in the USA and the world was very low. Many people lost their business, but during that time, we were more prosperous; we were building extra rooms and even another facility. God gave us favors with people around us, and the blessings were flowing continuously only through God's hands. God will cause your enemy to bless you. He humbles people who are proud and arrogant. In the worst crises, God will bless you. My example, when the enemy tried to ruin our business, God arose and scattered the enemy and gave us much more than the enemy tried to steal from us. The blessings came in the moment we least expected. God surprised us with victories each time the enemy attacked us. God will use even your enemy to help you in crises. You have heard many times that the enemy's strategies will become a ladder for you to step up in life, to be promoted. That is true.

When you walk in righteousness, holiness, and faithfulness, when there is no way, God will make a way for you. The prophet Jeremiah got everything. Jeremiah remained faithful when he was threatened. He was delivered because he loved the Lord. Jesus's disciples were in the middle of an unexpected storm with no hope for survival. Then Jesus appeared and calmed the storm when they did not expect Him to. During my storms and fearful situations, I did read Psalm 91 out loud, and I made it my personal prayer and I memorized portions of it to increase my faith in the Lord's provisions, that in the shadow of His wings I will have divine protection from my enemy and that the enemy will not come near me because His angels will guard me all the time. I knew that I could be at peace and rest in the shadow of the almighty. He showed Himself strong on my behalf many times during the Communist regime, and He was faithful and did it again in the USA when I was struggling with a new, challenging situation.

You can pray Psalm 91 as a powerful prayer that brings peace for you in Jesus's name. "Whoever dwells in the shelter of the Most High will rest in the shadow of the Almighty. I will say of the Lord, 'He is my refuge and my fortress, my God, in whom I trust.' Surely he will save you from the fowler's snare and from the deadly pestilence. He will cover you with his feathers, and under his wings you will find refuge; his faithfulness will be your shield and rampart. You will not fear the terror of night, nor the arrow that flies by day, nor the pestilence that stalks in the darkness, nor the plague that destroys at midday. A thousand may fall at your side, ten thousand at your right hand, but it will not come near you. You will only observe with your eyes and see the punishment of the wicked. If you say, 'The Lord is my refuge,' and you make the Most High your dwelling, no harm will overtake you, no disaster will come near your tent. For he will command his angels concerning you to guard you in all your ways; they will lift you up in their hands, so that you will not strike your foot against a stone. You will tread on the lion and the cobra; you will trample the great lion and the serpent. 'Because he loves me,' says the Lord, 'I will rescue him; I will protect him, for he acknowledges my name. He will call on me, and I will answer him; I will be with him in trouble, I will deliver him and honor him. With long life I will satisfy him and show him my salvation;" (Ps. 91:1–16 NIV).

God has a vision and a dream for you even in your crises for you to live in the great peace that you were created for. He has a plan, a future, and a hope for you to show you His salvation to fulfill your destiny. He has promises for you in His Word if you "feed your soul" with the Bread of Life, which is the Word of God.

PART IV

Designed for Blessings from Creation

God's Desire to Bless You

The only purpose God created and designed male and female on this planet is the desire to bless them and their seed after them from generation to generation through their obedience. After the fall in sin by the first family, God desires to see His creation obeying Him for their blessing to continue, as written in Deuteronomy. "Now it shall come to pass, if you diligently obey the voice of the LORD your God, to observe carefully all His commandments which I command you today, that the LORD your God will set you high above all nations of the earth. And all these blessings shall come upon you and overtake you, because you obey the voice of the LORD your God: Blessed *shall* you *be* in the city, and blessed *shall* you *be* in the country. Blessed *shall be* the fruit of your body, the produce of your ground and the increase of your herds, the increase of your cattle and the offspring of your flocks. Blessed *shall be* your basket and your kneading bowl. Blessed *shall* you *be* when you come in, and blessed *shall* you *be* when you go out. The LORD will cause your enemies who rise against you to be defeated before your face; they shall come out against you one way and flee before you seven ways. The LORD will command the blessing on you in your storehouses and in all to which you set your hand, and He will bless you in the land which the LORD your God is giving you. The LORD will establish you as a holy people to Himself, just as He has sworn to you, if you keep the commandments of the LORD your God and walk in His ways. Then all peoples of the earth shall see that you are called by the name of the LORD, and they shall be afraid of you. And the LORD will grant you plenty of goods, in the fruit of your body, in the increase of your livestock, and in the produce of your ground, in the land of which the LORD swore to your fathers to give you. The LORD will open to you His good treasure, the heavens, to give the rain to your land in its season, and to bless all the work of your hand. You shall lend to many nations, but you shall not borrow. And the LORD will make you the head and not the tail; you shall be above only, and not be beneath, if you heed the commandments of the LORD your God, which I command you today, and are careful to observe *them*. So you shall not turn aside from any of the words which I command you this day, *to* the right or the left, to go after other gods to serve them" (Deut. 28:1–14 NKJV).

You were created in His image, with the purpose to be blessed and to bless others. God designed His creation from the beginning with built-in features to be blessed when obeying His Word. The Word of God is the seed for your thoughts that will grow dendrites, will consolidate your memories, and will bring the blessings mentioned above. Emotions of hope from faith in the Word release chemicals, forming those blessing and memories for a long time. Memorizing scriptures helps to develop dendrites through the release of protein through gene expression, and the evil one will not snatch away the seed that was sown in your mind and your heart when you follow God's commandments.

◼ Generational Blessings Through Epigenetics

Your obedience in serving God will determine blessings for the next generations. Your children and your children's children will inherit those blessings. Now we know that is done at the microscopic level in our body through epigenetics. "Some epigenetic tags remain in place as genetic information passes from generation to generation, a process called epigenetic inheritance. Epigenetic inheritance is an unconventional finding. It goes against the idea that inheritance happens only through the DNA code that passes from parent to offspring. It means that a parent's experiences, in the form of epigenetic tags, can be passed down to future generations."[1]

Our Father in heaven changes the course of generational curses that are passed from generation to generation through the epigenetic mechanism, promising that those curses will no longer exist, as illustrated in the book of Ezekiel. "The word of the LORD came to me again, saying, 'What do you mean when you use this proverb concerning the land of Israel, saying: "The fathers have eaten sour grapes, And the children's teeth are set on edge"? '*As* I live,' says the Lord GOD, 'you shall no longer use this proverb in Israel. Behold, all souls are Mine; The soul of the father As well as the soul of the son is Mine; The soul who sins shall die'" (Ezek. 18:1–4 NKJV). The prophet Ezekiel prophesied about the coming of the Messiah, Jesus Christ, who will break the curse of sin and give humanity freedom, changing the curses of sin into blessings, how they were designed from the beginning, to those who believe in Him through the epigenetic mechanism that science discovered in the last decades.

Pastor, TV host, and author Larry Huch (whom my husband and I highly esteem), in his book *Free at Last: Removing Your Past from Your Future*, stated that "there's going to come a time when the fathers may eat sour grapes but the children's teeth will not be set on edge, when the curse will not be passed down from generation to generation. It doesn't have to be 'like father, like son.' Through the shed blood of Jesus Christ, we have a new and better covenant with God the Father. Through Jesus's blood, He forgives us of our sin and delivers us from our iniquity. God has redeemed us from the curses being passed on from one generation to the next. This redemption comes as we understand that the root of our problem is in the spiritual realm. As we apply God's Word and power in our lives, and as we choose to walk in righteousness and obedience to God, the chains of bondage will be broken. The freedom we have longed for can become reality!"[2]

God's blessings start with an invisible thought and dream that God put in your heart. We create dreams in our mind and heart that bring blessings for generation before we take actions to become reality. Follow your dreams, what God can do in your life when you live in obedience of His powerful Word. Keep trying when you face battles. God wants you to become a person of influence and to fulfill your dreams despise all discouragements and obstacles. God brings opportunities your way. The opportunity is never lost. The Lord wants to bring blessings in your life and the lives of your children's children. Take dominion over the dreams that God put in your heart. You must be bold and take dominion in the world because Jesus overcame the world. Keep your peace and rejoice in situations that you do not have control over. God created the world with power to reproduce the blessings. God wants us to be the channels of blessings for the world to reproduce physically and spiritually blessings in others through epigenetic mechanism.

The Word of God is the source of physical and spiritual blessings to spread the light to a world full of darkness. God's nature is to bless every person on earth. He created the earth with much wealth for humanity to enjoy. He also wants us to be creative and to be healthy. As I mentioned before, God created the earth with all the elements present in the body for that reason to live with a healthy body. You get the joy when you are blessed and when you bless those around you.

Blessings by Serving Others

Nothing can stop God to bless you when you bless others. God will do exceedingly abundantly everything you can ask or think. Nothing is impossible with God. Do not limit God with what He can do; the world cannot steal God's blessings from you. At an appreciation dinner event organized by PACS every year, I was invited to receive the Barbara Nelson Ward for serving others as a primary care provider in the PACS clinic, seeing the most vulnerable patients and minorities with multiple acute and chronic diseases who did not have access to the health-care system, volunteering for more than fifteen years one day a week.

Not many people knew about our dedication to sacrifice one day a week to provide free care to the most vulnerable population in

Portland and Vancouver area. But God knew, and He rewarded us beyond what we could ask for or imagine. By our doing good to others, blessings came over us. "But when you do a charitable deed, do not let your left hand know what your right hand is doing, that your charitable deed may be in secret; and your Father who sees in secret will Himself reward you openly" (Matt. 6:3–4 NKJV).

> My husband and I at the PACS appreciation dinner, October 2017, when I received the Barbara Nelson Award as a PCP at a PACS health clinic.

I experienced great joy and good feelings when my name was called as a recipient of that award. I was thinking, What will happen in heaven when the Master, our Lord Jesus, will give us the rewards for all our deeds on this planet, to serve others to enlarge His kingdom during our life on Earth? It will be glorious, not even comparable with any of the awards we win on this planet. What a joy it will be in heaven! Jesus said to those who served Him with a pure heart, "His lord said to him, 'Well *done,* good and faithful servant; you were faithful over a few things, I will make you ruler over many things. Enter into the joy of your lord'" (Matt. 25:21 NKJV).

That joy should be in our heart, starting here on earth. The joy of salvation is eternal. That joy of serving others can flood our hearts since we become Jesus's followers and doer of the Word. Since we become God's children when the blood of Jesus washes all sins with all curses away, we have divine protection through the blood of Jesus. He brings supernatural provision though the power of His blood. He brings salvation, healing, joy, and He washes all sins away and pours out His Spirit, which makes us feel the overwhelming emotions of hope, love, peace, joy, happiness, kindness, goodness, patience, faithfulness, gentleness, and self-control (Gal. 5:22–23). He is outpouring His Spirit to heal diseases, to break burdens and chains. The enemy is defeated when salvation comes. He brings blessings, prosperity, and success.

■ Blessings in Crises

God has a formula to walk the right way in victory during crises. Go back to the basic to win the battle when crises arrive. Your heart must be where Jesus's heart was when He died on the cross. When crises start, that is the time to start praising God in worship and prayers. Lift up your hands in worship. Praising brings the anointing for victory. The Holy Spirit, through praise and worship, flows from God's spiritual realm through your spirit. Your worship and praises in prayer put the Holy Spirit in motion. Change the way you pray. God wants you to walk in victory. Through prayer you can control your thoughts and the emotions attached to them. When you speak out the desire of your heart to praise the Lord in prayer, you hear yourself, and those words will trigger more thoughts of God's goodness and grace, which will increase your faith and hope more, which will bring encouragement and strength and emotions of peace and joy.

■ The Blessings of Sowing

To be blessed, you need to be a blessing. We hear many times that we reap what we sow. The will of God is to bless us to be a blessing and to rejoice in serving others. God told Abraham that He will bless people who will bless Abraham and his seed. "I will bless those who bless you, and whoever curses you I will curse; and all peoples on earth will be blessed through you" (Gen. 12:3 NIVUK). When we serve others in the name of Jesus, which is above all names, He will bless us. It is the seed that we sow that will bring blessings in our lives. People who do not sow seeds are cursed. But Jesus has the power to break curses and to release blessings over your life. The curses are broken in Jesus's name. "In that day their burden will be lifted from your shoulders, their yoke from your neck; the yoke will be broken" (Isa. 10:27 NIV). Christ Jesus broke the chains of slavery of sins and set us free from the bondages of sin. Sin brought curses over God's creation, but Christ came from heaven to break the curses created by sin. "It is for freedom that Christ has set us free. Stand firm, then, and do not let yourselves be burdened again by a yoke of slavery" (Gal. 5:1 NIV). Curses can be reversed when we sow seeds in Jesus's name.

God has a formula, a spiritual way to bless His people, so evident in Deuteronomy 28:1–14. Go in the presence of God in the name of Jesus to enter His blessings. From childhood, since I started reading the Bible, I understood this biblical principle that we reap what we sow, and I followed even in unpleasant circumstances under Communism. The Communist regime couldn't stop me from applying the Word of God in my life and to practice my faith and beliefs. Then I continued here in the US from the time my feet touched American ground. It gave me so much joy, and then the blessings were flowing and still flowing to these days in our life, exactly how God promised in His Word, and keep flowing in our daughter's life and the lives of her family and her children also.

Blessings in Giving

I experienced that joy from a very young age. When I was a teenager, I was moved by the Holy Spirit in my heart to give to the needy. The joy of giving overwhelmed my soul, which destroyed in me my desires for a selfish life. It was just for me at that time that Holy Spirit was teaching me that I can live a joyful life even when I have lived a simple life. The Lord loves the cheerful givers. Joy will cause you to give. Giving with joy at all times motivates people to not hold on to things in order to make yourself happy. Even as a teenager, I was overwhelmed by the love of Jesus Christ, which motivated me to share with the needy everything I had. Jesus's love was enough for the blessings to flow through us to those around us.

In Release Family Blessings: God's Plan for Your Marriage and Children, Larry and Tiz Huch wrote, "In order to bless us in every area, including our marriage, God has worked out a plan for us—a path that leads us to success in all aspects of life, including our relationships with our spouses. And His plan does not consist in a bunch of dos or don'ts. It's a bunch of 'get to's' and 'want to's.' His plan, which is laid out in the bible through the law, is really a path that leads us on the shortest route to the highest level of blessings possible. The law is meant to signify the pathway to all goodness and blessings."[3]

Designed for Victory

■ The Battle for Your Soul from Creation

From creation, Satan fights to hinder human destiny, by stealing the joy of salvation from people's heart and mind. "The heart *is* deceitful above all *things,* And desperately wicked; Who can know it?" (Jer. 17:9 NKJV). But God created man in His image with authority over all earth to overcome the wicked and deceitful thoughts. The entire hell rises up when God's children, the church, rise up with authority and determination. Christ, through the cross, gained back authority and the joy lost in the garden of Eden by Adam and Eve to Satan. The joy of salvation is ours. Tiz Huch, the author of *No Limits, No Boundaries: Praying Dynamic Change into Your Life, Family, & Finances*, stated that "our minds are the battlegrounds for spiritual warfare, and the battle is won or lost in our minds before it is won or lost in the physical world. I cannot emphasize strongly enough how important is for us to control our thoughts. Paul put it, we must 'take captive every thought to make it obedient to Christ' (2 Corinthians 10:5 NIV). When doubts and fear threaten to consume your mind, picture yourself actually pulling your thoughts into alignment with the Word of God. Pull down those thoughts that contradict God's will and His promises. Determine to resist and reject any thoughts that don't match God's promises. Then, picture yourself replacing those negative doubts with faith, confidence, and knowledge of His Word."[1]

The church was predestined by the Lord to overcome from day 1 to live with thoughts and feeling the emotions of the joy of salvation. He answers the prayers of the saints from the first day of prayer.

Jesus gave the church His spiritual DNA through the power of the Holy Spirit for greater things to be done in His name. When the Comforter will come, He will guide your steps. He will intercede for you, and He will give you wisdom, revelation, inspiration, and discernment to overcome the battle for the soul. We overcome through His blood. We regain legal position in heaven through the authority of Jesus Christ. We must believe by increasing our faith in the power of the blood of Jesus and rejoice in His salvation. Only through the blood of Jesus is the battle for the soul won.

Raise a Banner of Victory

Our life is hidden in Christ. Our life was emptied by the devil of our emotions, of love, peace, joy, and happiness. The Word of God was sent by the Creator to heal our emotions through the power of the Holy Spirit, to enable us to produce the characteristics of the fruit of the Spirit, to think like Jesus and have joy, peace, love, and kindness. The Word of God brings deliverance from our negative thoughts, which keep us in bondage from thoughts of fear and discouragement, causing us to feel the emotions of bitterness, sadness, and distress. The Holy Spirit is our helper in difficult circumstances and in hopeless situations and gives us victory so we have a testimony to build others' faith.

Many people fulfilled their destiny from the darkest places in their life. Many times, things do not look right, but God is at work in the most difficult situations. The pain of being rejected as a believer during the Communist system made me spend more time in the Word, praying more on my knees, seeking God's face and His presence through fasting, and I focused more on doing good deeds, like visiting the sick and lonely. God did build my character all those years under the Communist regime. Now I have a testimony to build the faith of others.

Joseph's example speaks loudly in Scriptures that God made him fruitful in his hard and difficult time. "For God has caused me to be fruitful in the land of my affliction" (Gen. 41:52 NKJV). God intervenes with His supernatural power in your sorrowful moments. He will cause you to be fruitful in the time of sorrow. In my sorrowful time, I was fruitful, I was working hard, and I was praying, seeking God on my knees, reading His Word, meditating on His promises day and night. My tears turned into joy. I was reading the Psalms on my knees when the enemy attacked me. I was seeking God with all my heart. God programmed your destiny in your DNA to be fruitful too. Your destiny is in you. He gives you the Holy Spirit to activate God's divine prescription for your life in you and to reach your full potential.

You will have a testimony after you go through a battle and a painful situation. We read in the Bible that Joseph's destiny was birthed in pressure to save the nation of Israel from dying from famine when God gave the dreams to the pharaoh about what is going to happen in the land. Moses's destiny was birthed in desert when God called him from the burning bushes and reveled Himself as the "I Am." My destiny was birthed because the pressure from the Communist system made me leave the country and travel to a country with Judeo-Christian values even though I had to face difficult situations. God takes your painful situation and turns it into a successful one and makes impossible things possible.

I grew up in country with almost no future due to the Communist regime. The darkness was so thick that I could not see the end of it except through faith that one day Jesus would return for His bride and we would be taken up to heaven, where Jesus is the light and our joy forever and ever and ever. But God took us out of that darkness and brought us in this great country with many opportunities, where He enlarged our territories in every area of our life. We were able to help our parents left in Romania, who were very poor, and our families and many needy people far away and here in this country.

He has many plans in your darkness and emotionally painful situations, so testimonies will be birthed. God brought destinies from nothing (embryology—every single life starts from one single invisible cell with a great destiny). All visible things are created from invisible things for a purpose. Israelites had to pass through the wilderness for a purpose, to see God's glory and to experience His presence. For them to fulfill their destiny, they needed to spend time in the desert to form their character. God gave them victory. He gives you victory in crises to become fruitful if you live in obedience of His Word. Blessings will flow when you delight in God's instructions. "Blessed is the one who does not walk in step with the wicked or stand in the way that sinners take or sit in the company of mockers, but whose delight is in the law of the LORD, and who meditates on his law day and night. That person is like a tree planted by streams of water, which yields its fruit in season and whose leaf does not wither—whatever they do prospers" (Ps. 1:1–3 NIV).

I had to make choices during the Communist regime either to walk in the steps of the wicked and to sit in the company of mockers or to delight in the Lord. During the Communist regime, there were many mockers of the Christian faith. Almost every day someone will approach me to make me turn my faith away from God. But they were in distress and tremored when they saw my strong faith in God's Word and when God's hand delivered me and made me prosperous and successful. We were planted by the stream of water to live.

He Will Use Enemies to Give You Victory

Crises come because of the sin in human life. God spoke to people to return and repent. "When the commander of the guard found Jeremiah, he said to him, 'The LORD your God decreed this disaster for this place. And now the LORD has brought it about; he has done just as he said he would. All this happened because you people sinned against the LORD and did not obey him'" (Jer. 40:2–3 NIV). But the fear of the Lord will make people obey His will. "Nebuchadnezzar king of Babylon gave command concerning Jeremiah through Nebuzaradan, the captain of the guard, saying, 'Take him, look after him well, and do him no harm, but deal with him as he tells you'" (Jer. 39:11–12 ESV).

Righteousness and holiness will bring the enemy to tremors. "I will plant her for myself in the land; I will show my love to the one I called 'Not my loved one.' I will say to those called 'Not my people,' 'You are my people'; and they will say, 'You are my God'" (Hosea 2:23 NIV).

You do not know whom God will use to help you out of crises. When you have the biggest problem, He will intervene miraculously with His strong, mighty hand. Crisis creates opportunity and a ladder for you to step up to fulfill your destiny. Communist crises made me decide to leave the country to move to the USA even if it was almost a-half-of-the-globe distance. And new crises started because I was not used to a different culture, different language, different environment, and different needs. Every day I cried out more to God for help, for direction, and He provided guidance step by step. "The cords of the grave coiled around me; the snares of death confronted me. In my distress I called to the LORD; I cried to my God for help. From his temple he heard my voice; my cry came before him, into his ears" (Ps. 18:5–6 NIV).

This is what God did for us and He will do for you when you go through crises and battle. "The LORD thundered from heaven; the voice of the Most High resounded. He shot his arrows and scattered the enemy, with great bolts of lightning he routed them. The valleys of the sea were exposed and the foundations of the earth laid bare at your rebuke, LORD, at the blast of breath from your nostrils. He reached down from on high and took hold of me; he drew me out of deep waters. He rescued me from my powerful enemy, from my foes, who were too strong for me. They confronted me in the day of my disaster, but the LORD was my support. He brought me out into a spacious place; he rescued me because he delighted in me" (Ps. 18:13–19 NIV).

One step at a time got me where I am now. From a Communist country first as poor child to becoming an economist there, to becoming a doctor in the health-care field in an unknown system; from almost homeless (sleeping at a friend's house) to becoming a businesswoman, founding, owning, and running multimillion-dollar business; from no English to becoming a writer; from a persecuted Christian not being able to communicate my values and beliefs to now speaking at national and international conferences from world stages; and from many times whispering my prayers in a bathroom to now giving prayers out loud under the power of the Holy Spirit, speaking in heavenly languages at conferences around the world. That is the Holy Spirit's work in me and His guidance step by step. Do not give up in crises. Fall on your knees and pray to the God of the heavens and earth, and He will find a way out of crises. His ways are perfect always. Obey Him; run to Him, not from Him.

Brenda Kunneman, in *The Daily Decree*, wrote, "If you recall the story of Gideon for a moment, he was in a time when he was seeing the dire circumstances all around him and wondered why God let so many bad things happen. Yet the angel that appeared to him did not acknowledge Gideon's perspective. He simply told Gideon to rise up as a man of valor and take action. Gideon still struggled to see himself with the ability to do anything, but ended up being the very person used to deliver Israel. Sometimes we see our abilities as limited and don't feel we can rise from the daunting challenges surrounding us, but God wants you to see yourself today as the warrior He has made you! Changes begin when we look inside, and despite the current circumstances we grit our teeth and declare, 'Rise up mighty warrior!'"[2]

God's Dreams for You

◾ Designed to Fulfill Dreams in Crises

Joseph's story in the Bible tells us that he was despised for his dreams given by God when he was even a child. He was rejected by his brothers to the point of death, when they wanted to kill him and his dreams with him. It appeared in the beginning, when his brothers decided to sell him to the Ishmaelite as a slave in Egypt, that the devil was fighting to stop Joseph from fulfilling his dreams and the destiny that God had for his life. The devil used lies, false accusations, false evidence, everything that was ugly and disgusting to kill Joseph's dream and destiny. But God watched every single moment over Joseph's life and turned all the devil's schemes in victory, not only for Joseph, but also for the entire nation.

Your dream is not lost in impossible circumstances when you take a stand against the enemy's schemes. "Put on the full armor of God, so that you can take your stand against the devil's schemes" (Eph. 6:11 NIV). I think about my dreams back in Romania when I was very young in Bucharest, and I vividly remember that I had a few dreams that I was flying in an airplane over Europe and over USA. Now, you need to know that I never left Romania during the Communist regime (we were not allowed to leave the country). They did not give passports for people to travel. I did not have one at that time. People were not allowed to have a passport except if they forced Christian people into exile in extreme situations. Like my best friend Ari, a schoolteacher, who became a Christian. When the principal of the school found that out, it made her lose her job, which was her only way to survive, to exist, so she was forced into exile.

So I did not know what my dreams meant at that time. I was sharing my dreams in secret with my best friends in Bucharest at that time, and they were laughing because that was impossible at that time to become reality. It became a joke among us that during the day, I was with them, but at night I was flying over foreign countries far away. Now, after being in the USA for about thirty years (I fly to Europe two to three times a year and different states in the USA for conferences frequently), I remind my friends about those dreams in my young age, when going out of the country was impossible and everything appeared nonsense. Now I know that those dreams were from the Lord, preparing me ahead of time, long before that happened, for a new life overseas. At that time, I did not have any intention to leave Romania. But God had a plan and was showing me those dreams. Indeed, I've had to fly unnumbered times over Europe and USA in the last twenty years.

A great example in the Bible of a fulfilled dream is Jacob's dream. God gave Jacob dreams about his future away from home. "Then he dreamed, and behold, a ladder *was* set up on the earth, and its top reached to heaven; and there the angels of God were ascending and descending on it. And behold, the LORD stood above it and said: 'I *am* the LORD God of Abraham your father and the God of Isaac; the land on which you lie I will give to you and your descendants. Also your descendants shall be as the dust of the earth; you shall spread abroad to the west and the east, to the north and the south; and in you and in your seed all the families of the earth shall be blessed. Behold, I *am* with you and will keep you wherever you go, and will bring you back to this land; for I will not leave you until I have done what I have spoken to you'" (Gen. 28:12–15 NKJV).

His dream seemed impossible at that time, but God watched over Jacob to fulfill his dream. Jacob was in Laban's house for twenty years, but during this time, God blessed him beyond Jacob's imagination. God was working at fulfilling His promises in Jacob's dream even when Jacob was in crises. He was fleeing from Esau, and God had a plan to bless him in unimaginable ways. All nations are blessed because of Jacob's dream, because through Israel, the Messiah came to save the world. Jacob did fight in prayer all night long, stating that he would not give up until he would be blessed. His fervent prayer changed all his future and the entire world's future through the nation of Israel. Through the nation of Israel, our Messiah was brought up to bring salvation for the entire world and to restore our relationship with our Father in heaven, the very purpose we were created in His image. Our relationships with the Father were broken in the garden of Eden through the disobedience of the first man, Adam. But they were restored in the garden of Gethsemane and the Garden Tomb by Jesus Christ.

Many times I did read Jacob's story, that he was a foreigner and worked so hard those twenty years. But God was with him and blessed him so much, as He promised Jacob in his dreams. God is faithful to watch over each one of us to fulfill our dreams and our destiny and the purpose that we were created for. God changes all circumstances through prayers. We have many examples in the Bible that, through prayers and petitions, God intervened in people's lives to fulfill their call here on earth. Here are just a few examples: Noah, Abraham, Jacob, Joseph, Nehemiah, Asa, Gideon, Esther, Elijah, Elisha, Daniel, David, prophets, Mary (Jesus's mother), the disciples, the revivalists, and the contemporary Christians.

Another great example is Jabez's prayer, which was a granted request. Jabez's dream was restored. "Now Jabez was more honorable than his brothers, and his mother called his name Jabez, saying, 'Because I bore *him* in pain.' And Jabez called on the God of Israel saying, 'Oh, that You would bless me indeed, and enlarge my territory, that Your hand would be with me, and that You would keep *me* from evil, that I may not cause pain!' So God granted him what he requested" (1 Chron. 4:9–10 NKJV). Jabez asked God in his prayer to be blessed, to have more provision for the kingdom of God to be expanded, to enlarge his territory, to have more influence, to reach out more people, to have God's hand with him for the supernatural presence of God in his life and for the divine protection for him to be kept from harm and from destruction.

In my life, I was inspired by Jabez's prayer, praying many times in the same way, and our territories have been enlarged in every area of our lives physically and spiritually. Prayers like Jabez's prayer changed circumstances in my life. You can change the name of your circumstances by declaring God's blessings. Jabez's dream and future were changed through simple but deep prayers. "Bless me, indeed." Jabez, in his desperation of a future full of pain, asked for blessings that will cause no pain and for his territories to be enlarged. His future was with no hope, no strength; he was discouraged, and the earth was sliding beneath his feet. Only God can bless indeed.

When you pray for God's will in your life, all power in heaven is released to bring God's perfect will into fulfilment, to bring His blessings over your life. You were created for blessings. Our bodies were not created for suffering and for problems. Blessings are available for you, for your children, and for your children's children when you need them the most, if you deposit in your heavenly account prayers, fasting, mercy, compassion, and good deeds in obedience of the Father's instructions.

Ask God to bless you "a lot." A while ago, I was invited to speak to a conference for mothers with children with disabilities organized by Star of Hope Romania/International almost every year. Several years ago, one time at a specific conference, the president of Star of Hope Romania announced that Star of Hope International from Sweden had decided to seize support for this program in Romania, and all those mothers were in so much distress that their hearts were broken for their children already in disadvantage due to their physical conditions and disability. Deep in my soul, I felt their pain, and I did not have solutions for them. By faith I encouraged them and told them about our hope in the Lord, and I told them Jabez's painful story in the Bible and about his victory after his short prayer to be blessed indeed.

At that conference, I was moved in my spirit by these mothers' desperate emotional pain and started to pray a fervent prayer for them to be blessed indeed. They started to cry out with a loud voice, "Bless us, Lord, a lot! Bless us, Lord, a lot! Bless us, Lord, a lot!" "Enlarge our territories, Lord!" The prayer time was so anointed that we hardly could stand on our feet. Something happened after that prayer. The president of Star of Hope International and the president of Star of Hope USA attended a conference of the parents/families with children with disability a few months after our anointed prayer, and their hearts were touched by these precious children and their families, and they announced later that their support would continue and they would open actually more projects and bless those parents and their children physically and spiritually with Alpha courses for them to get to know the Lord more to increase their faith in God and find hope in His mercy and grace for their life. God blessed them indeed and enlarged their territories, and more disabled children were helped through those new projects.

Do not look at your circumstances to be an obstacle in the blessings' ways. God's nature is to bless His creation. The earth is filled with His glory because His blessings on this planet never stopped. In heaven, angels are declaring God's glory continually, as the prophet Isaiah wrote, "And they were calling to one another: 'Holy, holy, holy is the LORD Almighty; the whole earth is full of his glory'" (Isa. 6:3 NIV).

Through prayer, with great faith, you can change your future. You can change what can happen in the next minute when you pray with great faith, because through faith you can command the mountain to move. Jabez prayed for his pain to move. Pain was his mountain, in the way of his blessings. He asked for enlarged territories. You can pray for more influence, more responsibilities, more opportunities, and more signs and wonders for God's kingdom. Everything that is in your sphere of influence and in your care can be blessed and be enlarged.

To illustrate, in our business at Tabor Crest, we asked for blessings every day for every resident/patient in our care, for their families, for every caregiver and their families. I did see blessings over them even though the environment looked so depressing, what with disabled people in wheelchair and bed-bound people needing end-of-life care and people dying when their life ended. We felt the shift in the atmosphere, which was filled with peace and joy because the atmosphere was saturated with prayers. The Holy Spirit was present in our facilities and filled people's heart with comfort and peace. I heard many testimonies from professional people, family members, visitors, and even our workers saying that they felt the peace of God when they came in our facilities, something they could not explain.

The caregivers who worked so hard caring for residents with challenging behaviors and the bed-bound, totally dependent, dying residents were saying that their job was easy because they knew we were praying for them. They experienced the blessings of God through prayers.

When I told one resident with multiple chronic diseases, including dementia, "Your face is radiating," he was smiling at my greeting and said, "I needed to hear that. That touched my heart." And he smiled more, rejoicing, even though he was crippled, spending his life in a wheelchair for many years. He was leaping of joy in his spirit and received a great peace. He started to ask us, "How may I help you?" which astonished the caregivers that he really wanted to help, convincing them that his spirit was lifted up, being encouraged by compliments he received. The seed of Christ in us that makes us valuable, the seed of greatness, is in us to move to a higher level in our spirit in our relationship with others, with great joy to fulfill the dreams that God put in our heart, mind, soul, and spirit.

God wants you to have dreams fulfilled, to have joy. Many young people go through crises in relationships, going through broken heart syndrome due to increased levels of stress. Jesus's soul was full of sorrow because of the weight of the sins of the world, to the point of death, and His Heart was broken so our broken hearts can be restored and healed. "He heals the brokenhearted and binds up their wounds" (Ps. 147:3 NKJV).

David was alone watching his father's sheep and learned how to manage stress and how to behave during crises in his youth. He learned how to sing praises to the Lord God, to worship Him. His life was different because the Spirit of the Lord was on him and in him. When you are alone, learn to praise God and worship Him. In God's presence, you are not lonely. You enter in God's spiritual realm in your spirit and feel that the entire heaven is on your side. Your power and victory are in your praises and in your prayers, which put in motion heavenly armies.

During high school in Bucharest, I was working to sustain myself since I was born in a big family with many brothers and sisters with many needs. At work, I was very tired sometimes from daily tasks. During my break time, I felt lonely and I went aside to rest. The Holy Spirit came over me, and I started to sing in the Spirit even during the hard work as an industrial painter at that time when I was a teenager, after my first vocational school. A huge burden was lifted off my shoulders. I felt like flying in that atelier. My mind was alerted by the spirit inside of me, and I was full of joy, praising God in a heavenly language. His presence was so real that my soul rejoiced in the Lord with unspeakable joy. My spirit received the Holy Spirit through that break prayer, and it was flowing through my body—even people around me noticed that transformation. The feeling of the joy of salvation in my heart and soul was real.

Hunger for Revelation About Your Future

Through prayers, God is revealing your dreams and works mysteries to fulfill them. Your territories are enlarged physically and spiritually when you pray without ceasing to fulfill your dream. "It was not by their sword that they neither won the land, nor did their arms bring them victory; it was your right hand, your arm, and the light of your face, for you loved them" (Ps. 44:3 NIV). The hand of the Lord changes every situation. He gives you favors with every person you work with or meet with in your business, community, society, and God uses them to fulfill your dreams and destiny.

Nehemiah prayed, and God answered his prayers. "So it was, when I heard these words, that I sat down and wept, and mourned *for many* days; I was fasting and praying before the God of heaven. And I said: 'I pray, LORD God of heaven, O great and awesome God, *You* who keep *Your* covenant and mercy with those who love You and observe Your commandments, please let Your ear be attentive and Your eyes open, that You may hear the prayer of Your servant which I pray before You now, day and night, for the children of Israel Your servants, and confess the sins of the children of Israel which we have sinned against You'" (Neh. 1:4–6).

God gave him favors everywhere he went for resources to build the wall. Nehemiah's prayer and heart's desire was God's will and

His plan to build the wall. God changes the law, the heart of King Artaxerxes, and those in charge to fulfill Nehemiah's dream to build the wall. He got three years of vacation, physical resources and materials, human resources, influence, protection, discernment, physical strength, boldness, and authority. He got discernment from God to discern the plans of the devil to stop him from fulfilling his call when the enemy used tricks and threatening words to intimidate and make him give up fulfilling his dream.

God has promises for your future. Your dreams are activated through prayers and fasting, through supernatural interventions. The hand of God changed circumstances for Daniel in the lion's den; for Shadrach, Meshach, and Abednego in the furnace of fire; for Esther in the king's house and in Mardoheu's house and for the Jewish people; for Ruth in Naomi and Boaz's house; for David in the battle with Philistines and King Saul's house; for Jacob in Laban's house and in front of Esau's revenge; for Gideon in the battle with enemies; for Asa in front of one million armed soldiers; for Ezekias's 180,000 soldiers, enemy's army, and more. The hand of God, who was with them, is also with each one of us as His creation and as His sons and daughters. When we do not take our eyes off Him, He will watch over us. Their stories were written in the Bible for our benefits, for us to be reminded from their example that the hand of the Lord changes circumstances, gives you favors, gives victory and success, and opens doors that no one can shut. "And to the angel of the church in Philadelphia write, 'These things say He who is holy, He who is true, He who has the key of David, He who opens and no one shuts, and shuts and no one opens'" (Rev. 3:7 NKJV).

All we need to know is that all circumstances are temporary and have an end. Put your dreams in God's hand, and He will last until all will be fulfilled for the joy that will last in eternity. He is there for you. He gives you signs to keep your faith up. You must keep your hope alive; do not let it die. Through fasting and prayers, Eliezer asked for a sign at the well, Gideon asked for a sign for the battle with the enemy, Nehemiah asked for a sign to build the wall, Ester asked for a sign and favors with the king in the palace, Ruth asked for a sign and a desire to become Boaz's wife, Elijah asked God to show His power to bring fire from heaven, Job asked to be healed and blessed again, David asked to recover everything, Solomon asked to build the temple, and so on. Jesus Christ asked for a sign to carry the cross to face death, to see the world saved and not perish eternally. "Looking unto Jesus, the author and finisher of *our* faith, who for the joy that was set before Him endured the cross, despising the shame, and has sat down at the right hand of the throne of God" (Heb. 12:2 NKJV).

Having the mind of Christ is God's purpose for humanity. Without the Spirit of Christ, humanity is unredeemed and spiritually dead. Every person needs to have Christ, the Spirit of Christ, to be redeemed. We must possess the Spirit of God to understand the things of God and to live like Christ. Our brain's thoughts must be the thoughts of Christ. Our nerve cells, the neurons (microcomputers) in our brain, must be in His possession. The Holy Spirit activates the thought of eternity placed in people's heart from creation and makes them a different person with a different personality living in the Spirit. Setting his or her mind on things above where Christ lives at the right hands of the Father. The Holy Spirit helps us grow in our relationship with the Father. The Holy Spirit brought God's energy to accomplish God's will by the powerful spoken Word, Jesus Christ, at creation. God promised His Spirit to come over every flesh and to give people dreams, prophecies, and visions about their future. "And it shall come to pass afterward That I will pour out My Spirit on all flesh; Your sons and your daughters shall prophesy, Your old men shall dream dreams, Your young men shall see visions. And also on *My* menservants and on *My* maidservants I will pour out My Spirit in those days" (Joel 2:28–29 NKJV). Pray for a hunger for God's anointing for a future filled with power to accomplish God's dreams and visions in your life.

Brenda Kunneman, in her book *The Daily Decree*, encourages us that "one of the key elements of the last days that Peter spoke about on Pentecost in Acts 2 was that God's people would experience the supernatural. Specifically he said that we would experience visions and dreams. Now, while we can't manifest these in our own power, because they are decided and distributed by God, we can ask that this last-days manifestation would have a place in our life. Again, it's as God wills it, but it wouldn't be in Scripture if it wasn't something He didn't want His people to experience. Ask the Lord today to allow you to experience last-days dreams and visions from heaven as He desires!"[2]

Revelation about your future comes when you live according to God's will. You can shine and carry the Lord's glory in your future with great revelation, and you will enjoy peace, love, happiness—love that brings more hope and more joy. He promises that the Lord's glory will appear over you when the Lord's light comes in the darkness of your circumstances. "Arise, shine, for your light has come, and the glory of the LORD rises upon you. See, darkness covers the earth and thick darkness is over the peoples, but the LORD rises upon you and his glory appears over you. Nations will come to your light, and kings to the brightness of your dawn" (Isa. 60:1-3 NIV).

Do not destroy the seed of revelation in you that has a divine origin. God programmed the ability to feel emotions in your DNA. When the Holy Spirit touches you, He activates that seed and makes it grow. He put the hunger for eternity in your soul. You need to accept that Jesus Christ has to live in you to light your path through the power of the Holy Spirit. He is your righteousness, your peace, your provider, your sanctification, your shepherd, your healer, your victory, your I Am, your everything. We need to be hungry for the Holy Spirit to achieve our great destiny.

You must keep dreaming, believing for God's visitation with great power to show His power and His glory. His glory is in the power of the Holy Spirit, and the Holy Spirit is His presence. The hunger in your soul gives birth to the desire for the Holy Spirit and His presence. The glory of God is the presence of God. You enter in intimacy with Jesus when the Holy Spirit comes and reveals Jesus to you. He reveals you His agenda and silences your agenda. When you surrender, the presence of God changes the atmosphere, changes your personality, your thoughts, your heart, your attitude.

You know when a person has been touched by the power of God and has been baptized in the Holy Spirit and has been in the presence of God. The power of the Holy Spirit and of His presence causes the transformation and causes miracles to happen. You cannot have benefits from the power of the Holy Spirit and His presence until you are touched by His power and understand the glory of his presence. God's presence touched me at work, and I was filled with joy and peace even in the middle of adversity in a Communist country. Get closer to God in intimate relationship with Him in your spirit when you are thirsty for revelation.

You get deeper in understanding, and in stillness you can disconnect from the noises of this world and can hear God because His power is lifting you above the circumstances you are in. You have a revival in your soul. Revival starts when you have a deep hunger and desire to see His glory. All revival is birthed from the deep desire to know the Lord more and from the hunger and thirst for the baptism with the Holy Spirit, the presence of the Lord. We must pray, "Show us Your glory."

There is a place for real fellowship with Christ. You will receive power when the Holy Spirit comes. You will have great revelation in your spirit and will show God to people around you. People will see God in your life. In my profession, I had the opportunity to comfort the dying patients and the families at the bedside of their loved ones passing away. Something happens when you show the real Jesus and His presence to the world, witnessing His power to heal, to restore, to comfort, and to bring joy and peace. You are fearless of the future when you have the power of God. His anointing touches those around you. Make a decision to shine for His glory. You are responsible for your actions. Arise, get up to bring joy for those around you and to bless them for action, and your future will be blessed.

In the Old Testament, Israel multiplied during their affliction. Affliction brought multiplication. Giving birth is painful, but the newborn baby brings unspeakable joy. There is a plan in the midst of your pain. Maybe you are lost in the painful situation and have no direction. God whispers to you in those difficult times that He is leading you to a great victory to comfort other people with the same comfort you received. You must look up, for your help comes from the Lord. Many times God used Christians to prophesy over me with revelation over my future, that He will bless me in my darkest moments. Those prophecies were fulfilled in my life, that God was with me in the darkest time. Darkness in your life builds your credentials, that you are a child of God, a daughter or son of the King of the universe.

In Egypt, God gave the Israelites favors and they became a great nation. Even when the Egyptians did not know the God of Israel, they had seen God's favor over His people. God gives you favor to be great for such a time as this. We did understand that when we were praying for business, community, city, society, nation to prosper, God made me and my family prosper. The favors of God were over our family all along the way to fulfill our destiny. God has a great destiny for you too. God is preparing a way for you to fulfill your destiny. God is looking for you to break limitations on your future when you are hungry for God. God works when things do not look right.

Smith Wigglesworth, in the book *On the Power of Scripture*, compiled by Robert Liardon, encourages us to "believe that Christ is enthroned in your heart to destroy the very principles of the devil in every way. Have the reality of this; build upon it by perfect soundness till you are in the place of perfect bliss. For this is perfect bliss: to know Him. Be so built in Him that you be not afraid of that comes on the line of all evil. You must have a fullness that presses out beyond. You must have a life which is full of divine. You must have a mind which is perfectly Christ. You must cease to be natural and begin to be supernatural."[3] Then he stated that "you are regenerated by the power of the Word of God, and it is in you as an incorruptible force, taking you from victory to victory."[4]

Created to Be the Voice of God

We were created to be the voice of God for influence. We must influence people around us and bring comfort to the hopeless people. God instructed Joshua to rise, to get up and pass Jordan. "Moses my servant is dead. Now then, you and all these people, get ready to cross the Jordan River into the land I am about to give to them—to the Israelites. I will give you every place where you set your foot, as I promised Moses" (Josh. 1:2–3 NIV). God is telling us to rise up and go over to a person in family, business, school, neighborhood, and hospital, to influence, to take spiritual dominion. At work, in the community, or in government, take spiritual control because Jesus gave it to us and it is already ours. We must get up and get it because it is ours for God's glory. You have influence. Silence makes you without influence and unable to interact with people. You are the product of your life and your environment. God can take anything and change it into something awesome. God puts people with wisdom around you. People who did not listen to wise advice ended up in terrible situation. Receiving wisdom, you become wise.

God will complete what He has started in you and with you. He is going to anoint you if you open your heart, and the Spirit of God will come over you with power to influence those around you. The Word of God is your treatment. If you take it like medicine every day, you will be healed physically and emotionally and will be able to heal others' emotions and diseases. Good news comes with power to influence those who receive it. Joy and gladness come with the news about receiving power. "But you will receive power when the Holy Spirit comes on you; and you will be my witnesses in Jerusalem, and in all Judea and Samaria, and to the ends of the earth" (Acts 1:8 NIV). The power of God comes on you and in you when you receive the Holy Spirit. The Holy Spirit is God's voice. God speaks to us through the power of the Holy Spirit.

Benny Hinn, in his book *Good Morning Holy Spirit*, emphasize that "you must come to this truth: The Holy Spirit is God. He is no less God then Jesus. He is no less than the Father. He's as much God as the Father and the Son. Jehovah is the name of the triune being-not the name of just one of them. The Father is called Jehovah. The Son is called Jehovah. The Holy Ghost is called Jehovah. When God the Father speaks, He speaks through the voice of the Holy Spirit."[1]

Do not let in influence from outside that conflicts with the Word of God. You must determine who will influence you. The Word brings conviction that builds your confidence so you do not lean on your own understanding. You must prepare and train your instinct to follow the Word of God. Do not lose your focus, your thinking, under pressure. You must practice to become who God wants you to be, and when the enemy brings pressure, you have a natural response. Make any effort to keep your self united in spirit, at peace with God longer; seek harder after God and do what is right, encouraging others through your great influence in doing good and in fellowship, as is written: "And let us consider how we may spur one another on toward love and good deeds, not giving up meeting together, as some are in the habit of doing, but encouraging one another—and all the more as you see the Day approaching" (Heb. 10:24–25 NIV).

Spiritual Upgrade

Spiritual Upgrade in a Deteriorating World

We live in a world where culture is continuously deteriorating. But the love of God to restore souls in the entire world was planned before the foundation of the world. We were in God's mind and spirit, with a destiny since creation. We were predestined before the foundation of the world to be in God's presence. "For we are His workmanship, created in Christ Jesus for good works, which God prepared beforehand that we should walk in them" (Eph. 2:10 NKJV). Sin took us out of God's presence, but the Lord Jesus brought us back. Our life is hidden with Christ in God. And we are seated in heaven with Christ Jesus. God sent the flame of holy fire that brings the flame of love because God is love. Leif Hetland stated at one of his conferences that "God is looking for fireplaces," meaning humans' hearts, where He will put His holy fire to burn with love. You were created to live in God's presence, to live with holy fire in his/her heart. In His presence is glory. When you enter in God's presence, in His glory, you enter in joy. Your heart is filled with joy. The joy of salvation is manifested.

His presence overwhelms you because of His love poured out on you. Many times in my prayers, I enter in God's presence and I sense the shift in the atmosphere. The same thing happens at conferences, and I see the changes on people's faces when the Holy Spirit touches hearts. I can read the expression of happiness radiating on people's faces, expressing the joy they receive in their heart from a fresh touch from the Holy Spirit. Tears of joy are rolling down on people's faces. That comes from inside, when the Holy Spirit is moving through people's heart and mind at the unconscious and conscious level. But to let God transform your mind in His presence is a conscious decision. Everything that God is doing is connected with your destiny, if you choose to allow His presence to manifest in you.

Fear and anger bring rejection and anger that pushes you to run away from God. But you have the greatest authority to run to God instead. You are rooted in love, and fear must leave. Fear, anger, and love cannot be in the same room. God's perfect love casts out fear. The goodness of God shows up in chaos when you fear the most. Running to God means you adore His presence. If you have His presence, you have everything. His presence changes everything. When you are changed, you become a changer. The joy of His presence brings light to the darkest places around you. People will see the light in those changed by the Spirit of God to be the light of the world. God restores the souls back to His presence, to His glory. God loves every single person from those approximately 7.7 billion people living on this planet at this time. God brings people in your life to be the answer to their prayers.

Upgrade Your Spiritual Life

An updated spiritual life is based on love and joy. The kingdom in me brings joy. In God's kingdom we are rich in faith. "Listen, my dear brothers and sisters: Has not God chosen those who are poor in the eyes of the world to be rich in faith and to inherit the kingdom he promised those who love him?" (James 2:5 NIV). God wants a deep love in our heart for one another to have an upgraded spiritual life. "Now that you have purified yourselves by obeying the truth so that you have sincere love for each other, love one another deeply, from the heart" (1 Pet. 1:22 NIV).

An upgraded spiritual life will be filled with the Holy Spirit, which fills us with the "oil of joy." "You have loved righteousness and hated wickedness; therefore God, your God, has set you above your companions by anointing you with the oil of joy" (Heb. 1:9 NIV). Joy is mandatory for an upgraded spiritual life to prevent physical and spiritual diseases. It is written to "shout for joy to the LORD, all the earth. Worship the LORD with gladness; come before him with joyful songs" (Ps. 100:1–2 NIV). Serve the Lord with gladness. God is our delight daily. "Then I was constantly at his side. I was filled with delight day after day, rejoicing always in His Presence" (Prov. 8:30 NIV).

Upgraded Through the Word

The Word sustains the weary. In our daily routine with high demands from the society, we live because of the high levels of stress that overwhelm us, making us extremely tired and weary. Stress therapists are advised to help weary people from stress to intervene with methods that will change their thought life: "In therapy sessions, experts might help their clients to identify the situations that seem to make them feel stressed, and they might teach them how to meditate, visualize or otherwise get away from the stressful thoughts without resorting to drugs. This kind of awareness can be incredibly powerful, and it could be just what some people need in order to recover. Similarly, therapists can also help their clients to process their prior sources of stress, so they won't always be dealing with old feelings and old concerns. Once people have the opportunity to put the past behind them and focus on the future, they might not be hobbled by feelings of nervousness and stress, and that might remove yet another pressure point that could lead to a relapse."[1]

The Word of God can make you identify the source of your stress and can transform your thinking as it contains "fountains of life and river of living water" that cause joy and peace in you for you to be able to overcome stressful situations, sparing your life from multiple diseases with complications and premature death. "The teaching of the wise is a fountain of life, turning a person from the snares of death" (Prov. 13:14 NIV). The Spirit of God is the anointing to comfort all who go through tough situation and mourning, to bind up the brokenhearted, to give oil of gladness when you are despaired and weary. God gives you power and authority to replace the negative old memories that bring rumination on the past mistakes and pain from hurting emotions that bring weakness and make you feel weary. Healing comes when you stop ruminating on past negative things and painful emotions. Physical restoration starts with restoration in your brain structures and your heart when you replace painful emotions with the fruits of the Spirit, making you feel love, joy, peace, and happiness.

In his book *The Pursuit of God*, A. W. Tozer describes that "any man who by repentance and a sincere return to God will break himself out of the mold in which he has been held, and will go to the Bible it-self for His spiritual standards, will be delighted with what he finds there. Let us say it again: The universal Presence is a fact. God is here. The whole Universe is alive with His life. And He is no strange or foreign God, but a familiar Father of our Lord Jesus Christ whose love has for these thousands of years enfolded the sinful race of men. And always He is trying to get our attention, to reveal Himself to us, to communicate with us. We have within us the ability to know Him if we will but respond to His overtures. (And this we will call pursuing God!) we will know Him in increasing degree as our receptivity becomes more perfect by faith, love and practice."[2]

Spiritual Upgrade Through Resilience

It is difficult in today's world to be resilient. The Bible speaks very loudly about resilience. Love of God is the antidote for fear. "For God has not given us a spirit of fear, but of power and of love and of a sound mind" (2 Tim. 1:7 NKJV). Where the Spirit of God is, there is love, because God is love. He replaces the fear memory in our brain with His love, casting out fear. When fear is allowed to reside in our mind, it will cause more stress and will cause disengagement ruminating over and over to the extreme learning hopelessness. The Word of God gives us prescriptions for resilience. "Do not remember the former things, Nor consider the things of old. Behold, I will do a new thing, Now it shall spring forth; Shall you not know it? I will even make a road in the wilderness. *And* rivers in the desert" (Isa. 43:18

NKJV). We have to admit that we were workaholics our entire life. I had that nice addiction to my business, working 24-7, performing multiple tasks and jobs as hands in providing care and managing the business during the day and on call during the night, being in charge twenty-four hours a day, seven days a week.

When God sent the best investor to our door to buy our business, we had to make that decision to sell the business in a matter of minutes while discussing the matter on the phone. While I was on the phone, my head was spinning; all kind of thoughts were rushing through my mind. I could not detach from my business after almost thirty years as the founder, the owner, and the operator. Deep in my soul, I had to whisper a short prayer. "Dear Father in heaven, please help me through the power of your Holy Spirit in Jesus's name. Lord God, help me." I was afraid to ask the investor for more time to think, because that opportunity will never come back to us. Also, my husband and I were not very young either; even though we were not ready to retire, it was too early for workaholics like us. I knew that my husband was fine with my decision.

But I looked up, and this verse from Isaiah 43:18 was typed on a piece of paper (placed on our refrigerator several months before that conversation took place on the phone) received when I attended a ladies' gathering. I received that verse as a reminder about that ladies' event. My eyes fell on those words. "Behold, I will do a new thing." I suddenly was leaping of joy inside even though I was worried about making such an important decision in less than twenty minutes. The battle started in my mind, but the Holy Spirit reminded me verse after verse, like "Be anxious for nothing," "Come to me you who are weary," "I will do a new thing," etc. I started to feel the peace of God that passes all understanding. God's living Word brought hope, peace, happiness, love, joy, thanksgiving, contentment, patience, and encouragement to my soul and spirit. I started to feel good in my body, having more energy, more motivation, being more dynamic, accomplishing more things in short time. The fruit of the Spirit was demonstrated in my attitude.

Use all opportunities when you go through trials to meditate on God's promises and produce the fruit of the Spirit to consolidate your good memories, to get stronger neurons, to prevent neurocognitive disorder (influencing others). Spiritual upgrades happen when Christ lives in you and has the power to attract you to have His character, His spirit, His DNA. The atmosphere is changed everywhere you go. Many times in my business, before I arrived in the facility, the helpers would report many patients being agitated, becoming aggressive and violent, even trying to attack the caregivers and other residents. As soon as I entered the facility, everybody would start to quiet down. Residents were relaxed and content, and the caregivers were smiling, feeling the change in the atmosphere. I heard them talking many times about this kind of change in the atmosphere upon my arrival in the facility. It was the peace of God that I was carrying with me at all times because of my prayerful life at the conscious and unconscious level.

The unconscious space in your mind needs to be occupied with love that brings hope and emotions as joy and peace from the fruits of the Spirit; in trials and in tempting situations, the Holy Spirit will bring those thoughts of hope from your unconscious mind, from the cortex in the brain in your conscious mind, and you are able to feel the emotions of peace, joy, and happiness and will spread them around to be felt by those around you. When you go through disappointments and lamentations, you must engage that hope in you to upgrade you spiritually and maintain your resilience.

PART V

Connecting Body with the Spirit

◾ Thoughts Connect the Body with the Spiritual Realm

"For she said, 'If only I may touch His clothes, I
shall be made well'" (Mark 5:28 KJV).

I vividly remember that when we visited Israel a few years ago
with Pastor Larry Huch's group, during our tour, we stopped at the
place of Migdal (Magdala), where Pastor Larry did read the passage
from the Bible about the story of the woman with blood issue. As our
thoughts went to that passage and we meditated on her story, everybody's eyes were full of tears. Our thoughts connected us with God's
spiritual realm in that moment, and His presence started to manifest
right away, activating our emotions with His powerful Word. We did
feel God's sweet presence in that place. Even though our eyes were
full of tears, we did feel the love of Jesus and the Holy Spirit's touch,
because we let our thoughts be connected with the Spirit of God in
that special place and let Him regulate our emotions.

The woman with blood issues in the Bible believed that Jesus's
purpose was to heal and restore. She thought in her head and said
with her mouth what she believed in her heart, and her thoughts of
hope and good emotions led her to action to touch Jesus's clothes,
and by her faith she was made whole. Her thoughts connected her
with the spiritual realm that Jesus lived in while on earth. Jesus came
from the spiritual realm and was carrying the kingdom of God with
Him. In His kingdom there were no diseases, pain, suffering, tears,
sadness, and discouragement. The Holy Spirit was resting on Him
and in Him to heal the sick, restoring the emotion of their soul to

263

make them whole. Talk of the Word of God and pray every single day out loud. Your thoughts of faith from the day are processed at night in your unconscious mind, stored away throughout your cortex as memories. When you worship, praising God, your faith is activated and the burden is removed. Pain will disappear, and you will have clarity in your thoughts. Your words will be different in your communication and actions because your thoughts connect you with God's spiritual realm.

Oppression can come from all directions in your life, from the negative news on television, internet, social media, and friends. Be determined to know God and believe to get delivered from your oppression. The woman with bleeding issue in the Bible was oppressed of her situation and of her disease but was determined to reach out to Jesus to connect to His spiritual realm and power to be restored physically and spiritually. Fear will leave you when you have faith and your thoughts are in connection with the heavenly Father and you have confidence in His powerful living Word and trust in Him. The all-powerful God opens the spring of water to burst from inside of you, as is stated in Jeremiah 17:5–8. "But blessed is the one who trusts in the LORD, whose confidence is in him. They will be like a tree planted by the water that sends out its roots by the stream. It does not fear when heat comes; its leaves are always green. It has no worries in a year of drought and never fails to bear fruit" (NIV). That is the prophecy for you and me, that when our thoughts are connected with God's spiritual realm, our neurons are planted near "water" and the "leaves are green always," meaning that we grow healthy neurons bearing the fruit of the Spirit.

That is God's prescription for long-term success. Trees planted along the riverbank are your thoughts' roots planted in the Word, the Living Water. The enemy gets in your home to create the environment of brokenness, sickness, diseases, trauma, financial problems, and divorce, and stepparents and stepchildren struggling to uproot your thoughts of hope, joy, and peace and promote negative thinking to bring discouragement and oppression and depression. Start right away to access the Living Water from the Word and replace the negative thoughts with constructive interaction, uplifting discussion, great resolutions, creative ideas, resolutions of arguments that cause painful emotions. Reconnect your thoughts with God's spiritual realm, communicating His powerful Word. You soul needs restoration. Science demonstrated that "the experience of positive emotions contributed, in part, to participants' abilities to achieve efficient emotion regulation, demonstrated by accelerated cardiovascular recovery from negative emotional arousal (Studies 1 and 2) and by finding positive meaning in negative circumstances (Study 3)."[1]

Build your life on the truth that God has a purpose for you even in your trial. Fight with spiritual pressure, not through resistance. God promised victory even in time of trials. Do not resist God's plan. I had many opportunities to resist God's plan in my life, but the Holy Spirit reminded me of the verse in the Bible that I must resist the devil, not God. With an open mind, I looked at the scriptures during all the uncomfortable situations and with all the changes I had to make in my life. Resist the devil and his strategies that make you resist God's plan. Resist what the world offers in order to obtain God's promises and to enter His spiritual realm. The devil comes with subtle actions and strategies to keep your mind preoccupied with worldly things even when you are a Christian. Sin will keep you from being a new creation in Christ to serve Him with a Christian walk, to worship God in spirit and truth.

Perseverance keeps your thought connected with God's spiritual realm, bringing victory. Egyptians wanted to keep the Israelites from going out to worship their God to connect with their Creator's spiritual realm. Moses was instructed by God to persevere in going back to the pharaoh even though he was humiliated and intimidated several times by the leader of the Egyptians. Moses did not give up in persevering to fulfill God's plan for the Israelites to be delivered from slavery and to worship God and their Father in heaven. The devil does not like it when you persevere in worship. The devil has strategies to create resistance to God's calling, against family, to steal the joy and happiness. Joy must be in the family at all times for continuing restoration and wholeness. Many people seek joy outside family when the joy in their family is missing. Run away from sin that destroys your soul and further destroys your entire family.

The Holy Spirit speaks to you to direct you and to guide you if you listen. He is speaking to you if you listen to His voice. He gives you power to persevere. You have the power of His Word. The Word is the weapon to fight every day every evil spirit. We are in a spiritual world. We hear many times that we are spirit, having a soul living in a body. Keep your spiritual eyes open at all times and your mind and thoughts connected with God's spiritual realm.

▪ Reprogram Your Thoughts and Desires on Him

Live with desire to know God daily for His glory. Look for Him every day and listen to His voice. Follow Him to go to higher places that you have no idea of. Desiring God is pleasing Him. It is pleasing God to have your emotions set to desire Him; He placed that desire in the human DNA from creation. You have His spiritual DNA built in your physical DNA. Do not build your life on social media, your superficial emotions, culture, easy fixes, wading in water, and addiction that leads to destructions. God's Word has better, safe fixes. Quiet water restores the soul. Hide the Word in your heart and do not sin against the Lord. When you have the Word inside of you, you cannot sin. You run away from destructive and seducing things of the world to avoid sin. The Holy Spirit is speaking, but many people do not listen to the voice of the Holy Spirit talking to their hearts and minds, and they end up in the darkest time of their life. Your thoughts can be reprogramming on desires to hear Him talking to you.

Live an honorable, authentic Christian life, practicing abstinence and purity with good morals. Do not use drugs, nicotine, alcohol. Promote clean relationship before marriage, and save sex after marriage. In your youth, respect other young girls and young boys. Those who haste to and run to the Holy Spirit's work will see measurable results. "Your children hasten back, and those who laid you waste depart from you. Lift up your eyes and look around; all your children gather and come to you. 'As surely as I live,' declares the

LORD, 'you will wear them all as ornaments; you will put them on, like a bride'" (Isa. 49:17–18 NIV).

Restoration Through Joy

Emotions of joy of the Lord bring restoration in our soul and spirit. The psalmist David cried out to God, "Restore to me the joy of your salvation and grant me a willing spirit, to sustain me" (Ps. 51:12 NIV). Thousands of years ago, David sinned against the Lord when he committed adultery with Bathsheba. Then the prophet Nathan came to tell him about the consequences of his sin of adultery. David suffered major depression because of the sin of adultery in his life. He loved the Lord and did not want to sin against him as he did when temptation came. In his distress, he asked the Lord to restore in him the joy of salvation to be able to overcome his painful distress and depression. Depression causes physical and emotional pain. David's joy needed to be restored in order to recover from the psychological distress and depression caused by his sin of adultery. Science demonstrated that "the neural processes of trait happiness are the opposite of those involved in depression/anxiety: 'rose-colored glasses' cause happy people to focus on positive cues while remaining oblivious to threats. Specifically, because negative affective styles have been associated with increased amygdala activation to negative stimuli, it may be happy people will not show this enhanced response, and may even show reduced amygdala activation to negative stimuli."[2]

When you look toward the Lord, your heart will be filled with joy. "Those who look to him for help will be radiant with joy; no shadow of shame will darken their faces" (Ps. 34:5 NLT). The First Christians were strong in their faith and lived a joyful life because they understood that the joy of the Lord was their strength. "They worshiped together at the Temple each day, met in homes for the Lord's Supper, and shared their meals with great joy and generosity" (Act 2:46 NLT). I remember as a child when fellow Christians stopped at our parents' house for fellowship and prayer. They were praising God full of joy and served meals with joy, eating together.

My parents shared their meals many times with strangers who were traveling through our village, not having place to stop to eat or sleep. Their hearts were filled with joy. Rejoice and be reassured that God has a solution for every situation. Our trials are not bigger than God.

Rejoice in the Lord Always

The secret for rejoicing is to leave all the worries in God's hands and to bring every situation in prayer with thanksgiving. That is a condition to get the peace of God and all our thoughts and hearts to be guarded in Christ Jesus. You must be excited about God's promises and decide to rejoice and change your disposition, to act enthusiastic. God wants you to be enthusiastic and have success. That was His plan for salvation and for success from the foundation of the world to make us happy and prosperous, to rejoice. He wants us to rejoice in health. Being full of joy and rejoicing promotes health. In 3 John 1:2, it is written, "Dear friend, I pray that you may enjoy good health and that all may go well with you, even as your soul is getting along well" (NIV).

People lose joy in sin or in sickness. Sin brings separation from God. You get in bondage because of your disobedience. Sins such as violence, murder, lying, sex before marriage, adultery, fornication, drugs, alcohol, stealing, anger, and unhealthy lifestyle are a choice people make every day. Then guilt is installed. Sins give people identity. Shame comes when people sin, then move away from God. They break relationship with the Creator. Jesus is our Savior and our healer, who can restore our relationship with our Father. He can remove all the bondage that keeps us from fellowship with God. He broke the power of sin. He holds the key for life. He sets us free from bondage of sin, anxiety, depression, discouragement, sadness, loneliness, rejections, adultery, drugs, and addictions. We must run to Him in prayer. Now, let's stop reading for a moment, close our eyes, and repent of every sin and ask for forgiveness and for healing. He is the only one who restores the joy of salvation when our sins are forgiven.

God is able and willing to forgive and to heal right in this moment. Practice excitement in your tone of voice and your walking with God. Jesus made you free from all bondages. Fill your mind with joy and enthusiasm. Every breath, every thought, every emotion, every action is the result of a choice you make right now. Jesus set you free already. In our memory care facility, a dear lady, a ninety-six-year-old former teacher with advanced dementia, was lying in bed, ready for her night's sleep. At bedtime, I used to visit the residents to make sure they were safe and lacked nothing for the night. So I visited this lady, and after I made her comfortable, I whispered in her ear, "Jesus loves you." Her face lit up as she got a big smile on her face, and she stated, "That made me so happy. Thank you for reminding me." Then she paused and, with a softer voice, stated, "You too." Her joy in her voice and face was so evident that it automatically made me feel the emotions of unspeakable joy that both of us were connected in the spirit with God's spiritual realm by this profound truth that Jesus loves us so we are able to rejoice always.

Overcome Obstacles with Joy

In our trials we did not lose our focus. With the joy of salvation in our hearts and mind, we overcame obstacles. We knew that all trials were temporary, and by faith we looked up at Jesus Christ and His promises, and He increased our faith greater than gold, as stated in 1 Peter 1:6–9. "In all this you greatly rejoice, though now for a little while you may have had to suffer grief in all kinds of trials. These have come so that the proven genuineness of your faith—of greater worth than gold, which perishes even though refined by fire—may result in praise, glory and honor when Jesus Christ is revealed. Though you have not seen him, you love him; and even though you do not see him now, you believe in him and are filled with an inexpressible and glorious joy, for you are receiving the end result of your faith, the salvation of your souls" (NIV).

Even people with impaired cognitions can rejoice in the midst of their loss and sorrow. Because I spent almost thirty years providing care directly to older adults with multiple chronic conditions and different kinds of neurocognitive disorder, automatically different scenarios come into my mind. I did see many of them; even in their suffering and disadvantaged situation, being in psychological distress, in their trials they still enjoyed life, smiling often. Science demonstrated that "people with advanced dementia can still enjoy life. Even if their language is impaired and they live in the moment, it should still be possible for them to live a life of pleasure and joy. A pilot study was conducted to learn more about these individuals' experiences, but because of the decline in their access to language, it was necessary to have others speak on their behalf. Analysis of findings was based on a hermeneutic approach inspired by Ricoeur (1981). Central findings were that all the interviewees emphasized humor and interacting with other people as a source of happiness."[3]

I can testify that I had the same observation when providing care to the elderly with different kinds of dementia. While interacting with them, I could see them smiling and rejoicing, with a pleasant expression on their faces, showing that even though they had lost everything, they were still fearless and able to rejoice. Some of them were still reciting verse from the Word of God and the Lord's Prayer, which gave them hope in their difficult times. Declare the Word of God. Speak what God speaks. God's promises are prophecies of His will for your life and your future. It brings hope for your future, increasing your faith, which casts out fear in life. That positions you to be in alignment with God's plan and purpose to fulfill your destiny and to be courageous. "Have I not commanded you? Be strong and courageous. Do not be afraid; do not be discouraged, for the LORD your God will be with you wherever you go" (Josh. 1:9 NIV). He is with you everywhere you are or everywhere you go.

Taught by the Spirit

The Holy Spirit works the same today how it worked a long time ago, if people have the same heart in unity. The Holy Spirit brings conviction, revelation, working miracles. Without the Holy

Spirit, there is no understanding of eternal life or things happening in heaven. The Holy Spirit does not keep secrets. He reveals the things of God to us. He will speak even through people with no formal education. As a young girl hungry and thirsty for the Lord, I went to small groups, in prayer meetings in very simple and small houses where people were living a very simple life. Many houses had the floor from dirt covered with used rugs, where we humbly knelt for prayers, and the Holy Spirit would come and speak to us through old Christians who literally did not know how to read. But when the Holy Spirit would come to give us instructions, their vocabulary was so eloquent, and anointed words came from their mouth, going directly to our hearts and minds. Unnumbered times, I felt the power of God when those people prophesied over me, that if you obey the Lord, He will bless you beyond what you can ask for or think of. Different prophets prophesied at different times in different locations the same thing over and over, that the Lord will bless me more than I can imagine if I will follow the Lord and love His Word.

Now, after more than forty years, I can testify that those prophecies were true, because they are fulfilled in my life. I never thought that God will pour out His blessings beyond my imagination. I remember vividly those prophecies coming through those persons through the Holy Spirit in a powerful way that they were even amazed. Who knows the future but God? Those words were alive in my mind, that I would be blessed even when all things were against me during Communism and when I arrived in the States with nothing. The Holy Spirit dropped ideas in my mind and was speaking to me as a "small voice," always teaching me which direction to go, what steps to take, what decision to make, even though my mind was bombarded with negative thoughts from all unfavorable circumstances. Now I understand why the prophet Isaiah stated, "Whether you turn to the right or to the left, your ears will hear a voice behind you, saying, 'This is the way; walk in it'" (Isa. 30:21 NIV). That verse was fulfilled in my life literally. The voice of the Holy Spirit is speaking today.

Develop a relationship with the Holy Spirit. The Holy Spirit will teach you all things. The Holy Spirit knows solutions for any situation in your life. The Holy Spirit gives you revelation through your mind and will remind you of all things and you will discover all things. Fellowship with the Holy Spirit can reach unthinkable things. The Holy Spirit moves inside of us, giving us wisdom, revelation, guiding our thoughts and steps. The Holy Spirit is not strange to the human's life. The Holy Spirit is God's power that came at creation with blowing, breathing, giving life to everything on the planet.

Boldness in the Spirit

The Holy Spirit makes you aware and gives you boldness. The presence of God will make you aware of things even in the middle of difficult circumstances. The Holy Spirit will help you work out your salvation with fear and trembling, filled with awe of who God is. He is holy. God is at work in you both to will and to work for His good pleasure. You must be in awe of His reverence. It is about His holiness. Put your eyes on the Lord in a way that chains will fall off you. Expect God to work in your life. Know who is God for you and be bold.

The fear of the Lord is needed for you to declare His Word with boldness. When Communists asked me about my faith, I felt the boldness come over me to answer with great courage that I am a follower of Christ. As soon as I declared that I believe in God and Jesus Christ is my Savior, I felt the power and authority that God gave me through His Word. The Son of God overcame death; God is ready to perform miracles in front of your enemy when you fear the Lord and proclaim that with boldness. Boldness will give you confidence and peace that will lead to growth and multiplication. "Then the churches throughout all Judea, Galilee, and Samaria had peace and were edified. And walking in the fear of the Lord and in the comfort of the Holy Spirit, they were multiplied" (Acts 9:31 NKJV). The Lord proves His work with signs and wonders in your life, and the power of the Holy Spirit heals the sick and casts out demons when you are bold.

Sharing the joy of your salvation needs boldness. "He proclaimed the kingdom of God and taught about the Lord Jesus Christ—with all boldness and without hindrance!" (Acts 28:31 NIV). The Spirit of God gives us power to overcome thoughts and emotions of timidity and fear. "For the Spirit God gave us does not make us timid, but gives us power, love and self-discipline" (2 Tim. 1:7 NIV).

Immersed in the Thoughts of the Spirit

The supernatural power of God is an incredible source to us to produce supernatural results and supernatural people to rejoice always. The Holy Spirit produces a people that pray in terrible situation with great faith that moves mountains and makes impossible situations possible. When the Holy Spirit comes, the atmosphere is changed. He whispers His breath over us, and something special happens. He creates a sweet atmosphere, bringing unspeakable joy. The Holy Spirit cannot be experienced in the worldly way. The Holy Spirit is a gift, a power to anoint for the sense of belonging and fellowship that embrace His anointing and His mighty work. He makes your work easy. When you are born again, the Holy Spirit leads you and guides you. You "fly" when your heart is filled with the Holy Spirit and full of joy. You enjoy the favors with God and favors with people. Favors with God helped people of the Bible get over their bad circumstances and be used for God's kingdom benefits. The Holy Spirit adopts people to God. The Holy Spirit holds everything together. What is inside of us matters.

When the Holy Spirit physically and spiritually passes the threshold of your physiology to get inside of you, you are immersed in the Spirit of God. From creation, the Spirit is wrapped in the body so we can be the person we were created to be with the fruit of the Spirit that we see outside as the result of the Spirit inside of us. His love, joy, and peace flow through each person and reach out those surrounding to be transformed too. The Holy Spirit positions you in God's presence. The Holy Spirit separates you from the world. When the Holy Spirit comes, you experience the fullness of God, a threshold of the glory. The body of Christ's specialties are the gifts given by the Spirit of God. The "whole body" fits together perfectly, like the human body with all systems, all the families on earth, as the body of Christ from the same Spirit that flows through each member of the body. "For this reason I bow my knees before the Father, from whom every family in heaven and on earth is named" (Eph. 3:14–15 ESV).

Cognitive Therapy

◾ Spiritual Cognitive Behavior Therapy

In health-care system, special therapists are using cognitive behavior therapy (CBT) to help patients cope with high levels of stress in life to change their underlying beliefs. For cementing ability, the power to forgive, to love unconditionally, to fellowship, for unity in family and community, Christ's followers are using what I like to call spiritual cognitive behavior therapy (SCBT). SCBT has been used since creation. You can see the transformation with eternal effects around the world when people use SCBT. The Holy Spirit does not let you be without fruit. The Holy Spirit changes you in a moment. His power is shaking you, and you know when He touches you. The Creator of the universe likes to live inside of you. You are transformed into a different person with thoughts like Christ's and with godly behavior. God loves you and wants to use you for His glory. Ask, seek, and knock, because He wants you to move in grace. Passivity is not a fruit of the Spirit. When the Holy Spirit is touching you, you move. You receive to pour it out, and seeds grow for others. But as with CBT, SCBT also takes discipline when lot of distractors and distraction surround you to get the living Word. The Word will disconnect you from the business of bad behavior of the world.

All of us are created in the image of God, but many live in confusion, asking a silent question, "Who am I?" People lose their identity and the perspective of life, what they were created for. Your identity is in Christ. You are a child of God, a new creation in Christ. Walk with confidence in your identity, fully filled with the anointing and God's breath in your lungs, and your spirit is enveloped in

His Spirit. Walk in the anointing that you are given fully, filled with Him. Christ lives in you. Christ is the hope of glory to meet the spiritual needs of the world. Empowered by the love of Christ, there is no reason and no purpose to live outside of Him. When you disconnect yourself from the living God, there is no salvation, no hope, no destiny, no joy, no purpose. SCBT takes discipline to create results.

When your sins are washed away and you are free from sins, your sins are forgiven, then joy overwhelms you. You focus on Christ. Your cognition is possessed by Christ, and you can do anything through Christ, who strengthens you. The Father likes your life because of the love for Jesus. Jesus was obedient to the Father. He empowered those around Him. We must empower those around us. You were created to connect with other human beings and engage in conversation to discover that we are different, that we have different purpose and different destinies and different social skills. When the Holy Spirit guides you, your cognition, your behavior, is changed, because dopamine is released as a result of your true joy because of His presence in your life that made you a new creation. SCBT works.

The world will be transformed only through the blood of Jesus Christ, the Lamb of God. We are adopted to the Father through the blood of Jesus because we are His creation. Each person on earth was created in God's image and longs for the Creator and is thirsty spiritually for His Living Water to satisfy the thirsty soul and spirit, thoughts, imagination, cognition, and conscious and unconscious mind. Jesus in us is the well of living water that springs, flowing to quench the thirst of those around us. The world around us is spiritually thirsty, spiritually dehydrated, needing living water to be restored. The world needs SCBT.

People live in the dark, lacking light, needing cognitive therapy. We can be recognized and focus our thoughts and imagination that Jesus became sin so we can become righteous. Jesus took our shame so we live a glorified life. He adopted us as sons and daughter when He became fatherless for a moment on the cross, crying out, "My God, My God, why did you forsake Me?" so we can have a Father. Fatherlessness creates confusion and much emotional pain in this world. Psychological distress and pain impair human cognition and paint a disfigured picture of life. They are huge obstacles in people's success in life. You must go through a process to get to success. God brings us to a process of testimony. God shows up in the middle of impossible situations to take possession of your mind and cognition to change your behavior to have a testimony.

Your testimony is a prophecy for other people who hear your testimony to be inspired and have their faith increased, and hope will rise inside and they start to experience joy.

You have to overcome criticism, opposition, demons, obstacles, resistance; you must go in the right direction to overcome obstacles. Disciples were filled with power to overcome obstacles because they did not lose the direction and their focus on Jesus, the Master of their faith. Many times your own thoughts and your cognition are an obstacle in your progression in life. Jesus went through all suffering before us. He knows the pain and the suffering. Through Him we are already victorious. Pray from the place of victory, peace, and rest and use SCBT to overcome the world.

Spiritual Cognitive Behavior Therapy for Spiritual Vital Signs

Emotional sickness is real and is painful and affects your soul, spirit, and body. The emotions in your body must be aligned with God's emotions in His powerful Word and let the Holy Spirit control them. Use SCBT to align your thoughts and emotions with God's will and desire for your life to function in the purpose for which you were created. The emotions in your soul will be restored when you are led by the Spirit and let the Holy Spirit take residence in your body. "Do you not know that your bodies are temples of the Holy Spirit, who is in you, whom you have received from God? You are not your own; you were bought at a price. Therefore honor God with your bodies" (1 Cor. 6:19–20 NIV). The purpose that you have a body is for the Holy Spirit to live inside.

When the Holy Spirit resides in you, your cup will overflow with His anointing. When you are anointed by God with the power of the Holy Spirit, symbolized by oil, your cognition is guided to the goodness of God and your behavior is changed, desiring more of God. And as the psalmist, you can declare, "You anoint my head with oil; my cup overflows. Surely goodness and mercy shall follow me all the days of my life, and I shall dwell in the house of the LORD forever" (Ps. 23:5–6 ESV). Your desires and cognition are led by the Spirit. You want more of His goodness and mercy. You want to be with the Lord forever. The Lord wants the enemy to know that with Him you are more than victorious, so the Lord spread the table in front of your enemy to show His glory. His presence changed the atmosphere.

God the Father desires to come to you through His Son, Jesus, and His power to dwell in you. Jesus entered through a closed door, and fear left when His peace flew from Him after His resurrection, and His disciples were full of joy and peace. He enters in your mind; thoughts and cognition are guided through His power, His peace, His provision, His passion. Your heart feels the joy. Jesus said, "I will be in you, a well of living water springing out in eternal life." We get what He has. You speak what God is doing to increase your faith and hope. Let your cognition be guided by the Holy Spirit, not about what the devil does, but what your heavenly Father does. When unhealthy fear comes, it will bring discouragement and make your hope disappear. When faith is replaced with fear from the work of the devil, your cognition, thoughts, and emotions are negatively affected. There is no benefit at all to give the devil credit for his work.

Spiritual Cognitive Behavior Therapy with Hope

Hope for eternal life brings joy. Inheritance prepared by Jesus brings joy. Your cognition and thoughts can be "washed" by God's Word, the Living Water, and can be renewed by the Holy Spirit, as emphasized in Titus 3:4–7. "But when the goodness and loving kindness of God our Savior appeared, he saved us, not because of works done by us in righteousness, but according to his own mercy, by the washing of regeneration and renewal of the Holy Spirit, whom he poured out on us richly through Jesus Christ our Savior, so that being justified by his grace we might become heirs according to the hope of eternal life" (ESV). People's cognition and behavior can benefit from the goodness and lovingkindness of God and the regeneration and renewal of His Spirit. "These things are excellent and profitable for people" (Titus 3:8 ESV). Living with eternity in mind brings the profit of a life changed for eternity. The joy of resurrection is an eternal joy.

Death brings sadness, separation. Death is devastating. Eternal death is more devastating. Destiny is dead, dreams are death and love, and peace and joy are lost. That is the reason most of us need spiritual cognitive behavior therapy. I have seen many people dying during my almost thirty years working in the health-care system and providing end-of-life care at the bedside of dying patients. I did see the entire dying process hundreds of times. It is emotionally draining both for the patient, the family, and the caregivers. Many living people are dead inside of them, with dead dreams and no hope. Even in the middle of a luxurious life and high achievements, the emotion of fear from the thought that one day you will die will be processed in your limbic system, including amygdala, and if you do not replace that thought with hope in everlasting life, your emotions, from the emptiness inside, will take over and will cause serious damage physically and spiritually. You can recognize the dying process through the vital signs of the body declining. The same thing happens with the spiritual death, that the spiritual vital signs are declining.

Do not let your hope and your dreams die. You have a destiny in Jesus Christ. When His Spirit lives in you, your joy is restored and your hope is revived, knowing that Christ lives in you by faith and He is the hope of glory, as is written. "Christ in you, the hope of glory" (Col. 1:27 NKJV). We will inherit eternal life because Christ lives in us and we are God's children. "And if children, then heirs— heirs of God and joint heirs with Christ, if indeed we suffer with *Him*, that we may also be glorified together" (Rom. 8:17 NKJV). Let this truth guide your cognition to benefit from the highest spiritual cognitive behavior therapy.

■ Spiritual Cognitive Therapy for the New Spirit

Through the Spirit of God, you receive a spiritual transformation, a new spiritual breath, a spiritual resurrection. From creation, humans carry God's breath in their lungs (temporary) but live in sin due to the sinful nature since the sin entered in the world through Adam and Eve's disobedience of God's instructions in the garden of Eden. But God chose to breathe again His eternal Spirit in those who obey Him and follow His directions in His living Word. Your breath is refreshed when He breathes again His spirit on you to revive you from the spiritual death of your soul because of the sinful nature.

He breathed over His disciples when their hearts were gripped by the fear of being alone and powerless in the face of the enemy and those who persecuted Jesus's followers. Their spiritual vital signs were revived. But they received power; new breath revived that new spirit, which is forever. In my profession, I see people breathing their last breath, and those who hope in the Lord have a peaceful death. When they get close to that moment, many of them express their faith with joy that a better life is waiting for them after the painful moments on this earth. They know that they will be in the presence of the Lord in a matter of days, hours, or minutes. You will be amazed what faith can do in people's heart about eternity.

Resurrection of Jesus changed everything. Jesus invented the spiritual cognitive behavior therapy through His resurrection power, and the spiritual vital signs are the demonstration. He brought joy in disciples' life and in those who followed Him. Those who got born again became new creation in Spirit through Christ Jesus. His resurrection brought healing, restoration, renewal, revival, and refreshing, which bring joy for eternity. Nobody can take that joy away from you. You are in charge of your emotions of joy.

King David, through God's Spirit, knew that he was in charge of his emotions. "I was glad when they said to me, 'Let us go to the house of the LORD!'" (Ps. 122:1 ESV). David said, "I was glad." David knew the joy of His presence when soaking in His goodness makes you glad. David knew that God's presence brings joy, is freeing souls from worries every day and from troubles of the world. His Word gives us hope, changing our thoughts and all emotions of deepest discouragement in our hearts and mind, causing joy that makes you feel good and strengthens you through a new spirit. That bring so much comfort. "Now may our Lord Jesus Christ himself, and God our Father, who loved us and gave us eternal comfort and good hope through grace, comfort your hearts and establish them in every good work and word" (2 Thess. 2:16–17 ESV).

During the earthquake in March 1977 in Bucharest, people were horrified with fear by the long violent shaking signaling the "end of the world." But the peace that I felt inside of me was from above, something I could not describe. It was His presence; the Holy Spirit inside of me filled my heart with joy and comforted me in that unexpected and disastrous earthquake. Any storm is calmed in His presence. Jesus, through His Spirit, is with you and in you in your storm to bring peace and joy, to calm your overactive brain, to reduce levels of cortisol, the stress hormone, and to release the right formula of the neurochemicals and hormones to prevent physical and spiritual sicknesses. In His presence, everything that seems lost is restored—your health, your joy, your destiny. Hope in our God will help you guard your heart and mind in the most outrageous storm and keep your spiritual vital signs stable.

Spiritual Cognitive Behavior Therapy: Guarding Your Heart and Mind

Many events affect your emotions, your feelings, and your heart. You can recognize that your emotions and feelings of love, joy, and happiness are healing your physical and spiritual diseases when you pay attention to your thoughts and your cognition. On the contrary, prolonged negative thoughts and emotions and feelings of constant sadness, anger, anxiety, and depression are destroying your health. You can measure that by your "spiritual vital signs." Spiritual vital signs help you assess your heart and mind. Abnormal vital signs will give signals to guard your heart and mind. Building walls to protect your mind from the enemy that comes to steal your joy. God builds a shelter, a refuge, and a fortress for you to dwell through your obedience. When you obey God's Word, God, in His faithfulness, will provide divine protection to shelter you from all fears, terrors, and destruction. "He who dwells in the shelter of the Most High will abide in the shadow of the Almighty. I will say to the LORD, 'My refuge and my fortress, my God, in whom I trust.' For he will deliver you from the snare of the fowler and from the deadly pestilence" (Ps. 91:1–3 ESV).

Before you guard your heart, you must guard your mind. What thoughts you let get into your brain, into your conscious and unconscious mind, will determine the feelings in your heart. You have the capability to select your own thoughts. You can resist those thoughts that bring psychological distress. "Submit yourselves, then, to God. Resist the devil, and he will flee from you" (James 4:7 NIV). Resisting the devil means guarding your mind from thoughts that lead you to activities that affect your emotions negatively.

In order to protect your heart, you must be careful about information from your environment that you collect with your eyes and ears and what information you store in your brain's structures and in your unconscious mind. Your heart is affected by your emotions and feelings caused by the thoughts influenced by the information from the world around you and your memory storage. This is the warning we read in the Bible: "My son, be attentive to my words; incline your ear to my sayings. Let them not escape from your sight; keep them within your heart. For they are life to those who find them, and healing to all their flesh. Keep your heart with all vigilance, for from it flow the springs of life" (Prov. 4:23 ESV).

Jesus Christ donated His blood when He died at Calvary for the sin of the world so we can receive His "spiritual resuscitation" and "spiritual blood transfusion," which brought us from death to life. He gave us eternal life through His death and resurrection. Only the blood gives life. For our sinful life and death in our transgressions, the world needed massive anointed and "holy blood transfusion" that only Jesus Christ, the Son of God, was able to donate at the cross. The enemy will strike with discouragement, doubt, despair, depression, and death. Only the joy of the Lord gives you strength. "Then he said to them, 'Go your way. Eat the fat and drink sweet wine and send portions to anyone who has nothing ready, for this day is holy to our Lord. And do not be grieved, for the joy of the LORD is your strength'" (Neh. 8:10 ESV). The joy of the Lord gives you strength to destroy the enemy. His joy will change your "spiritual vital signs."

God's Cognitive Behavior Therapy to Resolve Spiritual Signs and Symptoms

From the beginning, God created the body, soul, and spirit, a tridimensional being. When the body is sick, the spirit and soul are affected. When a human being is in psychological distress, the body is affected. Jesus Christ, as a person on this planet, healed every person tridimensionally. People of God in stressful situations in the Old and the New Testaments were encouraged to cry out, to pray, to trust God and His promises. People of God came to a place of victory and a place of peace when they put their trust in the Lord and His supernatural interventions. God intervened, and their hearts were filled with joy. They were singing, making music to the Lord in their hearts.

Today, thousands of churches are filled with believers every Sunday to receive spiritual food for their souls to increase their faith and trust in God, to keep their spiritual vital signs in balance.

That is the best spiritual therapy people receive in churches and cell groups for their soul and mind to build a strong resilience and overcome stressful situations, to promote a healthy balance and homeostasis. The Holy Spirit brings tridimensional healing and multiplication. Through all the trials in Romania and in the USA, we continue to believe that God exists and answers prayers. "But without faith *it is* impossible to please *Him,* for he who comes to God must believe that He is, and *that* He is a rewarder of those who diligently seek Him" (Heb. 11:6 NKJV). Then blessings will overflow and you experience increases, making you grow in strength and meaningful relationships with the Creator of the universe.

Measurable Spiritual Vital Signs

The manifestation of the power of God through the power of the Holy Spirit is measurable in the character and behavior of those that are touched and transformed in a supernatural way. They come from the darkest places to the light. Sadness is replaced with joy, fear with faith, anger and hate with love, discouragement with hope, disappointment and despair with trust, envy and jealousy with compassion, competition with collaboration. All positive changes are measurable and are seen in a transformed and spirit-filled life. Transformation happens in people's thoughts, in their mind, and in their emotional feelings, in their hearts and attitudes. Their quality of life is improved.

Measurable spiritual vital signs are recorded every Sunday in churches around the world through powerful testimonies of changed lives and every day in the life, affected by the touch of the Holy Spirit, the power that draws people near to the Father, giving them the fruitful experience, living a life to affect humanity and the history of the world. Jesus in them, through the power of the Holy Spirit, brings them in the presence of God to experience the transformation of their thoughts in their mind and feelings of emotions in their hearts, then the joy of salvation that brings the peace of God that passes all understanding. They experience His power. Their attitude is changed toward others to glorify God.

Control Spiritual Vital Signs with Enthusiasm

Enthusiasm and excitement in your action, speech, and thinking will bring you great joy in your heart that will change your "spiritual vital signs." My first job in the US was in a nursing home, providing care to the elderly. I had so much joy that I was leaping in the hallway of excitement that I could have a job and could work. My joy was so visible that each time someone called in for different motives and the facility was short of the caregivers, I was asked to cover for that person. I was working almost every day. Even when people had a hard time finding jobs, I was working two jobs because of my enthusiasm for work and for people around me.

Our Father in heaven is enthusiastic about us. It is His good pleasure to give us His kingdom. God gave us wisdom, gifts, skills, sound mind, health, power, and will because He wants us to prosper so we can help the fragile, disabled, disadvantaged, and marginalized to be able to finance His kingdom. (God gave Joseph wisdom to be prosperous for a reason, to bless the children of Israel [Gen. 48]). God wants to bless His children as we want to bless our children. They need God's blessings and protection from drugs, idolatry, alcohol, lies, corruption, perversion, greed, human trafficking, everything that is the fruit of the flesh.

Our children need God's blessings so they can rejoice in the Lord and their hearts can feel the emotions of joy. You cannot have joy under the curses. We must have the blessings of God on our lips for our parents and for our children, for the society and nation where we live. We must represent the God of Abraham, Isaac, and Jacob, the God who blesses His children when they walk in obedience. Our children must worship and go where the blessings of God are spoken and are flowing.

Cast out the kingdom of darkness and let the kingdom of light come into your life with joy, passion, and strong feelings of excitement, inspiring others. One time, a social worker from the state visited our business and did see my passion, my strong excitement at work, the zeal for life caring for others even in long hours, volunteering in community, and she stated, "She is a superwoman." Great joy and enthusiasm reveal great potential through the anointing power of the Holy Spirit, who makes us successful. Successful people have enthusiasm about life and are excited about opportunities and work that will motivate other people to enjoy their job and be enthusiastic about life. Joy is contagious and enthusiasm too.

God placed the mirror neurons in the human brain for that reason, to be able to communicate to your heart the feelings of other hearts and to learn from one another and make others become contagious themselves. Building a community with people happy and full of joy, enjoying bringing excitement in society where they live, serving others, promoting healthy attitude and behavior, will develop a healthy society. Nothing greater is achieved without enthusiasm. We cannot motivate others either without joy and enthusiasm.

Enthusiasm is a feeling of excitement. The definition of *enthusiasm* is "strong excitement of feeling: ardor," "something inspiring zeal or fervor," "belief in special revelations of the Holy Spirit."[1]

God in you creates enthusiasm. What is in God, Who created this universe, is in you. It becomes your personality. I have seen people being enthusiastic, talking about passing from this world into eternity. They have no regrets leaving this world behind, knowing that they will meet the Lord of Lords, the God whom they served with their whole heart. True Christians and strong believers are filled with enthusiasm. Providing care to dying people, I have the privilege to spend time at the bedside, observing unnumbered times how life on earth ends. One particular patient with advanced dementia was singing before her passing away, "Halleluiah, Halleluiah, Halleluiah. Bring revival, Lord. Bring revival, Lord." She was singing very loudly and with great joy on her deathbed. It gave me goose bumps hearing her voice rise toward heaven with such enthusiasm that morning, with her eyes gazing toward heaven.

I thought Jesus was coming right then. She was so clear in her thoughts. I knew she had advanced dementia and was not able to carry even a simple conversation. She was not able to process information at all. She did not recognize anybody around her, even the persons who took care of her for several years. She did not know her own name. But she knew the one she served her entire life. I knew she did love the Lord. She had so much joy in her soul passing into eternity. Usually, people are afraid of dying, fighting until the last second on their deathbed. Not with this strong believer, a giant of faith and great woman of God. Her physical vital signs were getting worse because her body was shutting down and all the cells were shrinking, getting ready for all the organs to fail, but her "spiritual vital signs" were at great levels and values when her soul and spirit prepared for her eternal home.

Spiritual Genetic Mapping

God, the Creator of the universe, mapped your genetic makeup with spiritual desires, and He breathed His breath in the human body to maintain great values of the "spiritual vital signs." He standardized our spiritual vital signs. The purpose was that we seek after Him. The purpose for us to be on this planet is to influence the world, to take the gospel to the nations, bringing the family, friends, nations in prayer for recovery. Do not grow weary. In the spiritual realm, we are "one" with the Father, the Son (Christ Jesus), and the Holy Spirit, which does not grow weary and does not faint.

The world is in great spiritual confusion because they do not see God. They are looking for things that are seen. God is Spirit, and with our human eyes we cannot see Him. God's face is hidden from humanity. Humanity can find Him in secret places and hiding places. He is there. He is working in your favor even when you sleep at night. God is not sleeping. "Indeed, he who watches over Israel will neither slumber nor sleep" (Ps. 121:4 NIV). When you persevere in prayer and fasting, you set your spiritual stage for victory. God is with you even though you do not see Him. You must have "spiritual eyes" to see Him. He answers your prayers when you do not give up in prayers. He said, "Call to me and I will answer you, and will tell you great and hidden things that you have not known" (Jer. 33:3 ESV). You have God's spiritual genetic makeup.

If you do not pray, things start to go wrong. You move in the wrong direction, making wrong decisions and mistakes that lead to isolation, separation, loneliness, discouragement, fear, anxiety, and depression. Do not take your spiritual eyes off Jesus Christ in any situation. Partner with God and do what He told you to do. He is calling us for repentance to restore our spiritual genetic makeup. Repentance and baptism break all limitations of your mind and your spiritual life. Obey by faith that will lead you in the presence of God, where you can be restored. The presence of God will make you whole. Your spiritual brokenness is healed. You are delivered from darkness and bondage. You do not ignore God anymore. Presence creates apostasy from ignoring God. We pass through times of apostasy, going away from God, but God's presence brings us back to Jesus. Jesus came to redeem us from the stages of darkness and to restore our spiritual genetic makeup. Darkness is gone when the light shines. Do not let the spiritual stage of the world influence your spiritual life. God creates a new spiritual stage for you when you seek Him with all your heart. He will empower you through the power of the Holy Spirit and will give you gifts to serve others through Him. You are created with a spiritual genetic makeup to live in light and with healthy spiritual vital signs.

Replace Emotion of Sadness with Gifts

The gift of the Holy Spirit brings unspeakable joy always, replacing emotions of sadness. We miss the joy because we miss the Holy Spirit, the perfect gift. All other gifts bring temporary joy. We are spiritually blind, ignoring the gifts of the Spirit. The gifts of the Spirit and the presence of God transformed millions of life. Those who came in His presence were convinced of their sinful nature through the power of the Holy Spirit. "But now I go away to Him who sent Me, and none of you asks Me, 'Where are You going?' But because I have said these things to you, sorrow has filled your heart. Nevertheless I tell you the truth. It is to your advantage that I go away; for if I do not go away, the Helper will not come to you; but if I depart, I will send Him to you. And when He has come, He will convict the world of sin, and of righteousness, and of judgment" (John 16:5–8 NKJV).

Separation brings grief, but the grief from separation is temporary. The Holy Spirit living in us produces the emotions of joy for eternity. He will never live us. It is God's gift to humanity. The Holy Spirit gives words of encouragement. The Bible is full of examples of people encouraged when we're touched and led by the Holy Spirit. The disciples and all who received the power of the Holy Spirit couldn't hold their joy of His presence. The Holy Spirit is teaching when you listen to His guidance. The joy of His presence continues day and night. God, the Creator, has the desire to be with His people. He created us to be with us, to dwell with us. He came on earth in flesh through Jesus Christ. The Son of God needed to come on earth, conceived through power of the Holy Spirit, to bring us back to His presence. The person in the Trinity became flesh through the power of the Holy Spirit. Because God loved us so much, He let His Son die on the cross for our sins and become cursed so we can be free from all our sins and curses. He gave us the most precious gift, eternal life, through His only begotten Son's sacrifice on the cross and through His resurrection. When you meet the Lord, you will have the gift of eternal joy. The joy of the Holy Spirit is the antidote for sadness from sin and curses.

Happiness in Humbleness

The Lord Jesus humbled Himself and was full of joy, serving others. He got the name above all names exalted by the Father. The joy to put others above you and be obedient brings joy in stressful situation. Do not live for what you prefer. Preferences lead to disobedience. God has a plan for you even where you are unseen. Most of us are unseen, not in the front line, not on the headline on the news. There are millions and millions of things done behind the scenes by the humbled servants of the Lord that do not make the headline of the news. But God takes notice of the unseen deeds and rewards those things done in secret. You get the joy from fulfilling your destiny and purpose on the unseen scene. As a humbled servant, every step you make is for a purpose, to inspire and to influence people for eternity and to advance His kingdom.

There is joy when you advance the kingdom of God, when the kingdom of God advances because of our impact. "To console those who mourn in Zion, To give them beauty for ashes, The oil of joy for mourning, The garment of praise for the spirit of heaviness; That they may be called trees of righteousness, The planting of the LORD, that He may be glorified" (Isa. 61:3 NKJV). God gives us joy to display His splendor because desperation, disappointment, and discouragement cause heaviness that hinders His praises.

■ Fear Is Not a Part of the Spiritual Genetic Makeup

Fear will keep us from praying for success. Fears keep us moving in the potential God gave us. When God gives you vision, fear cannot stop you. When God put the vision in our mind and head about a new facility, every demon in hell started to fight to stop that project. We had to say no to thoughts of intimidations, frustration, discouragement, fear, anxiety, and depression. We had the responsibility to fulfill that vision. We had to obey God's given thought. We partnered with God. He wanted us to be people of increase and success. Fear gripped our heart many times during this project because Satan wanted to delay and stop it to make us lose everything. Even the city came one time and placed a "Stop Construction" order on that property because they wanted to review the plans for that project one more time even though that plan was reviewed and was approved one time and the permits were ready to be picked up. We had to wait longer and collect more info and submit more paperwork. Every delay and every barrier was almost intimidating to make us back up and give up that wonderful project so God's plan for us to succeed and be blessed would end under the devil's attack.

But we knew that we had an assignment from God by faith. We trusted God. We had to go deeper in prayers, fasting and believing God's promises. We were encouraged by stories in the Old Testament. We knew God would show Himself strong on our behalf, as promised in 2 Chronicles 16:9. "For the eyes of the LORD range throughout the earth to strengthen those whose hearts are fully committed to him" (NIV). God wanted us to succeed in the vision He gave us. We did not allow fear to stop us. Satan wanted to defeat us, but God wanted to enlarge our territories, and we continued to work. With God on our side, we won.

Reverse Stress

Stress from Thoughts of Discouragement

It was demonstrated that "brain circuits involved in corticotropin-releasing factor-norepinephrine (CRF-NE) interactions during stress. NE neurons in the brain stem can stimulate CRF neurons in the hypothalamic paraventricular nucleus (PVN) to activate the hypothalamic-pituitary-adrenocortical axis and may affect other CRF neurons. CRF is the corticotropin-releasing factor."[1]

It is well-known that during periods of high levels of stress, we become more sensitive, since our amygdala is overactive. Stress can be increased by thoughts of discouragement from loneliness and isolation installed in our soul. We have the power to stop the stress response in our brain through our prefrontal cortex, involved in cognition and decision-making. "The prefrontal cortex is thought to play an important role in 'higher' brain functions. It is a critical part of the executive system, which refers to planning, reasoning, and judgment. It is also involved in personality and emotion by contributing to the assessment and control of appropriate social behavior."[2]

The prefrontal cortex enables you to make the right decisions, has executive functions to communicate with other brain functions and to inhibit the amygdala to stop the stress response through the parasympathetic nervous system. Science has discovered that through repetitive prayers and meditation, the parasympathetic nervous system is activated. That "produces a calm and relaxed feeling in the mind and body. People can learn to trigger their parasympathetic nervous system to immediately reduce their sense of anxiety and stress. This also lifts their mood, strengthens their immune system, and reduces their blood pressure"[3]

Overcome Stress and Burnout

Being overwhelmed and burnt out will lead to depression. But exercise regularly, find the career that fits you, and do what you are most passionate about. Do what you are called to do in life. Many people do not know what their call is. I often tell people that the call is where passion meets your skills. What you are good at doing. Keep in mind that your work and services bring benefits to others, then you will put more passion in your work. By doing your job, you are not just doing a job to make a living; you are actually serving the Lord by serving others that benefit from your work. The Lord will bless you because you bless others. Many times you do not know how much others are blessed by your work. Many will pray for you, and you do not even know when the blessings will chase you.

I pass by things and I pray to the Lord to bless those who contributed to the production of those things that I touch and use every day. Many times I drive on the freeways and bless the constructors and those who worked to build those nice roads so I can drive smoothly. I enter in a building, and I bless those who did build that building. If they pass away, I continue to pray for their families, children, and children's children, from generation to generation. This is just a small example of how you can focus on positive things. You go shopping, and pray for those present in the store and their families, even for those who built the shopping malls and their families.

I ask people to keep focus on good things. Do not focus on negative things at your work or in the community where you live. You must exercise when you are stressed and burnt out, because that will help your body release the healthy neurochemicals and neurotransmitters to improve your cognition and your circulation. Exercising at least 1.5 miles a day is equal with pharmacotherapy, causing your brain to release natural antidepressants as endorphin from the "chemical factory" in your brain. If you change your perspective when you are physically active, serving others, your body will release the same chemicals and will heal your brain and your body. Your life is influenced by your personality, genetic makeup, social relationship, behaviors, predispositions, temperament, and biological facts.

My husband and I worked hard in our memory care facilities to provide care to our patients with multiple chronic diseases, being in charge 24-7. We lived in the same facility for several years to give the best to our patients. Only to see their chronic conditions could make you feel burnt out. But every day we were happy that we were not in their shoes, spending our life in a wheelchair or being bed-bound, needing total care with all ADLs. We provided care with so much joy and were counting our blessings of being healthy and strong to serve those totally dependent adults. When you are burnt out, you cannot sleep. Sleep deprivation leads to depression, and for some people, that will lead to the extreme, even to suicidal ideation. When you are burnt out, that makes you depressed and increases the risk for inflammation, which suppresses the activity of the prefrontal cortex. Let's overcome stress through physical and spiritual interventions.

Chronic stress leads to pathology and diseases. Stress response is well-known as a defensive measure, the fight-or-flight response for human preservation. CRP inspires the hypothalamus to influence the adrenal glands to release corticoids to blood vessels, altering homeostasis, increasing sugar level, blood pressure, respiration, coagulation, pupil dilation, making the skin clammy, decreasing immunity, and making one unable to return to homeostasis. Residual stress activity increases neuronal death, increases infection, blood pressure, and ulcer, suppresses libido, muscle tension due to stress, and cytokines, causing preinflammatory activate stress system in the amygdala.[4]

Due to emotions of fear and sadness, the amygdala is hyperactive. The hippocampus's and prefrontal cortex's low activities driving CRF release an increased cortisol. Information comes from the environment, activating CFR, causing signs and symptoms as hypervigilance, getting startled, when the amygdala is activated by fear and becomes overactive. Chronic stress causes less flexibility and leads to chronic memory deficit, rigidity in memory, and impairment. Scientist Dr. George Koob, in *Calming Overactive Brain*, stated that stress causes pain and suffering, damage, and inappropriate emotional response.[5]

In chronic stress, fearful anticipation causes stress response. The amygdala, thalamus, hypothalamus, and locus coeruleus facilitate stress response; the dorsal raphe increases CRF, increases norepinephrine, and decreases serotonin. The amygdala gets activated by fear. Intense fear causes a person to be more sensitive, trying to avoid fearful situation. The person develops flashback, hypervigilance, nightmare, comorbidity, startle syndrome and is very vulnerable to drug addiction and alcohol to avoid the situation.[6]

Fear Activates Stress

Negative, impossible-to-change thoughts repeated over and over cause internalization in people's mind and hearts, feeding bad emotions. Depression is creeping in people's lives, especially those who are vulnerable due to high expectance for high performance, high bills and expenses, fear of competition for appropriate job, demanding jobs after graduation for younger generation, unmet needs at young age and adolescence. All those conditions affect their brain structures at a molecular level.

Science demonstrated that "macroscopic changes are supported on the molecular level by increased postsynaptic density-95 protein in the amygdala, consistent with stress-induced plastic changes and synaptic strengthening. Finally, we provide clinical evidence that strikingly similar structural network reorganization patterns exist in young adults reporting high childhood trauma and increased mood symptoms. Collectively, we provide initial translational evidence for a conserved stress-related increase in amygdala-centered structural synchrony, as measured by enhanced structural covariance, which is paralleled by a decrease in global structural synchrony. This putative trade-off reflected in increased amygdala-centered plastic changes at the expense of global structural dedifferentiation may represent a mechanistic pathway for depression and related psychopathology."[7]

Anticipation of bad and worse things to happen, panicking, negative expectation, lack of control, negative thoughts, rumination, and increased anxiety affect brain structures, leading to negative actions and unhealthy behavior. The amygdala in our limbic system is involved in bad emotions which expresses higher concentration of Cortico-tropin releasing factor, a neuropeptide responsible for behavioral responses to stress, that amplifies negative emotional state, decrease sleep due to rumination about negative thoughts, nasal obstruction, inflammation, heart diseases, impaired cognition, poor executive function, poor ability to concentrate, and poor ability to make decision—metabolic response to cortisol, increase insulin, lactic acid, trigger for panic attack, feedback from muscles, etc.

Stress response needs time to recover; but recovery is slow. If no recovery, the person is fragile, sensitive, experiencing flashbacks that will trigger more fear and anxiety. Emotional part does not go away. Researchers "hypothesized that lower-than-normal levels of neurotransmitters can lead to symptoms such as: feelings of sadness, helplessness, worthlessness, or emptiness overeating or loss of appetite insomnia or sleeping too much restlessness irritability a feeling of impending doom or danger lack of energy distancing yourself from others feeling numbness or lacking empathy extreme mood swings inability to concentrate thoughts of hurting yourself or others being unable to carry out day-to-day activities hearing voices in your head alcohol or drug misuse."[8]

Elegant Stress System Response to Escape Danger

Our Father in heaven, our Creator, placed in our body from creation an elegant stress response system to escape danger and for life preservation on earth. Dr. Brogaard stated that "healthy people possess levels of brain chemicals that lie within a certain normal range. When internal or external factors either deplete the brain of these chemicals or stimulate it to produce excess amounts, a chemical imbalance occurs. Imbalances in the brain's chemistry can give rise to mood disorders, learning disabilities, substance abuse and muscle weakness. The most easily noticeable imbalances in the brain's chemistry are imbalances in neurotransmitters that function as stimulants or inhibitors in the neurological system."[9]

We now know that an overactive brain causes the release of abnormal amounts of chemicals. Dopamine reward system is activated, triggers changes to produce dopamine release. There are many ways to increase dopamine levels naturally, by eating lots of proteins. Proteins are made up of smaller building blocks, called amino acids. Healthy nutrition as less-saturated fat, probiotics, beans, fresh vegetables and fresh fruits, exercise regularly, get enough sleep, listen to music, meditate.[10]

Negative emotions trigger the release of CRF, which activates the dynorphin complex in negative situations, decreasing serotonin neurotransmitters for depression, driven by CRF. Decreased serotonin affects sleeping, eating, anxiety, and further depression. Depression comes from isolation and rumination on depressive negative thoughts, making one feel unloved, unlikable, rejected, not accepted. Depressed spirits enter through those negative thoughts and feelings, and lack of fellowship and support system causes isolation. There is no joy. People are dealing with bad things in life that lead to depression. Depression is dangerous. Depressing spirits shorten life, causing lack of joy, lack of strength.

The Word of God gives us hope that helps people be encouraged and experience emotions of joy and peace. Achieve stability through changes that will help calm the overactive brain. Connect with heaven through prayer and fear of the Lord. The experience in our relationship with God and His presence determines what we will become in our soul, spirit, and body. A relationship with God will bring increased favor, blessings, and peace, physical and spiritual health. God uses the blessings to increase your influence. People who walk in the fear of the Lord will have open doors, multiplication, and comfort. Fear of the Lord brings us to Him. Abandon the worldly life to Him. Continue to walk in the presence of God for breakthrough in prayer and activate the elegant stress system response to escape dangerous fear and depression, building a strong resilience.

▪ Strong Resilience to Stress-Education System

To build strong long-term resilience, you must renew your mind and change the way you see life to avoid excessive worries. From my point of view, based on my own experience as a care provider, I believe that following Jesus's teaching is the best spiritual therapy in the world. Jesus's love and care for each human being is beyond comprehension. The education system must include Jesus's teaching in school curriculum to learn Jesus's way to manage stress and to build strong resilience by seeking the kingdom of God first, and the rest of the things we need every day for life will be provided by the Creator of heaven and earth. "Look at the birds of the air, for they neither sow nor reap nor gather into barns; yet your heavenly Father feeds them. Are you not of more value than they? Which of you by worrying can add one cubit to his stature? So why do you worry about clothing? Consider the lilies of the field, how they grow: they neither toil nor spin; and yet I say to you that even Solomon in all his glory was not arrayed like one of these. Now if God so clothes the grass of the field, which today is, and tomorrow is thrown into the oven, *will He* not much more *clothe* you, O you of little faith? Therefore do not worry, saying, 'What shall we eat?' or 'What shall we drink?' or 'What shall we wear?' For after all these things the Gentiles seek. For your heavenly Father knows that you need all these things. But seek first the kingdom of God and His righteousness, and all these things shall be added to you. Therefore do not worry about tomorrow, for tomorrow will worry about its own things. Sufficient for the day *is* its own trouble" (Matt. 6:26–34 NKJV).

When I arrived in the USA with no material and financial resources and speaking no English, with no family around me, I had to meditate on the Word from the Bible and trust Jesus's promises that He will take care of me and my family in every single situation. And He did. Later on, one time, I was invited to speak at a women's conference, and I was asked to share how we had been so successful in our life here in the USA since we came with no resources and spoke no English in a country where the competition is so great. My reply was that the secret for our success was that we did seek first the kingdom of God and His righteousness, and all other things we got were added to us. To illustrate, from the $400 that I gained in the first month of work, I sent to the needy half ($200). And we kept sowing since then in God's kingdom continuously with generosity, and God took care of all our needs. God is faithful, and He does not waste His promises. Anxiety and worries could aggravate our emotions and jeopardize our health and our well-being and affect our future. "Anxiety in a man's heart weighs him down, but a good word makes him glad" (Prov. 12:25). But the teaching of the Word of God has supernatural power to help us build a strong resilience that lasts for eternity.

Jesus Entered in Our World

Jesus entered our world spiritually at creation and physically in the flesh about two thousand years ago to feel our pain and to express our Father's love for us. To help depressed people, we need to get in their world and feel their pain. Many times, in taking care of people with neurocognitive disorder, including Alzheimer's and short-term memory loss, I was asked by professional people what made us successful in managing these people's behavior. My answer was always that these people live in their own world and we must enter in their world to help them. For example, one patient came in the office very upset and irritated, stating that it was her office and all of us must leave the office *now*. She became increasingly angry, starting to throw things at people and be physically and psychologically abusive and violent. With a calm voice, I approached her gently. I touched her shoulder and told her, "We all are working for you," and reassured her, "You are the boss" and "We will follow your directions." Her blue eyes got so big and her facial countenance changed, and with a big smile she received my statements and approved my proposal. Suddenly, the atmosphere in the office changed. She started to give us files and orders, and a calming environment was established. Everybody calmed down and relaxed. The picture changed in the moment I reassured her about our position, and we were able to move on with our tasks with her in our team. I entered her world and spoke her language. I could start to argue with her, and her anxiety could escalate so much to the point of her becoming more violent and aggressive that I needed to initiate the emergency response system. After that nonpharmacological intervention, the entire picture changed and we had a great time, laughing and enjoying our job.

I have seen the signs and symptoms of emotional pain of losing everything after a long time of hard work and many achievements in our patients' lives. When diseases hit people after a life spent in their profession, well-educated people will become frustrated and more confused. I had nothing to give but care with love, compassion, and understanding, and I valued who they were in the past, created in God's image. Jesus entered our world to show us the Father's love, to give us example, instructions, and direction on how to live life in a broken world. He felt our human pain from the deception of sin with its frustration.

One example is the woman at the well in John chapter 4. He understood the Samaritan woman and entered in her "spiritual world" when she arrived at the well frustrated and confused of the things in her world. Jesus felt her pain in her broken relationships with five persons, leaving her lonely, depressed, frustrated, and isolated. The woman at the well was depressed of her situation. Jesus knew her deep concerns and devastation. Love sees the pain. Jesus started a conversation, to connect with her, to give her hope, to give her "living water," to change her painful situation, to assist her in dealing with her emotions of depression, her loneliness, her isolation, her frustration with sin. Jesus approached her to help her deal with her reality.

Jesus reassured the Samaritan woman of the living water that will change her life forever. "Jesus answered and said to her, 'Whoever drinks of this water will thirst again, but whoever drinks of the water that I shall give him will never thirst. But the water that I shall give him will become in him a fountain of water springing up into everlasting life'" (John 4:13–14 NKJV). The "living water" is the medicine, the "pill" for your depression. The living water healed the Samaritan woman's depression and can heal anybody's spiritual and emotional diseases.

Jesus wants to enter your own world. When you meet Him, He gives you "living water" that bursts inside of you and changes your situation forever. His Word is the Living Water that activates your elegant stress response system and heals your depression, sadness, and frustration. When His living Word gets inside of you, as He promises, hope rises in your thoughts, in your mind and heart, and rumination on negative thoughts disappear, and you start to meditate at the Word of God when you make decisions to trust God's promises and drink from the Living Water. You start to look up to heaven, from which your help comes. He gives you life and more abundantly through His Spirit. He connects you with heaven with the Spirit of God. Jesus looked for opportunity for relationship to connect with people to do good, to spend time in prayer, study, and discipline.

The Most Powerful Network

A powerful network is extremely important to be able to manage stress from loneliness and suprasolicitation from life's daily demands. The Samaritan woman was networking with the King of Kings and the Lord of Lords without knowing and changed her life for eternity. "The Samaritan woman said to him, 'You are a Jew and I am a Samaritan woman. How can you ask me for a drink?' (For Jews do not associate with Samaritans.) Jesus answered her, 'If you knew the gift of God and who it is that asks you for a drink, you would have asked him and he would have given you living water'" (John 4:9–10 NIV).

God's purpose for creation was to create a network with humanity that will last in eternity. That dream was destroyed by Satan, and God sent Jesus Christ, His only Son, to repair and to restore the powerful network with heaven. The purpose for Jesus to network with humankind was and is to set our feet on higher ground with higher goals for eternal life. Networking with the right, influential people is a divine appointment that can catapult you on a higher position. Jentezen Franklin, in his book *Right People, Right Place, Right Plan*, stated that "faith people are the kind who fills your life. They draw you closer to being the person God created you to be. They are the ones who will be lovingly honest with you. They are strong when you are weak." Then he goes on saying that "we need to pray for 20/20 discernment in the world of the spirit to know the right people from the wrong people."[11]

Human life was created with a meaning and a purpose. Not only to exist, but also to exist to influence and to reach your full potential. Do not be alone. Gather people together; remove barriers, network to support one another. The Samaritan woman started an emotional and spiritual healing ministry as soon as she felt the healing power in her heart from the "living water" that Jesus gave her. Her ministry grew in a single day to hundreds in her village. She couldn't keep that for herself. Emotional and spiritual healing is a ministry. God desires for your ministry to get bigger.

When I initiate network meetings, I tell those who I invite for fellowship and prayer that they can approach me anytime with no protocol. Jesus receives you in His network any time of the day or night without protocol.

Eliminate Bad Memory

Rethink. You can block bad memories. Good memory can be reconsolidated and redistributed. Search for good memories in your brain, positive thoughts. God's promises are the most positive thoughts in the entire universe because He created us in His image with a plan in mind, written in His Word. The amygdala decodes emotions, communicates with the hippocampus, prefrontal cortex, and different parts of the cortex where memory is distributed. Your limbic system (including the amygdala) is the key part in brain for the stress system. The devil challenges human beings to enter in the body with thoughts of fear, anxiety, discouragement, negative thoughts, unbelief, anger, and bitterness by increasing levels of stress. Hope and faith are slowly reduced, leaving room for more fear and discouragement. The devil keeps us away from reading God's Word, keeps us occupied, angry, worried, and resentful, nurturing bad thoughts, ruminating them, and repeating them in our mind, not knowing that they become the food of our soul, being consolidated throughout our cortex, bringing more bitterness and more distress and more destruction.

In medicine, we recommend different ways to address people's emotions as focus on gratitude, practicing mindfulness to make you more aware of the moment and help you take a deep breath, training your brain to stay calm when bad emotions and bad thoughts are swirling in your mind. To boost happy hormones through joy, exercise, outdoor activities, smiling, giving hugs, being thankful and optimistic, not focusing on problems but on solutions. Be generous, giving to others to generate joy. All those interventions are actually biblical principles that will create neural pathways associated with joy, a feeling-good sensation from neurochemicals released in the body as serotonin, endorphin, dopamine, oxytocin, and other neurochemicals, helping to rewire the brain's structures to improve overall one's quality of life. Put the Word deep in your mind and heart, which brings joy and happiness.[12]

Science demonstrated that "we feel joy in our bodies because of the release of dopamine and serotonin, two types of neurotransmitters in the brain. Both of these chemicals are heavily associated with happiness (in fact, people with clinical depression often have lower levels of serotonin). If you're feeling down, simple activities like going for a walk in nature, petting a dog or cat, kissing a loved one, and yes, even forcing yourself to smile, can help those neurotransmitters do their job and raise your mood. So, when something you perceive as happy happens, your brain receives the signal to release these chemicals into your central nervous system (which consists of your brain and spinal cord)."[13]

The Purpose for Happiness in Depression

Joy is the best vaccine for depression. We know that joy is the antidote for sadness. Losing purpose in life brings negative thoughts, losing joy; people get burnt out in what they are doing and lose the purpose of life for what they were created. To bring joy to people around, you must have a purpose. Life has meaning even in tribulation. According to *Merriam-Webster Dictionary*, *tribulation* is "distress or suffering resulting from oppression or persecution," synonymous with "affliction, agony, anguish, distress, excruciation, hurt, misery, pain, rack, strait(s), torment, torture, travail, woe."[14]

To have increased joy when burnt out, and in tribulation, people must have a purpose in life. We belong to Jesus in tribulations and trials. We rejoice in tribulations and trials because our life has meaning when we trust in the Lord and believe the Word of God. Our soul is satisfied when we know that our hope is in the Lord and we are heavenly minded, living for our eternal life. Wealth and riches will not give meaning to our life. Even though we enjoy wealth and riches and we are satisfied with God's blessings and enjoy the fruits of our work, "to every man whom God has given wealth and possessions, he has also given him the ability to eat from them, to receive his reward, and to find enjoyment in his toil; these things are the gift of God" (Eccles. 5:19). But the ultimate meaning of life is to be saved by the grace of God, and when the life is over, we inherit eternal life through the blood of Jesus Christ, who died on the cross, rose again on the third day, and ascended to the right hand of the Father, interceding for us here on earth at this very moment. Study showed that "although life satisfaction was substantially higher in wealthy nations than in poor nations, meaning in life was higher in poor nations than in wealthy nations. In part, meaning in life was higher in poor nations because people in those nations were more religious."[15]

Consolidate the Word in the Brain for Joy to Remain

Get a mature heart to worship God. Read the Bible, His everlasting Word, rewiring your brain. Prepare your ear to hear from God. The Holy Spirit decodifies God's voice. Put on God's "spiritual" hearing aid. That means you must be intentional. It does not happen automatically. It takes preparation of the soul, spirit, and body, time in prayer, worship, communion, fasting, and meditating, by tuning on to the right waves and the right electromagnetic frequency on God's station. The Holy Spirit waves to hear Him when God is speaking. Many times we are not on the same frequency. In the atmosphere is a great competition at your ear due to all kinds of info dancing in the air, competing to get on screens, radio and TV channels, iPhone, internet, etc. All hell is trying to keep us from hearing from God, to distract us from the Word. Focusing on the Word and working on consolidating the Word in our memory storage help us prevent distraction and overcome distractors.

Life's worries choke God's promises in our brain structures, including our joy. We must change our focus according to Hebrew 12:1–2. "Therefore, since we are surrounded by such a great cloud of witnesses, let us throw off everything that hinders and the sin that so easily entangles. And let us run with perseverance the race marked out for us, fixing our eyes on Jesus, the pioneer and Perfector of faith. For the joy set before him he endured the cross, scorning its shame, and sat down at the right hand of the throne of God" (NIV). Focus on Jesus. Jesus focused on the Father's business, God's kingdom. If we do not stay focused, we get distracted and lose our purpose and joy. Without joy, we become sad, and depression creeps in as the enemy wants to steal, kill, and destroy neurons through toxic thoughts and toxic neurotransmitters "clouding" the connection in our reward system. To stay focused, we need discipline to pray every day. Let God's Word stir you up with discipline and a committed life until you hear clear from God. "In all your ways submit to him, and he will make your paths straight" (Prov. 3:6 NIV).

The joy of the Lord is the antidote for your depression. Joy is the best natural antidepressant. Antidepressants turn off "the switch" in our serotonin reuptake receptors, inhibiting the process of lowering the serotonin level. Joy naturally will turn off the switcher that contributes to depression and turns on the mechanism to release natural neurochemicals such as dopamine and serotonin and other neurochemicals in the bloodstream in the blood vessel conduits for our neurochemicals, with effects on our emotions, making us feel good, reducing emotions of sadness. Positive thoughts from memorized promises in the Word of God activate emotions and feelings experienced by the fruit of the Spirit. Loss of neurons in the hippocampus due to increased cortisol when stress level is high for a longer period, or alcohol consumption, shrinks the brain structure and reduces the capacity to consolidate memories. Stress decreases neurogenesis too. Neurogenesis process regenerates new neurons used in memory formation, learning, and exercise when our thoughts are positive.

You produce fruit when you persevere and produce healthy neurons in the brain. You are in the right season. Focus your energy for this season. God promised a safe path for you. "Then you will go on your way in safety, and your foot will not stumble" (Prov. 3:23 NIV). In faith we are doing what we're supposed to do, persevering. Perseverance finishes its work. Believers are called to stand and walk on "water," not to sink. Do not change your focus when worries are invading you, and do not let yourself sink deeper in more devastating fear, worries, anxiety, etc. You must keep your eyes on the Lord, with an optimistic attitude, focusing on tasks. He is the One who gives you grace to do it. Overcome challenges of the sea like Peter did about two thousand years ago. God asks you to do only what He gives you grace to do, not for what others are doing. Understand the season in your life. "To everything *there is* a season, A time for every purpose under heaven" (Eccles. 3:1 NKJV). If you do not understand the season in your life, it can drain your energy and create frustration, bitterness, jealousy, making you more aware of lacks than blessings. Count your blessings in this season to calm your overactive brain.

Know God's heart. Have a heart of submission, pursuing God's will and joy for that season. Follow the road to your purpose and destiny. The Lord finishes what He started. See God's intervention for that season. Ask for signs for reassurance. Rejoice with those who rejoice; mourn with those who mourn. God puts people in your path for the right season. See the value of the hands of God in others' lives. Develop relationship to provide support, pray for them, ask question, and determine them to give you access to their heart to be able to identify their needs and to help. Commitment, perseverance, and persistence bring great reward. God helps us achieve our goals together. Show vulnerability, sympathize for difficult cases, and promote trust. You have important roles to hold everything together when people are scattered. Show the love of God in any season. To produce fruits, to be ready to move to the next season. To have grace to "walk on the water" in the season you are in.

We have God's prescription for a discouraged world that sleeps, being away from God's desires and purpose. "How long will you lie there, you sluggard? When will you get up from your sleep?" (Prov. 6:9 NIV). Seek the kingdom of God first. People ask us how we got so many blessings: from nothing when we arrived in the USA to continuous great blessings. Our response is, "By seeking the kingdom of God first." You can become really blessed when you put God first and seek His kingdom first, and then He will give you the ability, favors, health, knowledge, and wisdom to prosper. He gives you favors with everybody around you when you follow the kingdom's principles in everything you do. He makes you successful and will fulfill the desire of your hearts and your purpose. Everything we do is for the kingdom of God. The kingdom is within us, and we carry the kingdom with us everywhere we go. He never left us alone as He promised.

Success is measured by what you accomplished. Your encouragement to others can bring measurable success in their life. Your thoughts as a child of God in your job, school, community, church, and nation will obtain measurable results in your blessings received as a result of your Christian walk and deeds. People are changed around you, being influenced by the blessings in your life. Jesus's transformation power is measurable in people's changed lives. Jesus believed in people before they deserved it. We must believe in people before they deserve it. Jesus died for us while we were sinners. We are anointing to bring encouragement for those around us to be strong and courageous. Our Father reassures us that He loves us with everlasting love. Courage is to pray and believe God's promises when fear, depression, anxiety, and negative thoughts are creeping in.

Meditate and talk to yourself the Word of God, His promises, which are real and bring measurable results. You are and become what is in your thoughts and imagination. I did imagine myself having a healthy family, living a Christian life, starting a business, owing and running a business that will grow, going to school to get my degrees, writing books, speaking at conferences, helping others, etc. Everything we accomplished physically, I had them in my thoughts before they became physically measurable in real life. Everything we see around us, before they came in existence, was God's given thoughts in people's minds. And before anything was created in the entire universe, it was a thought in God's mind and Spirit. There are about 7.7 billion people on this planet, and each one of us is the result of God's thoughts, since He said, "Let's make man in Our image," at creation. Those thoughts were placed in the first family's DNA. Then God drops in people's mind and parents' mind to reproduce. You accomplish what you see in your own thoughts and how you imagine what God can do for you. He demonstrated that He can do more than what we can ask or think.

Rumination on negative thoughts, unforgiveness, angry thoughts, and bad imaginations encumber your destiny. When you meditate on God's promises, your image about yourself and about what you can do is changed. You become the person God said you were created to be. God is thinking about you as being the most important person, because you are created in His image with His language, His plan, His blueprint, His will in your own DNA. God did see Israel as a prince. "And he said, Thy name shall be called no more Jacob, but Israel: for as a prince hast thou power with God and with men, and hast prevailed" (Gen. 32:28 KJV). God changed his name because God did see Jacob (when he was discouraged, lonely, afraid in distress) as a great and strong nation, Israel, with a new identity and a great purpose.

God sees you as a prince also and changed your name and your identity. You are a new creation; you were created in God's image, to be like God in your thinking, to have the mind of Christ (mirror neurons are placed in our brain to imitate Christ), and to grow from glory to glory. We were created for God's glory. We must reach that level in Christ. You are born to rule, to reign, destined for glory. Sin diminished and even canceled that, but Jesus redeemed that position for us by grace. "Christ has redeemed us from the curse of the law, having become a curse for us (for it is written, 'Cursed *is* everyone who hangs on a tree')" (Gal. 3:13 NKJV).

The Son of the mighty King restored the prodigal sons and daughters' royalty and their authority. Once you are restored, everything you have as a son of the King, you want to share to restore the prodigals in the world. God's beauty is in you, carrying the kingdom. You have the spirit of adopted children, heirs of Christ, heirs of the King; share the glory of the children of God. Creation reveals that we are born of His glory and for His glory. In every encouragement, clarity is needed, as heard from heaven. Encouragement brings life into a situation, strengthening, comforting; it is a gift from God. Any medical experience by every single person on this planet encounters heavenly intervention.

The healing process happens at unconscious level. Physical healing is programmed in every DNA. Physical healing does not happen at the level of consciousness. We have the ability to bring the healing thoughts in our consciousness from our unconscious mind to seek healing and restoration through the medical provider and directly from God through Jesus. The fullness of Christ will bring spiritual healing. A shift in atmosphere is felt when you receive Jesus, all of Him. Jesus resides inside of us, and we carry His apprentice on our DNA physically and spiritually to get grace enriched in every way, not lacking spiritual gift for physical and spiritual healing. The Holy Spirit gives anointing to support, encourage, and give confidence, hope, and healing through divine joy.

Changing the Unconscious Biases

To bring joy in other people's life, we must improve the way we react to their behavior. People react based on their unconscious biased background, memories in the past, thoughts culture, personal experience. Biases happen everywhere. No problem can be solved from the same level of consciousness. The science in postmodern society shows that paradigm must take place to flood the unconscious mind with constructive thoughts, then good attitude will come out from the unconscious mind. Spiritual and physical healing starts in our unconscious mind. We are unconsciously incompetent. Competence comes from the powerful Word of the living God and His promises.

He speaks to our unconscious level when in deep sleep to turn people from their wrongdoing and from perishing. "In a dream, in a vision of the night, when deep sleep falls on people as they slumber in their beds, he may speak in their ears and terrify them with warnings, to turn them from wrongdoing and keep them from pride, to preserve them from the pit, their lives from perishing by the sword" (Job 33:15–18 NIV).

Retrain Your Brain to Rejoice

To be full of joy, we must align our thoughts with God's, not with our biases. To bring joy to people around you, you must be full of joy. We must be transformational in emotional healing work. People commit suicide because of fear that they cannot overcome. Starting with a ray of hope will change minds and save lives. Encouraging people is the key. Encouragement increases confidence. Encouragement has roots in love. God is love. The Word of the living God has the most powerful message to bring encouragement over thousands of years to the entire world. The Word written in Isaiah 61:1–4 always brought much encouragement to my soul and spirit many times when I was in desperation, stating, "The Spirit of the Lord GOD *is* upon Me, Because the LORD has anointed Me To preach good tidings to the poor; He has sent Me to heal the brokenhearted, To proclaim liberty to the captives, And the opening of the prison to *those who are* bound; To proclaim the acceptable year of the LORD, And the day of vengeance of our God; To comfort all who mourn, To console those who mourn in Zion, To give them beauty for ashes, The oil of joy for mourning, The garment of praise for the spirit of heaviness; That they may be called trees of righteousness, The planting of the LORD, that He may be glorified. And they shall rebuild the old ruins, They shall raise up the former desolations, And they shall repair the ruined cities, The desolations of many generations" (Isa. 61:1–4 NKJV).

The Lord wants to bring restoration, to bind people's emotional and physical wounds to our ruined life through His anointing. He wants to repair our ruined families, community, nation, and generations. When the Spirit of the Lord comes on us, we have the same desire as the Lord had for our generation and the generations to come. The most powerful instrument is love. When people are sick, love is extremely important.

Reflecting on the prophecy written in Isaiah, the ultimate encouragement at the end of life is to lead the dying person to Jesus Christ to be saved for eternity. On one occasion, one of the patients with history of memory impairment and diabetes was declining, experiencing frequent minor strokes, and had multiple hospitalizations with little success to be stabilized at that time. This patient had outbursts of angry episodes, frequently using blasphemy, cursing, being violent and aggressive, hitting people with objects, and breaking doors. All the medications the patient was taking did not stop the progression of the diseases and did not calm the patient down. We ran out of solutions, and the situation got worse.

One day, I approached the patient and gently asked if the patient wanted to receive prayer. With a weak nod as a sign of agreeing, he made me understand that I could pray for him. I started to pray, asking the patient to say "Amen" at the end if the patient agreed with everything that was asked in prayer on the patient's behalf. I did pray a short prayer, asking the Lord's forgiveness of all sins on behalf of this particular person. At the end of the prayer, I was pleasantly surprised and amazed that I heard a strong "Amen" from the patient's mouth. I also was almost shocked the next second when he started to cry out loud uncontrollably. I had never heard such a cry before in my life. It was a wailing cry braided with joy as a delivered person of a heavy burden. I had never seen someone crying like that after a short prayer for salvation of a soul. The patient experienced the freedom from huge bondage of sins washed in the blood of Jesus and saved by grace for eternity in the last days of his life. The patient felt the joy of forgiveness. I could read that joy on his face and his actions and behavior. Shortly after that, the patient went to the hospital again and passed away from complications of multiple chronic diseases. I will never forget that moment of a saved soul experiencing that unspeakable joy. I did see the happiness on the patient's face in those few days left before the person passed away.

God is longing to forgive everybody, to bind up the broken-hearted, everyone who surrenders his life to Jesus. The world is starving for encouragement. The Word of God has the power of shaping cultures. We have the power to influence the world with encouragement, to speak words for life with eternal effect. Words have power. Jesus healed people with *words*. Impart words of encouragement to change the mindset of people, perspectives, views and to change the interactions with others. The Father wants us to use encouragement as a gift from heaven to bring joy in people's life.

God Speaks to Us Since Creation

God's prescriptions for health to be stress-free are to use imagination about the mind of Christ and hearing His voice. Jesus is painting our mind; He speaks through impression on our heart and brain. The Holy Spirit guides us in all truth. He speaks to us and tells us things. He brings His kingdom from heaven on us in a normal day and uses heavenly strategies. We must find deep secrets in His voice that build people up and release life. He imparts love to each person on earth. The enemy of your soul comes to kill, steal, and destroy, by killing hope, joy, happiness, and tries to empty your inside of hope, of faith.

The fight starts before you are conceived. But God, who created life, is the source of life and the source of love, joy, and peace. Connection with the source of love will enable you to be the resource for those around you who are not aware of God's resources. When you have true love, you have everything. Connect to the Father. Lift up your hands in natural worshipping in faith. Something happens inside supernaturally. Healing happens in your soul, then in your body. God, our Father, has more passion for our physical and spiritual health than we have. Because of the Word of Jesus and His spirit inside of you, you will be a "well of living water" springing out in eternal life. God is transformational. He created us so complex and empowered us with His love. Repentance in our heart brings transformation in our soul and spirit. See things from heaven's view because we are created with spiritual needs. The gospel reveals how we were created for God's glory and His kingdom.

The kingdom of the Lord becomes our kingdom. His knowledge fills the earth as water fills the sea. "For the earth will be filled with the knowledge of the glory of the LORD as the waters cover the sea" (Hab. 2:14 NIV). God is revealing Himself to the ends of the earth as never before. The advanced technology is used mightily to spread the Word of God everywhere. Moreover, Christians share their life testimonies through the internet, media, books, library, radio, TV, etc. Jesus breaks all barriers and uses all methods to reach out to His creation to save every soul and to give His peace through the power of the Holy Spirit. "On the evening of that first day of the week, when the disciples were together, with the doors locked for fear of the Jewish leaders, Jesus came and stood among them and said, 'Peace be with you!' After he said this, he showed them his hands and side. The disciples were overjoyed when they saw the Lord. Again Jesus said, 'Peace be with you! As the Father has sent me, I am sending you.' And with that he breathed on them and said, 'Receive the Holy Spirit. If you forgive anyone's sins, their sins are forgiven; if you do not forgive them, they are not forgiven'" (John 20:18–23 NIV). Many times, fear shuts the door. Jesus enters inside even with the door closed when you listen to His Word on your iPod, iPhone, social media, YouTube, internet, TV, radio or read a book in your quiet room to bring you peace. Jesus is Jehovah Shalom, our peace. He is the peacemaker. People everywhere around the world must receive His peace.

Jesus gives life. God's presence changes everything, restores soul, even when the doors of our souls are closed. We must share our experience with the Lord and must tell our story. Build memory stones with what God is doing and speak about what Jesus did and what He does and will do. You can see the future. We speak more about what the enemy did, and fear is building up and hope disappears. We must glorify God for His mighty work in our lives and leave no room for the devil and his lies. Our provisions are in Jesus. His anointing is among us today as he was about two thousand years ago. "How God anointed Jesus of Nazareth with the Holy Spirit and with power, who went about doing good and healing all who were oppressed by the devil, for God was with Him" (Acts 10:38 NKJV). He gave us His anointing, the power of the Holy Spirit, to guide us and do His work on this planet, to fulfill our assignment. "But you have an anointing from the Holy One, and you know all things" (1 John 2:20 NKJV). We are His anointed, representing heaven on earth. Jesus enters the room with the door closed, and His presence changes the atmosphere in people's hearts and minds, and all surroundings are changed. Fear is melting, leaving your hearts and minds. We are here to influence the next generation.

We get what He has—peace, joy, provision, passion, power to move on with our assignments. The seed is the Word. Things from the world interfere with your attention to God's Word, your purpose, your destiny. Paying attention to His Word is like following a prescription given for an acute or chronic disease. Our acute and chronic spiritual diseases are sins in our lives. God's Word brings sustainable results when we persevere and do not lose our focus. People are looking for instant gratification and fast food. But God asks us to persevere in everything we do and go through the entire process of sustainable results and a great victory. Prayer is the key that prevents interference with God's Word to work in your life at a deeper level.

Without prayer, there is no good harvest, like without antibiotics you cannot get rid of infection. The microorganisms will grow fast, and all interventions with antibiotics will fail and the patient dies from septicemia. Praying is talking to God, and it brings us in His presence, connecting us with His spiritual realm and His supernatural power. From creation, God wants a relationship with us to be in His presence. Through constant prayer, you build a reserve in your bank account to be sufficient in time of need for the next generation. God wants to bless all generations after us. Joel was inspired by the Spirit of the living God that He wanted to fill all people with His creation. "That I will pour out My Spirit on all flesh; Your sons and your daughters shall prophesy, Your old men shall dream dreams, Your young men shall see visions. And also on *My* menservants and on *My* maidservants I will pour out My Spirit in those days" (Joel 2:28–29 NKJV).

You pray privately, and He shows up publicly. Pray from your heart that the will of God will be manifested. "But you, when you pray, go into your room, and when you have shut your door, pray to your Father who *is* in the secret *place;* and your Father who sees in secret will reward you openly" (Matt. 6:6 NKJV). Ask God to interfere with your plans, finances, business, family, marriage and let His will be done. Talk from your heart to God and plead the blood of Jesus over any situation. With God there are no limits. Through prayer from your heart, build your relationship with God, praying in the Holy Spirit. You can start with the Lord's Prayer to connect with your Father in heaven, how Jesus taught the disciples to pray.

Reduce Stress Through a New Tongue That Can Be Controlled

The tongue reveals what is in your mind and the emotions in your heart. The tongue speaks from the heart. We speak what we feel. Our feelings are dictated by our emotions, and our emotions by our thoughts. Thoughts have emotions attached to them. It is like we are what we eat physically, so we are what we think and express spiritually. It is easy for people to focus on negative things that make people think painful thoughts, thinking negatively, creating emotions and feelings of pain, heaviness, distress, sadness, anxiety, depression, bitterness, insecurity, panic, and express them with our tongue, speaking words that can produce damage to our body, soul, and spirit. According to James, "The tongue also is a fire, a world of evil among the parts of the body. It corrupts the whole body, sets the whole course of one's life on fire, and is itself set on fire by hell" (James 3:6 NIV). "But no human being can tame the tongue. It is a restless evil, full of deadly poison" (James 3:8 NIV).

The tongue can be extremely dangerous when it uses words that stir up emotions of anger, bitterness, sadness, fear, threats, insecurity, unforgiveness, which trigger the brain's structures to release neurochemicals in our bloodstream and affect all the cells in our human body. All these emotions are processed in the amygdala, which cooperates with the hippocampus in the limbic system, creating the atmosphere in the brain to release neurochemicals that can destroy neurons and limit the communication with the prefrontal lobe, hindering the capability to make the right decisions, leading to neurocognitive disorders in time. It is a progressive diseases that can be stopped with the right attitude and the right thoughts. Using kind words that bring love and joy will trigger dopamine, oxytocin, and serotonin to be released to feel loved, accepted, forgiven, encouraged, reassured, confident, and happy and for the healing process to start. Even people with impaired cognition respond well to kind words and love. Humankind was wired for love and joy. Words and acts of kindness help these people feel the love and joy and reduce high levels of stress.

Our Tongue Must Be Under the Holy Spirit's Control to Reduce Stress

The fleshly words we express show the part of the mind that is not renewed. There is a constant war: flesh against Spirit and Spirit against flesh. The Holy Spirit's words work in your mind and bring from above fresh power with the desirable emotions of love, peace, joy, goodness, kindness, and patience, which create the atmosphere in our brain to calm the overactive brain and to restore the damaged area in the brain structures through a process called neuroplasticity. The Holy Spirit brings revelation, wisdom, discernment, power, understanding, knowledge, manifestation of power, and holy fire miracles, energizing us. The Holy Spirit makes you a different person because His power lives in you. The Holy Spirit fills all those who come thirsty and hungry and empowers people to take His message in the world. The blood of Jesus gives you authority to push the darkness away, to take dominion through the power of the Holy Spirit, and to speak the right words at the right time. Have the courage to use the authority that Jesus gave you according to Luke 10:19. "I have given you authority...to overcome all the power of the enemy" (NIV).

Watch Your Language

Dr. David Levy, in "Fear in Crisis—Part 1 (Coronavirus COVID-19) Help for Anxiety" on YouTube, speaks about "how much power your words have" and that "we have to be very careful what we say" since "death and life are in the power of the tongue," because our words give the power to fear when we speak negative words.[16]

Every human being has a place in the brain where forbidden words are stored, usually the bad language, swearing, blasphemous and obscene language, profanity, irreverent behavior that can be offending and intimidating, verging on bullying, and very unpleasant, giving the impression of lack of education and affecting negatively yourself and others. The human brain is a very complex organ in our body. Language process is in the left hemisphere, and the emotional content of a language is created in the right hemisphere. The cerebral cortex, the higher function of the brain, is where language is processed. Deep inside the brain take place emotions. The limbic system (involved in memory, emotions, and basic behavior) and the basal ganglia (involved in motor function and impulse control).[17]

I observed Christian patients with advanced dementia that will access those places with forbidden language and exhibit offensive and derogatory words and bad language, cursing others, which surprised the family members who knew them as very nice persons. Those habits can start in childhood when one is exposed to bad language. The brain has preserved ability for long-term memories. Memorizing the Word of God when you are young will benefit the language. The brain structures have the preserved ability for what you memorize at a very young age. For emotional memories, use the characteristics of the fruit of the spirit as love, joy, peace, and happiness at a very young age to experience good emotions in life. We have the capability to remember what we still have even at an old age. We can shift the thinking behavior to use what we have.

Restore God's Glory

Standing in the Gap to Restore the Glory

Iniquities abide in the world, keeping people in bondage and oppression, bringing spiritual blindness and deafness to prevent them from seeing God's glory and hearing God's voice. The Bible states about the environment that we will live in the last days. "But mark this: There will be terrible times in the last days. People will be lovers of themselves, lovers of money, boastful, proud, abusive, disobedient to their parents, ungrateful, unholy, without love, unforgiving, slanderous, without self-control, brutal, not lovers of the good, treacherous, rash, conceited, lovers of pleasure rather than lovers of God—having a form of godliness but denying its power. Have nothing to do with such people" (2 Tim. 3:1–5 NIV). We did meet this kind of people many times in Romania during the Communist regime, and in the USA, but we had to obey God's instructions to have nothing to do with them. Following God's direction is the key to distinguish His will for us and to bring restoration of His glory on God's people.

The house of God needs restoration. We must arise and speak with authority in the name of Jesus. The house of God needs restoration of the glory of God and the clouds of His presence to be in the middle of His people. We have to stand in the gap for every soul on this planet. God deals with rebellion in our life when we resist His call for prayers and fasting. Moses fell on His face to ask for salvation of Israel, pleading for mercy for the entire nation of Israel. Moses and Aaron stood between the dead and living, but 14,700 died in that day. They fell on their faces. "So Moses said to Aaron, 'Take a censer and put fire in it from the altar, put incense *on it,* and take it quickly to the congregation and make atonement for them; for wrath has gone out from the LORD. The plague has begun.' Then Aaron took *it* as Moses commanded, and ran into the midst of the assembly; and already the plague had begun among the people. So he put in the incense and made atonement for the people. And he stood between the dead and the living; so the plague was stopped. Now those who died in the plague were fourteen thousand seven hundred, besides those who died in the Korah incident. So Aaron returned to Moses at the door of the tabernacle of meeting, for the plague had stopped" (Num. 16:46–50 NKJV).

Incense represents the prayers of the saints. We are asked to stay between the living and the spiritually dead on our knees in prayers. Our prayers have power to enter in God's spiritual realm so God's spirit can touch people on earth and change people's mind and transform lives. Prayer is God's mystery to communicate with our hearts and to manifest physically His spiritual power in our physical world. "I looked for someone among them who would build up the wall and stand before me in the gap on behalf of the land so I would not have to destroy it, but I found no one. So I will pour out my wrath on them and consume them with my fiery anger, bringing down on their own heads all they have done, declare the Sovereign LORD" (Ezek. 22:30–31 NIV). It is our call on this planet to stay in the gap for human beings so God will have mercy in His great love and show His grace to save the lost.

Our eyes must focus on God, on what He is doing in the world today. When I decided to take a sabbatical year after forty-two years of hard work (in Romania, under the Communists, and in the USA, of working with elderly with multiple chronic conditions and challenging behaviors because of their different kinds of advanced dementia—a very demanding job 24-7), I asked the Holy Spirit to show me what He was doing in my life at the present time. My husband and I went to Europe with one desire, to take a break and rest and detach from our restless, long-hour jobs and the persistent, demanding work physically and psychologically. We had no plans for mission work in that sabbatical year at that time. Just to visit family, rest, and travel for leisure. I must confess that the Holy Spirit was at work in our lives that year more than the cumulated mission work we had of several years. Without planning, I did speak at multiple conferences, gathering, churches, radio interviews, and TV shows. I did about twenty book presentations in different locations that year without an established agenda or arrangement or schedule in advanced. We did mission work in very poor villages in Romania and free clinic, providing health care, medical supplies, etc.

I knew that was the work of the Holy Spirit. It was overwhelming to feel God's powerful presence in each gathering where I spoke. The power of God was felt also by people during the time of prayers. Each time we prayed in those congregations, the power of the Holy Spirit came in unusual way, touching every single persons with amazing love, comforting, restoring, healing, inspiring, giving revelation, discernment, understanding, overwhelming joy, peace, and happiness. I did see tears of joy rolling on so many faces. I fell with my face down at Jesus's feet, overwhelmed by His love, mercy, and grace. God is faithful and full of compassion for the souls, even in your free time or sabbatical year, like ours years ago. He shows mercy and grace. All glory is His forever and ever.

Altered Nociception

Pain Modulators from Creation and Altered Nociception

From creation, human beings faced physical and spiritual pain and suffering. Our human brain is involved in physical and emotional pain sensations. All pains have emotional experience, ongoing stress response, depression. People want immediate relief from pain, seeking help from prescribed and illicit drugs. But God placed pain modulators in our body from creation for us to be able to endure the pain created by sin and disobedience, but people conquered by fear of the emotions of pain run to medication and drugs, which can create more health problems and, for many, can be even lethal. Statistics tell us that "the opioid crisis is worsening. Over 42,000 Americans died of an opioid overdose in 2016, and government and public health officials are scrambling to find effective ways to reverse this frightening trend."[1]

We can train our brain with heavenly resources to restore the proper function of our reward system. Science demonstrated that "pain-induced maladaptation of reward/motivation circuits may be reversible with therapy, raising the possibility of recovery from chronic pain and restoration of normal affective/emotional and cognitive function. Finally, preemptive treatments could prevent anatomical and functional reorganization of brain reward/motivation circuits to inhibit the progression from acute to chronic pain, as well as associated comorbidities."[2]

Relief of pain is felt as a reward state. Our reward system can be restored because the Lord wants to heal our pain and bind our wounds and our health through our obedience of His Word to return to Him, to seek His face, and to humble ourselves before our Maker. "Come, let us return to the LORD. He has torn us to pieces but he will heal us; he has injured us but he will bind up our wounds" (Hosea 6:1 NIV).

Many times we feel physical and emotional pain due to distorted and altered nociception.

"The new mechanistic descriptor is defined as 'Pain that arises from altered nociception despite no clear evidence of actual or threatened tissue damage causing the activation of peripheral nociceptors or evidence for disease or lesion of the somatosensory system causing the pain.' The new designation could help to describe the pain that underlies many different chronic pain states, including fibromyalgia, complex regional pain syndrome, other types of musculoskeletal pain such as chronic low back pain, as well as visceral pain disorders such as irritable bowel syndrome and bladder pain syndrome. 'Nociplastic pain' is not a diagnosis, the task force emphasizes, but rather a way to understand the neurobiological workings of the nervous system that lead to pain when they go astray."[3]

The psalmist David, more than 3,400 years ago, wrote in Psalms that psychological distress from unconfessed sin and disobedience leads to physical and emotional pain. "O LORD, do not rebuke me in Your wrath, Nor chasten me in Your hot displeasure! For Your arrows pierce me deeply, And Your hand presses me down. *There is* no soundness in my flesh Because of Your anger, Nor *any* health in my bones Because of my sin" (Ps. 38:1–3 NKJV). Science discovered that "emotional state, degree of anxiety, attention and distraction, past experiences, memories, and many other factors can either enhance or diminish the pain experience."[4]

Science also describes "a recently identified mechanism of neuronal plasticity in primary afferent nociceptive nerve fibers (nociceptors) by which an acute inflammatory insult or environmental stressor can trigger long-lasting hypersensitivity of nociceptors to inflammatory cytokines. This phenomenon, 'hyperalgesic priming,' depends on the epsilon isoform of protein kinase C (PKCepsilon) and a switch in intracellular signaling pathways that mediate cytokine-induced nociceptor hyper-excitability."[5]

More and more studies show that our nervous system (which includes neurons involved in our thought formation and that produce different formula of neurochemicals and neurotransmitters according to the quality of our emotions based on positive or negative thoughts) is associated with pain regulation in our body. "Central sensitization is a condition of the nervous system that is associated with the development and maintenance of chronic pain. When central sensitization occurs, the nervous system goes through a process called *wind-up* and gets regulated in a persistent state of high reactivity. This persistent, or regulated, state of reactivity lowers the threshold for what causes pain and subsequently comes to maintain pain even after the initial injury might have healed."[6]

Central sensitization for many people with chronic condition is real, making people feel the pain. "It can occur with chronic low back pain, chronic neck pain, whiplash injuries, chronic tension headaches, migraine headaches, rheumatoid arthritis, osteoarthritis of the knee, endometriosis, injuries sustained in a motor vehicle accident, and after surgeries. Fibromyalgia, irritable bowel syndrome, and chronic fatigue syndrome, all seem to have the common denominator of central sensitization as well."[7] Our strong positive emotions can create the atmosphere in the brain to block emotional and physical pain from negative thoughts and their associated emotions.

Physical exercise helps decrease pain, increase function and weight control, increase natural endorphin for stress relief, emotional frustration, anxiety, and depression. Endorphin is the pain hormone with analgesic effect that activates the body's opioid receptors and helps us feel good. It was demonstrated that the nucleus raphe magnus in our brain can modulate the feeling of pain.

Nucleus Raphe Modulates Pain

Science described the function of our brain structures in experiencing pain that "pain modulation likely exists in the form of a descending pain modulatory circuit with inputs that arise in multiple areas, including the hypothalamus, the amygdala, and the rostral anterior cingulate cortex (rACC), feeding to the midbrain peri-aqueductal gray region (PAG), and with outputs from the PAG to the medulla. Neurons within the nucleus raphe magnus and nucleus reticularis gigantocellularis, which are included within the rostral ventromedial medulla (RVM), have been shown to project to the spinal or medullary dorsal horns to directly or indirectly enhance or diminish nociceptive traffic, changing the experience of pain."[8]

It is interesting that Jehovah Rapha, our healer, included raphe nuclei in our pain-modulatory circuit to modulate our physical and emotional pain. He knows our feelings when we are hurt. He placed the pain modulators, including the raphe nuclei, in our brain structure for healing our emotional and physical pain. The raphe nuclei are the largest location that contains neurons that produce serotonin; it synthesizes and spreads it to the entire central nervous system. Serotonin is the neurotransmitter that makes humans feel happy.[9]

When we hurt God's feelings, He is in pain toward us. God has emotions as we (His creation) have. God understands more than humans about our physical and emotional pain. That is why He calls on people to come to Him to be healed. In stressful situation, pain increases in intensity in the body. Even when we grieve, the Holy Spirit of God, through our attitude and behaviors, living in sin, is gracious and full of compassion. He will get angry when we ignore His instruction, but He is great in mercy. "The LORD *is* gracious and full of compassion, Slow to anger and great in mercy" (Ps. 145:8 NKJV).

God has solutions for His creation, humans, always, and does not punish forever those who return from their wicked ways, as is written in Hebrew 10. "'This *is* the covenant that I will make with them after those days, says the LORD: I will put My laws into their hearts, and in their minds I will write them,' *then He adds,* 'Their sins and their lawless deeds I will remember no more.' Now where there is remission of these, *there is* no longer an offering for sin" (Heb. 10:16–18 NKJV).

By activating God's laws and prescriptions in our brain, we get healing in our body, soul, and spirit. We are created to discipline our thoughts, redirecting them to the true reward when God's glory is revealed to preserve our reward system, exercising gladness and exceeding joy. The antidote for death is everlasting life with everlasting joy in the presence of God. Infusing our brain with thoughts of eternity is the most important intervention we can provide for people on earth. The Holy Spirit helps you through physical and emotional pain in the hardest time.

The Cure for Suffering

By living with Christ, with the hope of glory in you, even when you are suffering, you rejoice because the glory of God rests upon you. Your reward mechanism will be activated by using that knowledge and that truth about God's glory. You can experience exceeding joy when you consider that you go through trials as being a partaker to Christ's suffering. "Beloved, do not think it strange concerning the fiery trial which is to try you, as though some strange thing happened to you; but rejoice to the extent that you partake of Christ's sufferings, that when His glory is revealed, you may also be glad with exceeding joy. If you are reproached for the name of Christ, blessed *are you*, for the Spirit of glory and of God rests upon you" (1 Pet. 4:12–14 NKJV). Christ suffered for the glory of the Father. If you suffer for Christ, you suffer for God's glory. Do not stop serving the Lord when hurt. Hurts do not produce harm. God, the Creator, put genes in our body and placed neuromodulators, anti-inflammatory receptors, to be able to manage pain for our well-being, making our lives better.

Medical professional people give their patients strong advice and recommendation as new intervention to treat physical and emotional pain through mindfulness, a new way of thinking. Many patients want immediate relief from pain and run to clinics, ER, to get pain medication, and others run to the streets to get illicit drugs to make their life better. But opioids, narcotics, illicit drugs, and other strong pain medication can induce damage to the brain's cells and cause further confusion and decrease their functional ability.[10]

We need to find the source of pain through a careful history, blood work through labs, x-ray, ultrasounds, CT scan, MRI procedures, and address the pain and suffering carefully. Many times bad emotions lead to depression and serotonergic dysfunction, which causes modification in neuropathway, causing physical pain.[11]

Emotional pain needs different approach. In our modern life, it is recommended to use a biosocial approach to change behavior regarding emotional distress and stress management. The Word of God, inspired by the Holy Spirit, gave us the prescription, "not forsaking the assembling of ourselves together, as *is* the manner of some, but exhorting *one another*, and so much the more as you see the Day approaching" (Heb. 10:25–27 NKJV). Scientists are "studying man as a bio-social organism within a bio-social eco-system. 'Bio-social Psychology' is defined as the way in which adaptation to different biological environments results in the development of adaptive socialization processes, which influence particular habits of perceptual inference, personality traits, cognitive processes and psychological skills. The present paper describes the basic bio-social concepts of this approach. An analysis is also made of applications of the Bio-social approach to Environmental psychology. A review is also made of environmental stresses in modern life."[12]

In medicine and health-care system, we know that medications do not work in patients who do not take them; medications only work in patients who do take them. This is true for spiritual diseases, too, for persons who need spiritual treatment. God's promises (the best spiritual therapy) do not work in people who do not read them and apply them to their personal lives. Prayers do not work for those who do not pray; prayers work only for those who pray. God's promises work in those who read the Word with great faith and rejoice in the Lord. Also in medicine, medications treat signs and symptoms of diseases and prevent further damages. To prevent spiritual damage, people must take spiritual treatment for their spiritual diseases. When we grieve, we need biosocial treatment that will prevent isolation. God wants us to have a relationship and to connect with one another, "exhorting *one another*," encouraging one another (Heb. 10:25–27 NKJV).

God gave instructions through prophets more than two thousand years ago about "bio-social" therapeutic approach for the saints of all times and ages to get together to speak and meditate on God's name, to influence people's cognitive processes, personality traits, healthy habits of perception, and psychological skills. "Then those who feared the LORD spoke to one another, And the LORD listened and heard *them;* So a book of remembrance was written before Him For those who fear the LORD And who meditate on His name" (Mal. 3:16 NKJV). When you are overwhelmed with the fear of the Lord, you follow God's directions and instructions to connect with the body of Christ, to share God's goodness and His promises in His eternal Word.

It is documented in scientific literature that joyful social connection and happiness influence our body at the cellular level and, further, our soul and spirit. In psychology, it is well-known that social isolation, social disconnection, feelings of rejection, and loneliness leads to acute and chronic diseases. There is power in friendly, joyful relationships. In the Old Testament, it is written that God takes note of our fellowship when we fear Him and talk to one another, stay connected in fellowship (Mal. 3:16 NKJV). We mirror our friends (mirror neurons are at work) and we develop positive habits if we surrender to people who will lift us up and increase our social integration with people that have positive thoughts and the joy of the Lord.

Social stress changes expression of our genes that cause inflammation, how to manage inflammation in the body. If you feel social rejection, your body cannot fight inflammation. Chronic stress from loneliness causes inflammation, which leads to Alzheimer's, forming amyloid plaque in the brain, which decreases activities of daily living (ADLs) and increases heart diseases. We were created with the desire to belong, to desire a vital and authentic connection with one another and with God.

God gave instructions to His children to stay connected with one another in local churches to belong to the body of Christ. A strong connection with positive people, where you can feel accepted and belong to that community, will positively influence your immune system. Your faith will increase, and what you believe about love, and you will develop meaningful relationships, influencing your health. Healthy relationships feel uplifting and increase your energy, and you have a great sense of being yourself. It develops your identity, who you are, and you improve your belief system. Social connection influences our immune system. Interdependence promotes physical and spiritual health. Being whole means self-care, which implies doing work that has meaning in life. The desire to belong is built inside every single person. A longing to belong is a built-in feature in your DNA. Spirituality is an important factor in healing our physical body. The structure of the prefrontal cortex is unique to humans, who experience intelligence to sort thoughts of belonging and spirituality. Spiritual experience is critical to maintain health in the body, soul, and spirit.

Spiritual Nutrients for Our Soul

As a young girl early in life, in high school, I did read the New Testament five times. I was hungry and thirsty for the truth during the Communist era, when my brain was bombarded every day with Communists' lies that there is no God. I did study the Bible by myself, and all the revelation and inspiration was directly from the Holy Spirit, who taught me how to live a Christian life and how to apply the Word in that hostile environment and every circumstance under the Communist regime. My life was changed completely when I started to live by the Word and applied His teaching in my daily life. My faith increased, and my thinking was different, my actions were different, and my attitude was different. I looked at people around me with more compassion, loving those unlovable.

Instead of looking at the Communist environment all around me and people who were discouraging me every day, mocking my faith in Christ, I did choose to believe the Word of God and live by the teaching from the Bible. I could be easily burnt out, lose sleep, be more concerned of what they were saying, have conflicts in conversations, have increased anxiety, feel lonely, have stressful relationships, and have depression. But I had hope in God's Word. That hope gave me courage, confidence, joy, peace, happiness, which made me calm and relaxed, to the point that people around me could not understand what was the source of my character, which added value to my professionalism. I was more flexible, not competing with others, always willing to help, thankful and content. Even the Communist leaders trusted my character and entrusted me with special tasks in my profession as an industrial painter first, and then as economist after my graduation from ASE Bucharest.

Even during the Communist regime, God gave me favors with people around me. I did read about Joseph's temptations and his attitude toward sin in the Bible, and I learned that was written for us, too, to learn how to behave in the middle of temptations and how to look up to our Father's instructions and follow them. I also did read Esther's story, and I learned how to fast three days and three nights and be able to escape all the Communists' ridicules and psychological distress caused by persecutions. Jesus's life and suffering on earth were the most powerful examples for me in my early age, starting in my childhood.

I did build a strong resilience, feeding my spirit and mind with God's Word and following the Word. My strategies were shifting my focus on positive emotions, gratitude toward God and people, optimism, passion, compassion toward others, helping the needy and disabled people from an early age.

I was mindful and realized that life has meaning and purpose, and God helped me develop skills to solve problems, conflicts. He gave me abilities to cope with difficult situation. Only the power of God made me the person I am today. The power of God is in His Word. His Word never fails. The Word of God is the Bread of Life and gives spiritual nutrients to nourish our spirit. We must feed our soul and mind every day. When our starving soul is consumed with doubt, it is like living with the brain in a cloudlike atmosphere of disbelief, being frustrated, discouraged, unhappy, and angry.

The Scriptures come alive in your mind and heart to clear the "cloud" of cortisol from stress from excessive worries and the fear of death that traps people's mind and hearts. The Word of God is alive and has power to transform the mind, performing "spiritual mind surgery," taking out thoughts that are damaging the body, soul, and spirit and replacing them with thoughts that bring joy, happiness, hope, and peace. Meditating on the Word of God gives us new, fresh revelation and creates new influence in your mind, connecting your positive thoughts and giving you power to live again a joyful life. The Word of God has the power to transform your life and to change your mind completely to become a new creation in Christ.

You must believe that Jesus Christ has the power over every situation in your life and His anointing, through the power of the Holy Spirit, makes everything possible. He gives life more abundantly, and you can live again. Death is not your final destination. "Jesus said to her, 'I am the resurrection and the life; he who believes in Me will live even if he dies, and everyone who lives and believes in Me will never die. Do you believe this?'" (John 11:25–26 NKJV).

Healing Power in Your Healthy Thoughts

We speak our thoughts, and we act on our thoughts. The most outrageous spiritual battle in the entire universe is the battle for the neurons involved in our thinking process in our brain and heart. Negative thoughts will connect with other old negative thoughts already in our memory, spread in our cortex, and will amplify our stress level, which will further cause the stress hormone levels to go up and cause inflammation throughout the body. From that, it is the saying "Inflammation is the mother of all diseases," because inflammation causes all conditions in the body, including neurocognitive disorders. Also, "fear of death is the mother of all religions," because due to fear of death, people seek spiritual help when closer to the end of their life. But to prevent the second death because of our sins, we need the right religion to be cleansed from our sins, to do the atonement, and to have salvation through the blood of the Lamb of God, Jesus Christ, who gives eternal life to those who believe in His death for the sins of the world and in His resurrection, which He gives to everyone who believes in Him. We set our hope in Him and in His resurrection power, which will raise us from the death by faith that influences out thoughts.

We are what we think, we think what we express, and that is the expression of our thoughts through our emotions, our behavior, and our actions. Our thoughts become measurable when we act upon them and are materialized in our behavior as a physical and visible manifestation of our invisible thoughts. We have automatic negative thoughts (the seed from the devil). There is a negative dialogue going on inside of us continuously. The Bible says, "Keep your heart with all diligence, For out of it *spring* the issues of life" (Prov. 4:23 NKJV). We must guard our hearts continually. Negative thoughts are formed in our unconscious mind from our exposure in the past to fear, anxiety, bad news, bad behavior, emotions of anger, grudges, madness, unhappiness, unforgiveness, bitterness, uncertainty, disbelief, doubts, etc. We live in a world with an adversary. His work in people is measurable in people's behavior. The damage he does to people's brain and body is measurable by the physical, mental, and emotional conditions that we observe around us and in the world.

The results of the power of the Word of God are measurable through our changed behavior and personality and the characteristics of the fruits of the Spirit. The Word of God is not an abstract teaching or theology. When you read the Word of God, the information we see with our eyes, and when we read it aloud, we hear the Word, and it will pass the threshold in our brain and will become electrical impulses and action potential. They will travel through our axons and dendrites, passing through synapses, activating neurochemicals (such as serotonin, endorphin, oxytocin, dopamine, etc.), causing protein synthesis and gene expression, altering our DNA, making us godly persons with godly character living a righteous life as new creation in Christ. Those neurochemicals will be released based on increased faith and hope, which will create the atmosphere in the brain to feel emotions of joy, peace, happiness, self-control, kindness, patience, goodness, faithfulness, love, and compassion. Our belief system and how we believe influence our gene expression through the epigenetic mechanism and our behavior. We do need to guard our heart and not let unbelief and doubts and negative thoughts destroy our being and our godly character (the peace of God will guard our mind and hearts).

Science discovers that there is a strong connection between our heart and brain. Our heart sends signals to our brain through the neural pathway.

You Are in Charge

◢ You Are in Charge of You Heart and Brain Connections

Kay Metzger, RN, BSN, cardiac nurse manager for about thirty-eight years, spoke at an International Women's Conference and presented in a unique way "open-heart surgery," emphasizing that we are in charge of the connection between the heart and the brain. "God opens the eyes of your heart," according to the scripture written in Ephesians chapter 1. "May the eyes of your hearts be enlightened in order that you may know the hope to which he has called you, to riches of His glorious inheritance in His holy people" (Eph. 1:17–18).[1]

Our heart is connected physically to our brain through the preganglionic and postganglionic neurons of the autonomic nervous system.[2] "Research indicates the heart is far more than a simple pump. The heart is, in fact, a highly complex information-processing center with its own functional brain, commonly called the *heart brain,* that communicates with and influences the cranial brain via the nervous system, hormonal system and other pathways. These influences affect brain function and most of the body's major organs and play an important role in mental and emotional experience and the quality of our lives. In recent years, we have conducted a number of research studies that have explored topics such as the electrophysiology of intuition and the degree to which the heart's magnetic field, which radiates outside the body, carries information that affects other people and even our pets, and links people together in surprising ways."[3]

We are created to carry God's breath of life, His energy in our body, and His thoughts in our mind. When the positive thoughts from our faith are expressed, we influence people around us through our positive attitude. Same thing happens with those with negative thinking. They can spread hostility, hate, anger, madness, discouragement, and unhappiness, causing you to suffer emotionally. I have seen this phenomenon in my profession and in my Christian walk in life. Only the Holy Spirit can control our thoughts when we meditate on God's instructions in the Word. We carry God's Spirit in us. Christ lives in us, and people can feel the influence. I cannot emphasize enough the we carry God's glory everywhere we go, because "to them God willed to make known what are the riches of the glory of this mystery among the Gentiles: which is Christ in you, the hope of glory" (Col. 1:27 NKJV).

When I was praying to get baptized with the Holy Spirit, I wanted to know the prerequisites to get heaven's attention. I heard the spiritual advisers who were simple people in the village where I grew up saying that you must clean your vessel first. The Holy Spirit cannot live in a dirty vessel. Indeed my "vessel" was "dirty" with negative thoughts, angry, bitterness, envy, and jealousy at a very young age, with all the characteristics of the fruit of the flesh. I had to work on those things to recognize them, confess, and repent, not doing them again. Through fasting and prayers, I was able to get closer to God's heart and enter His spiritual realm through fervent prayers. From a very young age, every person needs to guard his or her heart.

Science has now discovered that we must destabilize negative thoughts from our unconscious mind to bring them in the conscious mind, then destabilize them and replace them with positive thoughts that bring hope, love, joy, peace, and happiness. That is very encouraging, showing that the Word of God is the therapy for us all. The hope of salvation that our sins can be washed in the blood of Jesus Christ, the Lamb of God, and we can have our name written in the book of the Lamb when we confess our sins and negative feelings. We bring them in our conscious mind and destabilize them, then we can replace our negative thoughts from our sinful nature with God's love, joy, peace, and happiness. The joy of salvation will be installed. That will bring healing power in your heart and entire body.

We hear often the advice "Do not spend time around negative people." They carry negative thoughts and spread their negative energy, which can affect your emotions, your mood, your faith, and your behavior. In my profession, I had to spend time with patients that did not follow my prescriptions and those written by other prescribers, and over and over we had to reinforce the need to follow a healthy diet, exercise regularly, be active, take the medication as prescribed, and follow up for labs, procedures, etc. The burden from those patients came over me many times. I realized how hard it is to function under the burden of not obeying God's orders and His eternal prescriptions in our life.

Those emotions will drain the energy out of you, and your soul and spirit will be dry and "dehydrated" as your body gets dehydrated when you do not drink enough water, and it affects all the systems in your body to the point that you can faint. People can die from severe dehydration because your kidneys will shut down, causing all the other organs to shut down, and there will be no blood filtration. The toxins will increase and cause hypovolemic shock, affecting the entire human being. Just to put that in a simple way, spiritually our souls and spirit suffer from "spiritual dehydration" when we "do not drink" from the Living Water, which is the Word of God.

◾ Free Living Water for the Soul: The Word of God

Physical dehydration leads to lethargy from accumulated infiltrated toxins and can cause serious health problems, even death. What happens in our physical body naturally happens in our spiritual being. When we lack spiritual food and spiritual drink for our soul and spirit, spiritual starvation and dehydration happen. That will lead to accumulation of toxins in our soul and spirit and lead to spiritual death. We must rehydrate our soul and spirit with the Living Water. Jesus invites us all on this planet, including you, to come and drink from Him. In John 7:37–38, it is stated, "On the last day, that great *day* of the feast, Jesus stood and cried out, saying, 'If anyone thirsts, let him come to Me and drink. He who believes in

Me, as the Scripture has said, out of his heart will flow rivers of living water'" (John 7:37–38 NKJV).

When you water your soul and spirit with the Living Water, your soul will bloom. The toxins in your spirit will be cleansed, and your mind will be filled with thoughts nourished by faith, hope, and joy; you get rehydrated, your spiritual energy is back, and you are a new person. From your heart will flow rivers of living water, and you have the energy. And you can water those around you; they can be energized also. "The righteous shall flourish like a palm tree, He shall grow like a cedar in Lebanon. Those who are planted in the house of the LORD Shall flourish in the courts of our God. They shall still bear fruit in old age; They shall be fresh and flourishing, To declare that the LORD is upright; *He is* my rock, and *there is* no unrighteousness in Him" (Ps. 92:12–15 NKJV).

The Living Water, the Word of God, flows through our brain to wash negative thoughts that whither your neurons and your gray matter from the years of drought and spiritual dehydration. Trusting in the Lord and His miracle-working power, believing His powerful Word, will cast out fear, discouragement, discontent, and bitterness from rejection, loneliness, and isolation that produce toxic formula of neurochemicals, destroying neurons in the brain. Trusting the Lord brings hope that "waters" your thoughts with encouragement that brings joy unspeakable from the living water that flows continually, rehydrating your mind and quenching the "bad fire" in your brain that causes inflammation from unhealthy increased amount of cytokines due to bad thoughts from high levels of stress from bad emotions such as worries, fear, and anxiety, leading to degenerative diseases in your body, brain, soul, and spirit, affecting your eternity.

The Living Water for the Neurons

The Word of God is clear about our needs for the Living Water in order to be healthy physically and spiritually. "But blessed is the one who trusts in the LORD, whose confidence is in him. They will be like a tree planted by the water that sends out its roots by the stream. It does not fear when heat comes; its leaves are always green. It has no worries in a year of drought and never fails to bear fruit" (Jer. 17:7–8 NIV). When we trust in the Lord with great confidence, we feed our mind and brain with God's Word, maintaining healthy neurons in our entire body.[4] "I will never forget Your precepts, For by them You have given me life" (Ps. 119:93 NKJV). That means God's Word, which is the Living Water, gives life through healthy neurons in our brain structures.

We have seen already that the best medication for healthy neurons is the Living Water—that is, the Word of God—which is God's love shown to humankind. If it is not working, increase the dose of the Word, because the maximum dose has no limits. I will add that an increase dose of love taken with a mega dose of joy, with great and strong faith, will decrease the stress hormone cortisol, will prevent inflammation in the body, and will increase the neurotransmitters to the right formula of serotonin, oxytocin, dopamine, endorphin, and other neurochemicals that promote health for the body, soul, and spirit. That is a holistic approach to prevent physical and spiritual diseases. Transformation and reprogramming your thoughts and mind are possible through the Word of God and the power of the Holy Spirit. At the base of all creation is the Word. Man lost connection with the Creator due to the sin that entered in the world, but reconnection with our Holy Father is now possible through the power of the blood of Jesus and the power of the Holy Spirit. The blood of Jesus is the antidote for sin of any kind, and the Word can water our thoughts to keep our neurons healthy and "green."

Our Creator gave us hope to be able to reconnect with His divine power through the thoughts in our mind and neurons. Hope is created in us by our positive thoughts that are coming from positive life experience of ourselves and others. Hope rises up the most from biblical examples of men and women of faith who trusted God, and He showed up mightily in their lives and worked miracles through His mighty power and showed His glory by giving them marvelous victories in impossible circumstances. "For everything that was written in the past was written to teach us, so that through the endurance taught in the Scriptures and the encouragement they provide we might have hope" (Rom. 15:4 NIV). Reading stories of victory in the Living Word of God and living according to God's promises in His powerful and divine instructions in the Word give us hope, and we are encouraged to not give in and not give up when situations seem too difficult to manage in our own strength.

Prevent the Arthritis of the Brain

The enemy comes with voices of desperation, anger, failure, worry, broken relationship, rejection, guilt, weakness, disease, fear of the unknown, fear of death, uncertainty, unforgiveness, and anxiety, which cause emotions of bitterness. Those voices that we hear every day will cause depression and confusion and will increase the stress hormone cortisol and other neurochemicals, cytokines, and hormones that increase the inflammation process in the body, causing degenerative diseases and "arthritis of the brain," destroying neurons.

Increased inflammation causes damages in the brain cells (neurons), microglial cells that surveil the cells, taking care of the neurons, releasing cytokines to protect them, imitating the inflammatory process. But chronic inflammation from chronic stress and fear causes to attack itself and destroy them, and dysfunction of the immune system turns to attack itself, causing autoimmune diseases by increasing inflammation more, causing depression to increase, leading to sluggish action, panic attacks, psychosis, fluctuation in thyroid function, causing encephalopathy in the thyroid, which influences the brain negatively.

"The main mediators of the inflammatory response, proinflammatory cytokines, such as interleukin (IL)-1β, interleukin (IL)-1 receptor antagonist (RA), interleukin (IL)-6, tumor necrosis factor (TNF)-α, and interferon (IFN)-γ, have been recently shown to communicate with the brain and affect neurotransmission, neuroendocrine activity, and brain structure and functions, thereby inducing emotional, cognitive, and behavioral changes (Haroon et al., 2012). If the inflammatory response remains unresolved, the chronic release of pro-inflammatory cytokines can promote pathology, including depression."[5]

Our neurons are involved in our thinking process and in releasing neurochemicals in the body according to electrical impulses and information circulating in our mind and brain.[6]

God is speaking to us every day through our mind and thoughts and information circulating through our neurons. We have the capability to be selective when so many voices compete for our ears, bombarding our five senses with overwhelming information. We must be selective and intentional about our hearing, refusing the voices of discouragement that cause much distress. Tune in to the Holy Spirit channel for good news. Good news comes from the Word of God. We are His creation. He knows how we are made. You need to spend time in the Word of God. Memorize verses with His promises. When the voice of diseases with discouragement come, we must hear that God is Jehovah Rapha, our healer, which will increase our hope and faith in His healing power, and we'll have peace in our heart that He is watching to fulfill His Word and promises in us when we make our thought obedient to Christ.

The good news comes from God. Tune in to His frequency channel. The communication line is open since the creation of the world. The Holy Spirit is present to decodify His voice for us as the radio decodifies electromagnetic waves in audible and understandable sounds. We encounter millions of voices in our generation. But we know to resist and to turn away those strange, destructive voices. "Do not be deceived: 'Evil company corrupts good habits'" (1 Cor. 15:33 NKJV).

You have prescriptions written in the Word of God: "Incline your ear, and come to Me. Hear, and your soul shall live" (Isa. 55:3 NKJV). The voice you hear can make you take actions that influence next generations. The sword of the Holy Spirit is in your hands. When voices of the world are competing for our ears, we are facing an army of spirits fighting for our neurons in the brain's structures, leading to "arthritis of the brain." "Is your brain on fire with inflammation? The brain doesn't hurt like an inflamed knee does, so it's hard to know if inflammation is happening. However, the brain communicates inflammation in how it makes you feel. One of the most common symptoms of brain inflammation is brain fog, that feeling of slow and fuzzy thinking. Other common brain inflammation symptoms include depression, anxiety, irritability, anger, memory loss, and fatigue."[7]

Chronic stress from thoughts of fear, worries, anxiety, anger, and frustration increases the inflammatory process in the brain and the body. Increased sugar from bad eating habits, bad fats, lack of exercise, hidden infections, and hidden inflammation causes premature aging. God gave us prescriptions to age in an optimal way. Our immune system is programmed by our Creator to respond to an insult to heal the body and to repair itself. But chronic insult (through our behavior and bad attitude in managing stress) to our immune system will cause an inflammatory response, leading to memory loss, arthritis, heart diseases, diabetes, depression, neurocognitive disorder, and other degenerative diseases, including premature aging.

Inflammation will leak in the brain and will affect the prefrontal lobe, which will decrease our performance in daily activities and cause poor decision-making. It will cause "arthritis of the brain," with unclear thoughts and difficulties performing tasks. Systemic inflammation is the root of depression, the inflammation from the "gut." It gets in our bloodstream, then in the brain, suppressing the activity of the prefrontal cortex. Increased inflammation causes "fire in the brain," affecting the cell's danger response, the microglia, which takes care of the neurons (the nervous cells involved in thinking).

Microglia release cytokines to protect the neurons, but chronic inflammation itself destroys them, causing dysfunction in the immune system, turning against itself and attacking its own cells, causing autoimmune diseases with increased inflammation, which causes depression, sluggish actions, panic attacks, psychosis, and fluctuations in thyroid function that interacts with the brain, leading to encephalopathy. All chronic illnesses are autoimmune, persistent inflammation. "The brain and gut communicate in a bi-directional manner. Disturbances in the brain from either physical or psychological stress affect gut function, while imbalances in the gut environment can produce behavioural and neuro-chemical changes. The gastrointestinal system contains its own nervous system—the enteric nervous system. It is through this system, and a nerve called the vagus nerve, along with endocrine (hormones) and immune pathways, that researchers believe the gut communicates with the brain."[8]

Microbiome That Affect the Brain

Science demonstrated that alteration of microbiome has an effect on the brain through the vagus nerve. "Through these varied mechanisms, gut microbes shape the architecture of sleep and stress reactivity of the hypothalamic-pituitary-adrenal axis. They influence memory, mood, and cognition and are clinically and therapeutically relevant to a range of disorders, including alcoholism, chronic fatigue syndrome, fibromyalgia, and restless legs syndrome. Their role in multiple sclerosis and the neurologic manifestations of celiac disease is being studied. Nutritional tools for altering the gut microbiome therapeutically include changes in diet, probiotics, and prebiotics."[9]

It is recommended to adhere to a diet that reduces inflammation. "The types of food you eat affect how much inflammation you have. Get plenty of fruits, vegetables, whole grains, plant-based proteins (like beans and nuts), fish rich in omega-3 fatty acids (such as salmon, tuna, and sardines), and healthier oils, like olive oil. Also eat foods with probiotics, like yogurt (just check that it doesn't have too much sugar). Limit saturated fats, found in meats, whole-fat dairy products, and processed foods."[10]

Depression affects the gut microbiome by increasing inflammatory cytokines, alters intestinal permeability, controls gastric acid output, shifts the balance of immune cells, alters the tryptophan metabolism, influences neuroinflammation, affects the activity at the hypothalamus and pituitary level, affects the adrenal output, alters the executive function in the brain's prefrontal lobe, and affects the reward system.[11]

Holistic Health in the Bible

To have a healthy body, soul, and spirit, we must address the whole body with holistic medicine.

"Holistic medicine is a form of healing that considers the whole person—body, mind, spirit, and emotions—in the quest for optimal health and wellness"[12] Dr. Avery M. Jackson III, a well-renowned neurosurgeon, in his book *The God Prescription: Our Heavenly Father's Plan for Spiritual, Mental, and Physical Health*, stated, "In medical school, we are taught to investigate only the pathology of illnesses and diseases—in other words, the structural and functional deviations from the normal that constitute disease or characterize a particular disease. The impact of spiritual and mental/emotional health on physical health is not typically investigated. In my opinion, this approach addresses only one-third of the human condition. There is both anecdotal and empirical evidence that demonstrates the significant connection among these three components. Physical disease and illness often appear as the result of mental, emotional, and spiritual issues. As medical practitioners, however, we cannot heal these attributes of the three-part human. Only God can. But He has imparted the capability of healing these components, both through self-care and the intervention of trained surgeons and other medical practitioners. Can you improve your physical health simply by having a positive outlook, attitude, and mind-set? Yes! It's really about your beliefs. What you think about will affect your emotional and physical health. When you feel sick and discouraged, it creates a downward spiral. But if you can turn that negative mind-set around and think positively, you can experience healing. Divorcing His living and life-giving Word, His essence, from the act of "turning the negative mind-set around" will yield less than complete and lasting results."[13]

All systems of the body are affected by the soul and spirit conditions and the quality of our thoughts, decisions, behaviors, and actions because they are connected to the brain. Our eyes, ears, nose, mouth, tongue, throat, glands, lungs, heart, stomach, liver, pancreas, intestine, gallbladder, kidneys, bladder, sexual organs, muscles, bones, all tissues, every cell in every system (the entire body) are connected to the brain.[14]

Addressing the body, soul (mind, emotions), and spirit is extremely important in obtaining optimal health physically and spiritually to increase resilience, decrease stress, reduce inflammation, and improve your immune system. People need to get spiritual help to understand who we are at a deeper level. Develop a life force inside at deeper level, connecting us with the heaven. You go within yourself, acknowledge that spirituality is real, and you will be healed faster. Spiritual health starts with positive attitude, engaging in daily activity with the body, soul, and spirit, using emotions and feelings about what is your calling. It gives you greater sense internally when you pursue with a sense of purpose. God brings unexpected opportunity that makes you more fulfilled and feel happier.

Emotional health starts when you evaluate your emotions, which make you feel anxious, fearful, shameful, guilty, bitter, depressed, draining your energy in your daily life, increasing your risks for many diseases. Purpose gives you meaning in life and hope that will prevent physical and spiritual diseases. You cannot ignore your emotions from your thoughts. You need to face fear. You can write your feeling on a piece of paper. Through writing, you externalize emotions; you destabilize those bad memories from bad thoughts and negative emotions, to be replaced with God's promises and meanings in life. What goes in must come out physically, emotionally, spiritually.

If they do not come out, they cause diseases. Spiritually, confession brings healing to your emotions according to James 5:16. "Therefore confess your sins to each other and pray for each other so that you may be healed. The prayer of a righteous person is powerful and effective" (NIV). Acknowledge your emotions and feelings. Do not be afraid to talk about them; do not run away from your emotions. They are connected to everything in your body, your physical health, and your spiritual being. Change your sorrow into joy to optimize your health. As you need to minimize chemical use, toxins from environment for your physical health, so also do you need to minimize spiritual "toxins" of your soul and spirit.

■ Toxicity of Sin in Body, Soul, and Spirit

Pollutions of sin will intoxicate your spiritual life and bring physical diseases. Sin is all around us. Spiritual pollutions come from every direction. Our soul and spirit are fed with "garbage," and only the Word of God has the power to detoxify our thoughts and our mind and body. We need to be washed with the Word, which has the cleansing power in our life in the "living water."

The desire of the flesh manifests in many ways. You live in the flesh that is not dead. You need to come to Jesus daily to be cleansed from those toxic emotions. Only in God's presence can you be holy, when the anointing is touching you. Distractions of the day depart you from God's anointing. Without anointing, there is no touch from heaven. Focus on the presence of God, worshipping in your spirit. God talks to us every moment. We need to fear God in order to hear when He speaks. The fear of God brings wisdom, revelation, understanding, which brings peace and joy.

He wants you to meet Him face-to-face, to have an encounter with the Son of God, to keep you strong in the worst moment. When you truly meet Jesus, he becomes real to you. Nobody can shake your faith that He is the Messiah, your Savior. The Holy Spirit helps you make your election sure. He is leading you to repentance, which sets you free from the weight of sin and brings peace to your overwhelmed soul. It is like a job doing something about it every day. He predestined us for salvation before the foundation of the world, when the Lamb of God was slayed in His heart. Christ was committed before creation to give His life to save humanity from the toxicity of sin. God's promises became ours through Jesus Christ at the appointed time, as is written in Galatians 4:4. "But when the fullness of the time had come, God sent forth His Son, born of a woman, born under the law" (NKJV). You acknowledge publicly that He is Jesus, your Lord. The knowledge of the Lord gives you peace.

Reset Your Mind

Reset your mind with hope from God's promises every day. Create a routine, like when you wash your face in the morning, you must reprogram your mind to wash distracting thoughts and replace them with who God is for you, as your heavenly Father, who cares for you. In *Find Your Peace*, I gave an example of my meditation and prayer in the morning, which brings me so much power and energy for the day and for several days of my life. I start with the Lord's Prayer, acknowledging who God is for me and praying in the Spirit.[15]

Turn your intentions in daily practice to have a daily routine, praising God in prayer and meditation at His great power, which is available to you right now. When you have a wellness routine with meaningful purpose to have a healthy life physically and spiritually, as healthy diet, eating-well habits, daily exercise, reading the Word of God daily, you worship Him with your attitudes. Mindset is a collection of attitudes that affect the body, soul, and mind. Avoid excessive stress. Just allow enough normal daily stress that keeps you engaged.

True Mindfulness Is Powerful

If you face challenging situations, use gratitude, counting the blessings from those challenges. Use gratitude and appreciation, which gives you energy for the day. We always had challenging patients in our memory care. Often, discharge planners called us from hospitals to refer to us the most challenging patients. We could say no to them and admit only easy patients needing easy, light care. My husband and I considered dealing with the most challenging cases as countless blessings, not only meeting the needs of someone that is difficult to manage, but also carrying the burden of those families that their loved ones were so devastated from the diseases and now rejected by many facilities. Yes, we had to work harder and longer hours, but we rejoiced in our spirit that those families' burden was lightened by our attitude and actions.

Several years ago, one patient in particular, a distinct former history professor, was admitted in the hospital with severe restlessness, not sleeping at all day and night for several days in the hospital. His single daughter was devastated because nobody wanted to admit him in a long-term facility due to his constant restlessness. He needed to be discharged from the hospital, and they had no place for him to be moved. When we met his daughter, her eyes were filled with tears from sadness and desperation. So we decided to admit him in our memory care facility. When people asked us how we were able to manage those challenging cases brought even from psychiatric units, we replied that we counted every case as "a privilege and an opportunity" given to us to show God's love and to meet the needs of these challenging residents physically and spiritually.

We prayed and meditated at God's goodness toward us, giving us health and strength, and counted our blessings to be able to provide such a high level of care to others. That brought us peace, joy, and happiness deep in our soul, knowing that our purpose was to help the most challenging people. Family members were surprised when they saw the changes in their loved ones many times. In our facility, they were more content, smiling frequently, were more comfortable and at peace, with improved quality of life. We gave them "the best of medicine, the best of care, and the best of Christ," as they allowed a tridimensional approach, caring for their body, soul, and spirit.

Discover your gift, how to live your life using your gift to bring joy to people. Purpose is evolving, and shifting happens every season of your life. I discovered that I had compassion for the elderly when I was a teenager, not even in high school, in Romania. I did see older people working hard in the field with primitive tools and then came home to prepare food for themselves and family and for their cows, sheep, horses, etc. But they never forgot to attend prayer meetings late in the night in the weekend and throughout the week. I did watch my grandfather, who was a strong believer in Christ, praying three times a day on his knees. I heard him praying aloud in his bedroom, asking the Lord to send "holy fire" in his soul and spirit and those around him. He was not afraid of Communists. People passed by his house and heard him praying out loud, and their hearts were gripped with fear.

He was a widower, and I went to help him with some house-work. There was not much I could do at that very young age, but only visiting him brought him joy and made a huge difference in his life. Later in Bucharest, during my high school, I started to visit old people who could not get out of their houses. One time, an old lady with "elephant legs" was hardly moving because of pain in her swollen lower legs. When I visited her, she was so happy. One time she stated, "Rodicuta"—she used that name to show her love for me—"I was watching through the window, and when I saw you coming, my pain went away." I went on with my education in Bucharest to become an economist, and I worked in a big company there, but deep in my soul I knew that I had a different call on my life.

When I arrived in the USA and visited my friends who were operating an adult foster home with very old people with multiple chronic conditions, and when I was introduced to those old residents, I knew right away what I would do in this country. I started to help right away, and since 1990, I have been involved in the health-care system, taking care of thousands of adult patients with multiple acute and chronic conditions to the end of their life. But my favorite ones are frail old people who are weak and vulnerable. I love the geriatric population more. My heart is with this special group of people because of their vulnerabilities. That was my deep calling since I was a little girl, and it was clearly demonstrated later in my life. That call was placed in my DNA, and God brought that to pass. The Holy Spirit brings clarity as we obey and follow His guidance. The brain does not like uncertainty or surprises. Every thought in our brain affects the body. Our body is tuned in our thinking every moment of our life. Even our energy to fulfill our destiny is dictated by the power of our thoughts and our mindfulness.

Reset Your Feelings Through the Mind

Reset Your Brain for Heaven

I have seen many dying people as a care provider, and I realized that dying people with hope are at peace. One example of my experience is with Mr. G, when he passed away, and it illustrates that truth. He was very advanced in his dementia and was close to death. He was in distress one day during my routine visits and rounds. I stopped by to provide comfort and emotional support, and he grabbed my hand, but not like he did many times, repeating in a hurry, "Let's go, let's go," pulling me after him to walk in the hallways. This time, he grabbed my hand gently with his hand and placed it on his forehead and whispered with a sweet tone of voice, but with a sort of urgency, "Please pray for me." That action of his melted my heart. That moment was so precious. Deep in my heart, I was so moved, knowing that he had advanced dementia with behavioral disturbance and severely impaired cognition, but he knew that prayer would help him regain his peace. After a short prayer, I did sense that peace in his heart, and he was relaxed, content, and happy. I observed many times that nonbelievers are dying with no hope. They are struggling in their deathbed. We have many medications, like painkillers, for the physical pain, but they cannot kill the pain of the soul and spirit.

▪ Reset a Lifestyle of Gratitude

Reset you brain by developing a habit of gratitude and coming with the attitude of exaltation in His Name, a style of worship in the kingdom of God to proclaim the excellence of the King of Kings. Worshipping by giving Him thanks, honor, praises, obedience, as a new creation, proclaiming what God did in our life. "Therefore, if anyone is in Christ, he is a new creation; old things have passed away; behold, all things have become new." Obeying is greater than sacrifice. Let God know that you appreciate what He has done for you. Hold on to His Word when you do not see Him at work. Heaven is roaring with gratitude, praises, and exaltation. "*The* four living creatures, each having six wings, were full of eyes around and within. And they do not rest day or night, saying: 'Holy, holy, holy, Lord God Almighty, Who was and is and is to come!' Whenever the living creatures give glory and honor and thanks to Him who sits on the throne, who lives forever and ever, the twenty-four elders fall down before Him who sits on the throne and worship Him who lives forever and ever, and cast their crowns before the throne, saying: 'You are worthy, O Lord, To receive glory and honor and power; For You created all things, And by Your will they exist and were created'" (2 Cor. 5:17 NKJV).

The enemy's strategy is to blur your vision through worries, increasing the cortisol level, clouding your mind to not see what God is doing in your life so you can give Him glory that He desires and deserves from His creation, His promises that bring hope, that you are never alone on this planet and that you will live forever, making you bow down and worship Him regularly, making that a part of our lifestyle. In God are power, glory, riches, healing, wisdom, perfect peace, and forgiveness.

"And I heard a loud voice from heaven saying, 'Behold, the tabernacle of God *is* with men, and He will dwell with them, and they shall be His people. God Himself will be with them *and be* their God. And God will wipe away every tear from their eyes; there shall be no more death, nor sorrow, nor crying. There shall be no more pain, for the former things have passed away.' Then He who sat on the throne said, 'Behold, I make all things new.' And He said to me, 'Write, for these words are true and faithful.' And He said to me, 'It is done! I am the Alpha and the Omega, the Beginning and the End. I will give of the fountain of the water of life freely to him who thirsts'" (Rev. 21:3–6 NKJV).

Using the five senses to accumulate info from the outside world and to activate memories from the unconscious mind with info stored in the past to bring up in our speeches and words, controlling what gets in our brain through those five senses, will help us control our memory storage. The Holy Spirit helps us repair the "broken wall" in our mind from the corruptions of the world and to wash our mind with the Word to partake His divine nature. "As His divine power has given to us all things that *pertain* to life and godliness, through the knowledge of Him who called us by glory and virtue, by which have been given to us exceedingly great and precious promises, that through these you may be partakers of the divine nature, having escaped the corruption *that is* in the world through lust" (2 Pet. 1:3–4 NKJV).

Gentleness is a supernatural quality of the Spirit, a fruit that gives you power to endure persecutions and to walk in humility, accepting God's will to work in your mind and spirit. You never lose the battle in your mind and spirit when you have the fruits of gentleness and humility. I had to be subject to rules and authority during the Communist regime. It was painful to listen to their criticisms and ridicules humiliating Christians' faith with rude and harsh words. But I knew they were wrong in their unbelief, but gentleness in me did not leave place for pride or arrogance or revenge. I was feeling unworthy of God's grace to endure that kind of persecution for my faith in God. Jesus Christ, through the power of the Holy Spirit, was living in me and gave me wisdom and understanding and reminded me that we all are sinners but I was saved by grace. To be filled with the Holy Spirit is supernatural. The Holy Spirit is a gentle person, bringing conviction of sin and repentance. The reward of memorizing God's Word will build wisdom and instructions for life, as it did for me. Reset your brain with God's Word.

The Word Is the Answer

The world is wounded, lonely, broken, but the answers for the world's questions are in the Word of God. Fear catastrophize the worst results. You can be confused and disturbed in trials when fear takes over your brain. Persevere in His Word, for nothing is impossible with God. God's plan is always connected to our obedience of His Word and willingness to take the risk to make a stand for the truth. He will direct your path. "Trust in the Lord with all thine heart; and lean not unto thine own understanding. In all thy ways acknowledge him, and he shall direct thy paths" (Prov. 3:5–6). The quality of life on this planet depends on your trust and your obedience of God's instructions and His standards in the Word.

God's Word is God's story. He is the author of creation, science, and our life on earth. God includes our life in His story by His grace. God always speaks through His Word. The Word of God recreates your life, changes, transforms you, and you see life differently when you know His Word and meditate day and night at His instructions and reshape your identity. It becomes part of your genetic makeup and who you are. Make the Word a part of your life to direct your life to make the right decision. In spite of those who wanted to destroy, it helps you navigate through difficult times and even persecution. Search for the Lord and spend time with God in the Word and devotion time; obey the Lord's instruction and His standards for life and pray to the God of your life. Keep your eyes on Him through it all. Lift your eyes, hands, and voice, worshipping God, and encourage one another.

The Word of God was written over 1,600 years by over forty different authors, inspired by the Holy Spirit. It started about 3,400 years ago, writing the Word of God, the eternal book, to transform human life. The results and outcomes of the power of the written Word of the living God are measurable. We do not need to take the Word of God to the laboratory, because the world we live in is God's laboratory, with billions of lives being transformed over thousands of years. Billions of Bibles are distributed to change people's life, to be transformed and renewed, and to live with eternity in mind, to make the right decision for the future and for eternity. The joy comes when you have the promises in His Word that all sins are forgiven and God is healing your physical body and your emotional and spiritual wounds.

The Word of God brings healing in your body, soul, mind, thoughts, emotions, and spirit. God works in a miraculous way to bring healing and restoration even when you do not understand. He knows your body, mind, soul, and spirit's functions. He works at the microcellular level of those trillions of cells, the building blocks of your body, with DNA residing in those cells. God, through the power of the Holy Spirit, controls the cell's functions, giving instructions on how to multiply, repair, reproduce, heal and restore, and dispose unhealthy particles, when to die through apoptosis, to regenerate them. He put His Spirit in you. The spirit of truth lives in you. He is your healer. He promised in Jeremiah 30:17, "'I will restore you to health and heal your wounds,' declares the LORD, 'because you are called an outcast, Zion for whom no one cares'" (Jer. 30:17 NIV).

You are children of God, restored and healed physically and spiritually by the blood of Jesus and the power of His Word. You are anointed to bring light in every dark situation. You walk in that anointing, that power to be the light of the world. True Light lives in you to light the world and bring healing and restoration. Jesus *is* the light of the world and called each one of us to be the same. He said, "I will be with you." Praise Him and shout for joy; walk in confidence that His anointing will be with you. He gave you the assurance that His Spirit will be with you. Let people around you see the light that God wants you to be in your school, community, social media, family, and friends. He did not give us the spirit of fear, but love. He gave us power and an anointed mind. It is written, "For God has not given us a spirit of fear, but of power and of love and of a sound mind" (2 Tim. 1:7 NKJV). God gave us dominion, control over crises and circumstances. You do not have to fear but remember the Lord and keep His law. "In the night, LORD, I remember your name, that I may keep your law" (Ps. 119:55 NIV).

Speak the Word for Your Brain

Agreement with God's promise will build resilience, and you know that the Lord is on your side. We have the example of David and Goliath. David spoke the Word in front of the enemy. "I come in the name of the Lord." He encouraged himself with words filled with hope, knowing the name of the Lord. He used the name of the Lord by faith in battle to kill a giant. David was in complete agreement with God's promises in His Word. His faith was increased when he aligned his thoughts with God's Word. David was not led by emotions of fear, discouragement, insecurity, doubts, disbelief, intimidation, or abandonment, facing the giant of his life by himself. David was led by the Spirit of God through faith in the name of the Lord and killed the giant. It does not matter how big the giant is when you come in the name of the Lord.

The Righteous Live by Faith; Through Faith We See Unseen Thoughts

By faith, you are calling things, that they are not as they were, to create hopeful situation by speaking the Word. The calling creates things because the words of the mouth have power to create. Negative words keep you out of "the promised land," out of God's blessings, prepared for us here on earth and in heaven. Words create your future. Your tongue guides your life. Only what God says is true. Negative generation perish. Positive people live to fulfill their destiny and God's plan. David's words encouraged him to move with power, to destroy God's enemy, when naturally there was no hope for the entire nation of Israel. "He who guards his mouth preserves his life, *But* he who opens wide his lips shall have destruction" (Prov. 13:3 NKJV).

By speaking the word of encouragement and acting in faith, you build a strong resilience. Through strong resilience, you create light out of darkness. People can see that your light is shining when you recover quickly from your difficult circumstances, tragedies, trauma, serious financial problems, and severe broken relationships in the family. In medicine, specialists are recommending alternative techniques, like prayer and meditation. But those techniques are God's prescriptions, written about 3,400 years ago to rewire our brain, to change the brain's structures, performing neuroplasticity to see things through God's eyes, as David did when he faced the giant. You can make changes in the brain by meditating on God's promises day and night, to build a strong resilience in the face of the enemy. Science demonstrated that "those with enhanced stress resilience mechanisms have the ability to adapt successfully to stress without developing persistent psychopathology. Notably, the potential to enhance stress resilience in at-risk populations may prevent the onset of stress-induced psychiatric disorders."[1]

In emotional storms, people destroy neurons in the brain due to increased cortisol level—too high—the stress hormone that is raised during stressful time. Through epigenetic mechanism, gene mutation, protein synthesis during emotional stress, the next generation can be affected. Maternal stress hormone cortisol crosses brain barriers and emotions, toxic exposure to anger, madness, and early neglect affect the brain. "You shall not bow down to them or worship them; for I, the LORD your God, am a jealous God, punishing the children for the sin of the parents to the third and fourth generation of those who hate me, but showing love to a thousand generations of those who love me and keep my commandments" (Exod. 20:5–6 NIV).

Every seed you plant spiritually multiplies in your souls and spirit as the natural seeds multiply in the ground from generation to generation. If your spiritual seed is joy and peace, it will multiply in many physical and spiritual blessings, but if your seed is anger, madness, negativity will multiply in physical lack through increased sickness and diseases translated in generational curses. Everything multiplies in the appointed time by God. Blessings are prescribed for you if you obey and follow God's prescription to influence generations to come.

Mind Infused with the Word of God

The Word of God changed what you think about who you are. You are what the Word of God says about you. Change the way you think about God. God is love. He loved the world so much that He sent His only Son to save every soul. He infused His love in our DNA from creation when He breathed life in the human body. His spirit and His love remained in human beings since then. He wants to communicate with the world, to fellowship with you, to be involved in your life in His immanent characteristic as a God that sustains the universe, the Father of all creation, demonstrating the characteristics of the fruit of the Spirit at all times. He did not cause chaos in the world, diseases, cancer, poverty, divorce, destructive behavior, drugs, alcohol, adultery, perversion. The devil only comes to kill, steal, and destroy through our ways of thinking and acting when we do not fear God. He is the Father who loves His creation more than we love ourselves, and He wants to intervene in our lives to change our thinking through His Word.

His instructions in His powerful Word must infuse our brain structures and neurons to become part of us, completely transformed in a new person and a new creation in Christ through the power of His Word. It is God's pleasure to bless His creation with more than enough. The earth is filled with His glory through His continuous love, continually creating goods to satisfy us. Everything created on this planet is through God's ideas, given to people with gifts of imagination and creation as their Creator, who created everything from the beginning and continues to create through His creation, demonstrating His holiness. He is holy and wants His children to be holy. His holiness is our goal and purpose in life. "But as He who called you *is* holy, you also be holy in all *your* conduct, because it is written, 'Be holy, for I am holy'" (1 Pet. 1:15–16 NKJV).

Through His Word we are changed to become like Him. Our success in life is directed by Him and accomplished by the strength we receive from above. God gives us new ideas, knowledge, understanding, visions, dreams, revelation, and discernment to walk in God's way. He ordains our steps to fulfill our destiny. "The steps of a *good* man are ordered by the LORD, And He delights in his way" (Ps. 37:23 NKJV). He teaches us to pray until there is a momentum and until there is breakthrough, when He will step in the situation to bring victory, restoration, healing, prosperity, so we can fulfill our assignment given by God on this planet. I reflect on everything we accomplished on this planet that was through prayers. Sometimes we had to pray and received the answer right away; sometimes we had to pray and wait for the answers several years. But we never gave up. God led us step by step when we did not see victory or success coming right away. We continued to persevere in prayers, and in the same time, we worked physically very hard in our business until breakthrough happened in our finances, business, family, education, profession, etc.

In my book *Find Your Peace: Supernatural Solutions Beyond Science for Fear, Anxiety, and Depression*, I invited the reader to ask God for forgiveness in order to receive salvation and eternal life through Jesus Christ. I will cite it here again that "if you are not sure if you are saved, and not sure where you will spend your eternity, do not wait for that incurable diagnosis to force you to come to the Lord. You can lift your hands toward heaven right now and say from the bottom of your heart: Father God in heaven, I sinned against You. I recognize and confess all my sins, since I was born until today. Please forgive all my sins and wash them away with the precious blood of the Lamb. I bring all my sins to the cross. Cleanse me with the precious holy blood that was shed by the Lamb of God, Your Son, and Jesus Christ. Come into my heart through the power of the Holy Spirit and be my personal Lord and Savior. Transform my life. Today I want to start a new life with You, Jesus Christ, who died on the cross for my sins, was resurrected on the third day and ascended to heaven, and who is sitting at the right hand of God, the Father, the Creator of the universe, to intercede for me, my family, and the entire world. Thank You. In Jesus's name I pray. That powerful prayer will change your spiritual DNA and make you a new creation in Christ Jesus. You will receive unspeakable joy and peace—and no stress!"[2]

Holy Spirit Brings Comfort from Beginning to End

Death hurts. I spent about thirty years of my life providing care for people dying from different kinds of diseases and from old age. I observed the dying process. I watched family members, close relatives, friends, observing how their loved one was dying slowly, inch by inch. You can feel death approaching literally. Telling a dying person about Jesus will bring joy to that person, even on a death-bed, and to the family gathered to surround their loved one dying. Hopelessness and heaviness disappear when the Holy Spirit came in the room where we prayed.

One morning, the family of Mr. G was gathered in his room, surrounding his bed. He was very close to passing, and his dear wife of more than sixty years, with their six children, filled with grief and nervousness, were waiting for his end. I joined them for a few moments, and we all were prompted in our spirit to join hands in prayer that morning to lift Mr. G in prayer in his last moments on earth. He was a man who loved prayers. We raised our voice as one and asked God for His mercy and grace in the last moments of Mr. G's life, over which none of us had control. The presence of God was gently felt by each one of us when "electricity" started to flow in waves through our human body. Tears were rolling down our faces. Each of us started to cry instantly, being touched by the Holy Spirit. Hope and peace filled our hearts. The atmosphere changed the moment we started to pray. Literally we felt the electricity flowing through our bodies. Through tears we looked at one another, knowing that only the power of the Holy Spirit could do something like that in a room full of people grieving the loss of one dear person in their life, ushering him to the gates of heaven.

Dr. Crandall, cardiologist and heart transplant surgeon, in one of his speeches at the Medical Healing Conference, with hundreds of doctors and medical professionals, stated that in medicine, we will truly help patients when we "give people the best of medicine and the best of Jesus," to provide natural and supernatural healing. The family of Mr. G received healing of their painful emotions when Mr. G breathed his last breath. I saw tears of joy on their faces. They forgot about their grieving pain, focusing on what God was doing, touching their hearts and souls and spirits. They were even talking about that moment all day long after that experience with the staff and caring, professional people visiting that day from different agencies, coming to get report on his care at our facility that day. The body is the shell that hides the soul and spirit. At the end of life, the soul and the spirit leave the shell with the last breath and instantly enter in the presence of the Lord. "We are confident, I say, and would prefer to be away from the body and at home with the Lord" (2 Cor. 5:8 NIV).

Loneliness creates crisis, isolation, and depression. People seek network to support each other. People seek healing, health, for their emotions, which affects their physical body also. Science demonstrated "that certain positive emotions speed recovery from the cardiovascular sequelae of negative emotions."[3]

Scientists demonstrated that "social support buffers associations between anger and metabolic risk factors. Field studies monitoring daily events and ambulatory blood pressure also show that perceived support and positive interpersonal interactions buffer the link between negative affect and increased blood pressure. Perceived support dampens daily rumination and negative affect in trait ruminators, indicating that perceived support has both psychological and physiological benefits in those who tend toward negative affect in general and anger in particular."[4]

We learned already that exposure to stressful situations, physical diseases, and painful emotions from unhealthy fear, anxiety, unforgiveness, anger, bitterness, isolation, loneliness, depression, negative thoughts, lack of hope, and unhappiness affect our brain structures, like the amygdala and hippocampus. Lange C and Irle E. stated, "Evidence is increasing that amygdala and hippocampus show significant structural abnormalities in affective disorders. Two previous studies found enlarged amygdala size in subjects with recent-onset major depression." "Compared with control subjects, depressive subjects had significantly larger (+13 %) amygdala volumes and significantly smaller (-12%) hippocampal volumes."[5]

We can reverse stress and its complication by reflecting on the truth that the purpose of creation is to bring glory to the Creator and to help others find Him for the same reason, to bring glory to our sovereign God here on earth and then in eternity. Only the Holy Spirit of God gives that confidence when we receive His promised power. It is important that we gain confidence that we are created in God's image with purpose on this planet to be filled with the Holy Spirit, to serve God and serve others as we show our love to God and to others.

Greg Berglund, MD, MDiv, in his book *This Mountain: You Shall Say to This Mountain, 'Move From Here to There,'* stated that "there are some ways by which we position ourselves to receive this gift of the Holy Spirit. James 4:8 says 'Draw near to God, and He will draw near to you.' We can initiate drawing near to God by confession and repentance of sin. We draw near to Him when we are aware of our need for a Savior, when we pray in the name of Jesus who gives us access to the Father, when we read God's word and choose to believe those words. Faith comes to us by the hearing of God's word. Without such faith, it is impossible to please God. Additionally, we draw near to God by doing the words of God recorded in the Bible. This places us in a position before God's throne of grace to receive help and mercy. The Spirit of God sees a sincere heart seeking after Him. He begins an inner work bringing confidence before Him, not based on our performance. God gives righteousness to us, based on the work of Jesus for our salvation. We are forgiven and freed from sin through faith and trust in Jesus Christ. His vicarious sacrifice pays the penalty for our sin. The Spirit of God works this assurance of salvation in a way that only He can do in the heart and soul of one seeking Him. He confirms these truths in our hearts so that you know that you know that you have eternal life, that you are a child of God."[6]

Reset your brain for heaven, and your limbic system will be preserved due to the joy of salvation. You were created in His image, with a purpose to belong to the body of Christ, to fellowship and communicate with its members, and to inherit eternal life. During our journey on this planet, we hoped to be in a better place. Your soul and spirit will never die. Set your mind on heaven. Live heavenly minded. Jesus lived heavenly minded for Himself and for every single person living on this planet. He offers each person the way and the chance to go to heaven. Death has been defeated so you will never die. "Jesus said to her, 'I am the resurrection and the life. He who believes in Me, though he may die, he shall live. And whoever lives and believes in Me shall never die. Do you believe this?'" (John 11:25–26 NKJV). The joy of the resurrection power is in you to defeat fear of death, depression, and anxiety. Heaven is waiting for you; the greatest feast is in heaven. Jesus made reservation for you for that feast in heaven. Your name was written in the book of the Lamb. You need to accept His invitation.

Jonathan Cahn stated in his book *The Oracle,* "The voice of God would say to you this… I have known you from the beginning, from before you took your first step, before you breathed your first breath, before you were even conceived. I have seen all your tears and have known all your sorrows and wounds and pains, all your longings and hopes, all your fears, your dreams and heartbreaks, your burdens and weariness, your times of asking Me why, your cries of loneliness and emptiness, your times of separation, your mourning for what was lost, your weaknesses and failings, your wanderings, your sins and shame… And I have still loved you with an everlasting love… And now I call you to leave the darkness and all that is passed and all that I never willed or purposed for your life…that the days of your separation would come to an end. It is time now to return. It is time to come home…to enter the inheritance of blessing you never knew but were born to enter. It is time for your Jubilee. Come to Me. And I will not turn you away but will receive you. And I will wipe away all your tears. I will forgive all your sins. I will heal all your wounds. And I will turn all your sorrows into joy. And you will forget your days of darkness and wandering, the days of your separation. And I will make all things new."[7]

Come to Him who created you in His image with a unique purpose to prepare during this temporary life on earth, in this earthly body, carrying the eternal soul and spirit, to enjoy eternal life with our Creator and Savior and to give Him glory forever. He is worthy.

References

Part I

Chapter 1

1   Dr. Avery M. Jackson III, *The God Prescription Our Heavenly Father's Plan for Spiritual, Mental, and Physical Health* (Kindle Edition, 2018), 116.
2   https://ghr.nlm.nih.gov/primer/basics/gene, accessed December 21, 2019.
3   Dr. Guillermo Maldonado, *Created for Purpose* (New Kensington, Pennsylvania: Whitaker House, 2019), 26.
4   https://ghr.nlm.nih.gov/primer/basics/dna, December 21, 2019.
5   https://ghr.nlm.nih.gov/primer/basics/cell, December 21, 2019.
6   https://www.gettyimages.com/detail/photo/fetus-with-dna-umbilical-cord-royalty-free-image/183878409?adppopup=true
7   Grant R. Jeffrey, *Creation: Remarkable Evidence of God's Design* (Colorado Springs: WaterBrook, 2003), 44–47.
8   Ibid.
9   http://scienceline.ucsb.edu/getkey.php?key=3059, accessed February 3, 2020.
10 http://scienceline.ucsb.edu/getkey.php?key=3059, accessed February 3, 2020.
11 https://en.wikipedia.org/wiki/Eros_(concept), accessed December 17, 2019.
12 Dr. Scott K. Hannen, *Stop the Pain: The Six to Fix. A Complete Six-Step Approach to Detect and Correct the Cause of Chronic Pain and Suffering.* (Trilogy Christian Publishers, 2019), 27.
13 https://answersingenesis.org/human-body/from-dust-to-dust, accessed December 24, 2019.
14 https://toxtutor.nlm.nih.gov/08-006.html, accessed December 24, 2019.
15 https://answersingenesis.org/human-body/from-dust-to-dust, accessed December 24, 2019.
16 https://www.hsph.harvard.edu/news/press-releases/fruit-vegetables-breast-cancer, accessed March 23, 2020.
17 Grant R. Jeffrey, *Creation: Remarkable Evidence of God's Design* (Colorado Springs: WaterBrook, 2003), 36.
18 Phil Mason, *Quantum Glory: The Science of Heaven Invading Earth* (Maricopa, Arizona: XP Publishing, 2010), 29.

19 https://training.seer.cancer.gov/anatomy/cells_tissues_membranes/cells/structure.html, accessed March 22, 2020.

20 https://ghr.nlm.nih.gov/primer/basics/cell, accessed December 21, 2020.

21 Dr. Paul Brand and Philip Yancey. *Fearfully and Wonderfully Made* (Zondervan, 1980), 14.

22 https://ghr.nlm.nih.gov/primer/basics/dna, accessed December 22, 2019.

23 https://www.news-medical.net/life-sciences/What-are-Mitochondria.aspx, accessed March 22, 2020.

24 https://www.medicalnewstoday.com/articles/320875.php, accessed April 18, 2019.

25 Dr. Avery M. Jackson III, *The God Prescription: Our Heavenly Father's Plan for Spiritual, Mental, and Physical Health* (Kindle Edition), 11.

26 Phil Mason, *Quantum Glory: The Science of Heaven Invading Earth* (Maricopa, Arizona: XP Publishing, 2010), 294.

27 https://manwithoutqualities.com/2018/02/28/double-helix, accessed March 22, 2020.

Chapter 2

1 https://en.wikipedia.org/wiki/Executive_functions, accessed November 2019.

2 T. D. Jakes, *Instinct: The Power to Unleash Your Inborn Drive* (New York, New York: Faith Word. Hachette Book Group, 2014), 261.

3 https://quizlet.com/394745592/areas-of-the-brain-diagram, accessed March 22, 2020.

4 https://www.bbc.co.uk/science/humanbody/body/factfiles/nervecellsand-nerves/nerve_cells_and_nerves.shtml, accessed December 2019.

5 Christopher Bergland, "How Do Neuroplasticity and Neurogenesis Rewire Your Brain?" https://www.psychologytoday.com/us/blog/the-athletes-way/201702/how-do-neuroplasticity -and-neurogenesis-rewire-your-brain, accessed July 26, 2019.

6 https://fherehab.com/neuro-rehabilitative-services/eeg-brain-mapping, accessed December 31, 2019.

7 Jentezen Franklin, *Right People, Right Place, Right Plan. Discerning the Voice of God* (New Kensington, Pennsylvania: Whitaker House), 27–28.

8 Phil and Diane Comer, *Raising Passionate Jesus Followers: The Power of Intentional Parenting* (Michigan: Zondervan Grand Rapids, January 2018), 56–57.

9 Phil Mason, *Quantum Glory: The Science of Heaven Invading Earth* (Maricopa, Arizona: XP Publishing, 2010), 291.

10 Ibid., 297.

Chapter 3

1 http://onradiology.blogspot.com/2010/07/human-eye-anatomy-diagram.html, accessed March 22, 2020.
2 Grant R. Jeffrey, *Creation: Remarkable Evidence of God's Design* (Colorado Springs: WaterBrook, 2003), 39–40.
3 Ibid., 40.
4 https://www.linkedin.com/pulse/20141021062211-151652777-william-shakespeare-once-aid-the-eyes-are-the-window-to-your-soul/

Chapter 4

1 https://www.webmd.com/cold-and-flu/ear-infection/picture-of-the-ear#1, accessed March 22, 2020.
2 Phil Mason, *Quantum Glory: The Science of Heaven Invading Earth* (Maricopa, Arizona: XP Publishing, 2010), 142.
3 John Bevere, *The Baith of Satan: Living Free from the Deadly Trap of Offense* (Charisma House, 2004), 1.
4 Phil Mason, *Quantum Glory: The Science of Heaven Invading Earth* (Maricopa, Arizona: XP Publishing, 2010), 140.
5 Ibid.
6 Ibid., 141.

Chapter 5

1 http://www.myhealth.gov.my/en/loss-sense-smell, accessed March 22, 2020.
2 https://www.bbc.co.uk/science/humanbody/body/factfiles/smell/smell_animation.shtml, accessed November 27, 2019.
3 https://www.researchgate.net/figure/The-human-brain-The-colored-part-is-considered-part-of-the-limbic-system_fig7_220795664, accessed March 22, 2020.
4 Kandhasamy Sowndhararajan and Songmun Kim, "Influence of Fragrances on Human Psychophysiological Activity: With Special Reference to Human Electroencephalographic Response," *Scientia Pharmaceutica*, 84 (4) (2016), 724–752.
5 https://www.ncbi.nlm.nih.gov/pmc/articles/PMC5198031, accessed August 3, 2019.
6 https://en.m.wikipedia.org/wiki/Christian_meditation, accessed April 17, 2019.

Part II

Chapter 6

1 https://thebrain.mcgill.ca/flash/i/i_03/i_03_cr/i_03_cr_par/i_03_cr_par.html, accessed December 28, 2019.

2 https://www.researchgate.net/figure/Dopaminergic-pathways-in-the-brain_fig3_284786249, accessed March 26, 2020.

3 https://neurohacker.com/what-is-dopamine, accessed July 31, 2019.

4 Ibid.

5 https://www.neuroscientificallychallenged.com/blog/know-your-brain-reward-system, accessed August 14, 2019.

6 https://learn.genetics.utah.edu/content/addiction/rewardbehavior, accessed November 2019.

7 https://learn.genetics.utah.edu/content/addiction/rewardbehavior, accessed March 26, 2020.

8 T. D. Jakes, *Instinct: The Power to Unleash Your Inborn Drive* (New York, New York: Faith Word. Hachette Book Group, 2014), 268.

9 Dr. Ananya Mandal, MD, "Dopamine Functions," https://www.news-medical.net/health/ Dopamine-Functions.aspx, accessed August 15, 2019.

10 Shaneen Clarke, *Dare to be Great: Forget Your Past! Live Your Dream* (Charlotte, North Carolina: LifeBridge Books, 2009).

Chapter 7

1 Dr. Caroline Leaf, *Who Switched off My Brain? Controlling Toxic Thoughts and Emotions* (Improv, Ltd. Thomas Nelson Publishers, 2009), 133.

2 WA Cunningham, NL Arbuckle, Jahn A. Mowrer, AM Abduljalil, "Aspects of neuroticism and the amygdala: chronic tuning from motivational styles," *Neuropsychologia*, 48 (12) (October 2010), 399–404.

3 https://www.ncbi.nlm.nih.gov/pmc/articles/PMC4482114, accessed January 8, 2020.

Chapter 8

1 Lisa Bevere, *Without Rival, Embrace Your Identity and an Age of Confusion and Comparison* (Michigan, Grand Rapids: Revell-Baker Publishing Group, 2016).

2 Dr. Emilia Arden, cardiologist, "Philadelphia Romanian Penticostal Church," *Christian Medical Conferences* (October 12, 2019) https://mail.yahoo.com/b/search/keyword=VhJMFCgOYaP5xAxjTqWUbfStvQ---A&accountIds=1/messages/ACH5eUJMkz9fXaHc Agz8OEvRBwg?showImages=true&offset=0, accessed March 29, 2020.

3   https://www.ahajournals.org/doi/full/10.1161/CIRCULATIONAHA. 107.760405, accessed February 19, 2020.

4   Dr. Caroline Leaf, *Who Switched off My Brain? Controlling Toxic Thoughts and Emotions* (Improv, Ltd. Thomas Nelson Publishers, 2009), 40–41.

5   Marina Eliava, Meggane Melchior, H. Sophie Knobloch-Bollmann, Jérôme Wahis, Miriam da Silva Gouveia, Yan Tang, Alexandru Cristian, Ciobanu, Rodrigo Triana del Rio, Lena C. Roth, Ferdinand Althammer, Virginie Chavant, Yannick Goumon, Tim Gruber, Nathalie Petit-Demoulière, Marta Busnelli, Bice Chini, Linette L. Tan, Mariela Mitre, Robert C. Froemke, Moses V. Chao, Günter Giese, Rolf Sprengel, Rohini Kuner, Pierrick Poisbeau, Peter H. Seeburg, Ron Stoop, Alexandre Charlet, and Valery Grinevich, "A New Population of Parvocellular Oxytocin Neurons Controlling Magnocellular Neuron Activity and Inflammatory Pain Processing," *Neuron*, published online January 22, 2016 doi:10.1016/j.neuron.2016.01.041)
Eliava et al., "Love Hormone Oxytocin Relieves Pain," *Neuroscience News* (Max Planck Institute, 2016) https://neurosciencenews.com/pain-oxytocin-neurology-3808, accessed July 28, 2019.

6   Dr. Chauncey Crandall, *Raising the Dead: A Doctor Encounters the Miraculous* (FaithWords. Kindle Edition, 2010), 158–159.

7   L. J. Cottrell, "Joy and happiness: a simultaneous and evolutionary concept analysis," e-Pub (April 27, 2016).

8   Leif Hetland, *Transformed by Love* (Peachtree City, Georgia: Global Mission Awareness, 2015).

Chapter 9

1   https://www.lawattractionplus.com/2015/01/the-pharmacy-of-brain.html, accessed March 28, 2019.

2   https://www.lawattractionplus.com/2015/01/the-pharmacy-of-brain.html

3   Ibid.

4   Ibid.

5   https://courses.lumenlearning.com/boundless-ap/chapter/water-balance, accessed April 26, 2020.

6   https://courses.lumenlearning.com/boundless-ap/chapter/water-balance, accessed December 22, 2019.

Chapter 10

1   https://www.nicabm.com/how-anger-affects-the-brain-and-body-infographic, accessed January 6, 2020.

[2] Dr. Emilia Arden, cardiologist, *Christian Medical Conferences* (Portland, Oregon, October 12, 2019) https://mail.yahoo.com/b/search/keyword=VhJMFCgOYaP5xAxjTqWUbfStvQ---A&accountIds=1/messages/ACH5eUJMkz9fXaHcAgz8OEvRBwg?showImages=true&offset=0, accessed March 29, 2020.

[3] R. Lampert, *Circulation 2002* (October 1).

[4] Eli Puterman, Elissa S. Epel, Aoife O'Donovan, Aric A. Prather, Kirstin Aschbacher, and Firdaus S. Dhabhar, "Anger Is Associated with Increased IL-6 Stress Reactivity in Women, But Only Among Those Low in Social Support," *International Journal of Behavioral Medicine*, 21 (6) (December 2014), 936–945. https://www.ncbi.nlm.nih.gov/pmc/ articles/PMC 4406249, accessed March 18, 2020.

[5] https://www.ncbi.nlm.nih.gov/pmc/articles/PMC4406249, accessed March 18, 2020.

[6] https://www.ncbi.nlm.nih.gov/pmc/articles/PMC4406249, accessed March 18, 2020.

Part III

Chapter 11

[1] Martin Clarke, London (August 8, 2018) martin@themartinclarkegroup.co.uk.

[2] Dr. Rodica Malos, *Find Your Peace: Supernatural Solutions Beyond Science for Fear, Anxiety, and Depression* (Lake Mary Florida: Siloam. Charisma Media/ Charisma House Book Group, 2020), 117.

[3] Ibid., 138–139.

[4] J. Ryan Lister, *The Presence of God: Its Place in the Storyline of Scripture and the Story of our Life* (Wheaton, Illinois: Crossway, 2015), 65.

Chapter 12

[1] Kris Vallotton. *Destined to Win: How to Embrace Your God-Given Identity and Realize Your Kingdom Purpose* (Nashville, Tennessee: Nelson Books. An imprint of Thomas Nelson, 2017), 185.

[2] https://www.healthline.com/human-body-maps/frontal-lobe#1, accessed April 15, 2019.

[3] Dr. Don Colbert, MD, *Reversing Diabetes* (Lake Mary, Florida: Siloam. Charisma Media/Charisma House Book Groups, 2012), 214.

Chapter 13

1 Bill Johnson, *The Supernatural Power of a Transformed Mind: Access to a Life of Miracles* (Shippensburg, Pennsylvania: Destiny Image Publisher, 2005), 104.
2 Dr. Guillermo Maldonado, *Break Through Prayer: Where God Always Hears and Answers* (New Kensington, Pennsylvania: Whitaker House, 2018), 143–144.
3 John G. Lake, *Your Power in the Holy Spirit* (New Kensington, Pennsylvania: Whitaker House, 2010), 117–118.

Chapter 14

1 Michael Koulianos, *Holy Spirit: The One Who Makes Jesus Real* (Shippensburg, Pennsylvania: Destiny Image Publisher, Inc., 2017), 173.
2 Dr. Chauncey Crandall, *Raising the Dead: A Doctor Encounters the Miraculous* (FaithWords. Kindle Edition, 2010), 183–185.
3 https://twitter.com/crandallmd/status/1155112362921205 76
4 Michael Koulianos, *Holy Spirit: The One Who Makes Jesus Real* (Shippensburg, Pennsylvania: Destiny Image Publisher, Inc., 2017), 57–58.

Chapter 15

1 Lloyd C. Douglas, *The Robe: The Story of the Soldier Who Tossed for Christ's Robe and Won* (HijezGlobal. Kindle Edition), 173.
2 Jack Hayford, *The Beauty of Spiritual Language: Unveiling the Mystery of Speaking in Tongues* (Gateway Press, 2018), 260.
3 https://discernthetime.files.wordpress.com/2013/10/spectwvt.jpg, accessed February 22, 2020.
4 https://discernthetime.wordpress.com/2013/10/04/speaking-in-tongues-medical-study-proves-its-the-holy-spirit-praying, accessed February 22, 2020.
5 John G. Lake, *Your Power in the Holy Spirit* (New Kensington, Pennsylvania: Whitaker House, 2010), 256.
6 Ibid., 258–259.

Chapter 16

1 Source: Compiled by Ben Malcolmson, assistant to the head coach Seattle Seahawks (March 8, 2019).
2 https://www.oneclearmessage.com/mirror-neurons, accessed February 22, 2020.

3 https://www.scientificamerican.com/article/london-taxi-memory,   accessed March 26, 2020.

4 https://highexistence.com/thoughts-program-cells,   accessed   February   23, 2020.

Chapter 17

1 Kris Vallotton. *Destined to Win: How to Embrace Your God-Given Identity and Realize Your Kingdom Purpose* (Nashville, Tennessee: Nelson Books. An imprint of Thomas Nelson, 2017), 12–13.

Chapter 18

1 Derek Prince, *Shaping History Through Prayer and Fasting* (New Kensington, Pennsylvania: Whitaker House, 2002), 40.

2 Ibid., 71.

3 Dr. Scott Hannen, *Stop The Pain. The Six to Fix* (Tustin, California: Trilogy Publishing Group, 2019), 270–271.

Chapter 19

1 Beth Moore, *Living Beyond Yourself. Exploring the Fruit of the Spirit* (Nashville, Tennessee: Life Way Press, 2004), 85.

2 Benny Hinn, *Good Morning Holy Spirit* (Nashville, Tennessee: Thomas Nelson Publisher 2004), 53.

Chapter 20

1 Brenda Kunneman, *The Daily Decree* (Kindle Locations 1758–1763: Destiny Image, Inc. Kindle Edition, 2019).

2 Bill Johnson, *Face to Face with God: Get Ready for a Life—Changing Encounter with God* (Lake Mary, Florida: Charisma Media/Charisma House Book Group, 2015), 16.

Chapter 21

1 https://healthybrains.org/brain-facts, accessed January 4, 2020.

2   C. Faye, JC Mcgowan, CA Denny, DJ David, "Neurobiological Mechanisms of Stress Resilience and Implications for the Aged Population," *Current Neuropharmacology*, 16 (3) (March 5, 2018), 234–270.

3   https://www.gotquestions.org/Christian-mindfulness.html, accessed March 20, 2019.

4   https://www.sciencedaily.com/releases/2013/12/131208090343.htm, accessed November 2019.

5   https://www.integrativepractitioner.com/practice-management/news/inflammation-could-be-the-cause-of-all-disease, accessed November 2019.

6   https://www.mayoclinic.org/tests-procedures/meditation/in-depth/meditation/art-20045858, accessed January 5, 2020.

7   RA Fabes, N. Eisenberg, "Regulatory control and adults' stress-related responses to daily life events," *Journal of Personality and Social Psychology*, 73 (5) (November 1997), 1107–1117.

8   https://www.pinterest.se/pin/255720085069960967, accessed March 27, 2020.

Part IV

Chapter 22

1   https://learn.genetics.utah.edu/content/epigenetics/inheritance, accessed January 5, 2020.

2   Larry Huch, *Free at Last: Removing Your Past from Your Future* (New Kensington, Pennsylvania: Whitaker House, 2004), 190.

3   Larry and Tiz Huch, *Release Family Blessings. God's Plan for Your Marriage and Children.* (New Kensington, Pennsylvania: Whitaker House, 2012), 33.

Chapter 23

1   Tiz Huch, *No Limits, No Boundaries. Praying Dynamic Change into Your Life, Family, and Finances* (New Kensington, Pennsylvania: Whitaker House, 2009), 105.

2   Brenda Kunneman, *The Daily Decree* (Kindle Locations 446–450: Destiny Image, Inc. Kindle Edition, 2019).

Chapter 24

1   Benny Hinn, *Good Morning Holy Spirit* (Nashville, Tennessee: Thomas Nelson Publisher 2004), 66–67.

2   Brenda Kunneman, *The Daily Decree* (Kindle Locations 1182–1187: Destiny Image, Inc. Kindle Edition, 2019).

3   Smith Wigglesworth, *On the Power of Scripture* compiled by Robert Liardon (New Kensington, Pennsylvania: Whitaker House, 2009), 188.

4   Ibid., 189

Chapter 25

1   https://dualdiagnosis.org/stress-relapse, accessed January 8, 2020.

2   A. W. Tozer, *The Pursuit of God. The Human Thirst for Divine* (Camp Hill, Pennsylvania: Christian Publication, Inc., 1993), 66–67.

Part V

Chapter 26

1   Michele M. Tugade and Barbara L. Fredrickson, "Resilient Individuals Use Positive Emotions to Bounce Back From Negative Emotional Experiences," *Journal of Personality and Social Psychology*, 86 (2) (February 2004), 320–333.

2   William A. Cunningham and Tabitha Kirkland, "The joyful, yet balanced, amygdala: moderated responses to positive but not negative stimuli in trait happiness," *Social Cognitive and Affective Neuroscience*, 9 (6) (June 2014), 760–766.

3   Person M. Hanssen, "Joy, happiness, and humor in dementia care: a qualitative study," *Creat Nurs*, 21 (1) (2015), 47–52.

Chapter 27

1   https://www.merriam-webster.com/dictionary/enthusiasm, accessed February 10, 2019.

Chapter 28

1   Dunn AJ, Swiergiel AH, Palamarchouk V., "Brain circuits involved in corticotropin-releasing factor-norepinephrine interactions during stress," *Annals of the New York Academy of Sciences*, 1018 (June 2004), 25–34 https://www.ncbi.nlm.nih.gov/pubmed/15240349, accessed March 27, 2019.

2   https://www.dnalc.org/view/2099-Prefrontal-Cortex-.html, accessed August 15, 2019.

[3] Terry Hurley, "Activating the Parasympathetic Nervous System to Decrease Stress and Anxiety" (2018) https://canyonvista.com/activating-parasympathetic-nervous-system, accessed August 15, 2019.

[4] George Koob in Calming an Overactive Brain.

[5] Ibid.

[6] Ibid.

[7] YS Nikolova, KA Misquitta, BR Rocco, TD Prevot, AR Knodt, J. Ellegood, AN Voineskos, JP Lerch, AR Hariri, E. Sibille, M. Banasr, "Shifting priorities: highly conserved behavioral and brain network adaptations to chronic stress across species," *Translational Psychiatry*, 8 (1) (January 22, 2018), 26.

[8] https://www.healthline.com/health/chemical-imbalance-in-the-brain, accessed August 15, 2019.

[9] Berit Brogaard, "Brain Chemical Imbalance Symptoms" https://www.livestrong.com/ article/192253-brain-chemical-imbalance-symptoms, accessed August 15, 2019.

[10] https://www.healthline.com/nutrition/how-to-increase-dopamine, accessed August 15, 2019.

[11] Jentezen Franklin, *Right People, Right Place, Right Plan. Discerning the Voice of God* (New Kensington, Pennsylvania: Whitaker House), 51.

[12] https://hippocratesinst.org/rewire-brain-generate-joy, accessed August 15, 2019.

[13] https://www.healthline.com/health/affects-of-joy#1, accessed August 15, 2019.

[14] https://www.merriam-webster.com/dictionary/tribulation, accessed February 2019.

[15] S. Oishi, E. Diener, "Residents of poor nations have a greater sense of meaning in life than residents of wealthy nations," *Psychological Science*, 25 (2) (February 2014), 422–430.

[16] Dr. David Levy, MD, neurosurgeon, "Fear in Crisis—Part 1 (Coronavirus COVID-19) Help for Anxiety," YouTube, accessed March 28, 2020.

[17] https://people.howstuffworks.com/swearing4.htm, accessed August 16, 2019.

Chapter 30

[1] https://www.nsc.org/home-safety/safety-topics/opioids/prescription, accessed January 16, 2020.

[2] https://www.ncbi.nlm.nih.gov/pmc/articles/PMC4301417, accessed January 18, 2020.

[3] https://www.painresearchforum.org/news/92059-whats-name-chronic-pain

[4] https://www.ncbi.nlm.nih.gov/pmc/articles/PMC2964993/

[5] https://www.ncbi.nlm.nih.gov/pubmed/19781793

[6] http://www.instituteforchronicpain.org/understanding-chronic-pain/what-is-chronic-pain/central-sensitization, accessed January 18, 2020.

7 http://www.instituteforchronicpain.org/understanding-chronic-pain/what-is-chronic-pain/central-sensitization, accessed January 18, 2020.

8 https://www.ncbi.nlm.nih.gov/pmc/articles/PMC2964993, accessed January 18, 2020.

9 Mark Thompson, "Neurological Mechanisms of Sleep" https://www.mattress-advisor.com/ how-neurological, accessed April 13, 2020.

10 https://www.psychiatry.org/patients-families/addiction/opioid-use-disorder/opioid-use-disorder, accessed January 18, 2020.

11 https://www.frontiersin.org/articles/10.3389/fpsyt.2019.00286/full, accessed January 18, 2020.

12 https://onlinelibrary.wiley.com/doi/abs/10.1080/00207598208247454, accessed March 8, 2019.

Chapter 31

1 Kay Metsger, RN, BSN. "Open Heart Surgery" message at International Women's Conference published on May 17, 2019 in YouTube, accessed March 29, 2020.

2 Mirnela Byku and Douglas L. Mann, "Neuromodulation of the Failing Heart. Lost in Translation?" *JACC: Basic to Translational Science*, volume 1, issue 3 (April 2016) http://basictranslational.onlinejacc.org/content/1/3/95/F1.

3 https://www.heartmath.org/research/science-of-the-heart, accessed March 15, 2020.

4 Brooks Hays, "New bioimaging technique offers clear view of nervous system," *Science News* (August 22, 2016) https://www.upi.com/Science_News/2016/08/22/New-bioimaging-technique-offers-clear-view-of-nervous-system/8881471888418/

5 Viktoriya Maydych, "The Interplay Between Stress, Inflammation, and Emotional Attention: Relevance for Depression," *Frontiers in Neuroscience* (2019) https://www.ncbi.nlm. nih.gov/pmc/articles/PMC6491771, accessed March 18, 2020.

6 "The Human Memory: Brain Neurons and Synapses" (September 2019) https://human-memory.net/brain-neurons-synapses.

7 http://www.naturalfoundationshealing.com/brain-fire-symptoms-brain-in-flammation, accessed April 18, 2019.

8 https://mindd.org/connection-leaky-gut-leaky-brain, accessed March 18, 2020.

9 https://www.ncbi.nlm.nih.gov/pmc/articles/PMC4259177, accessed March 17, 2020.

10 https://www.webmd.com/women/ss/slideshow-what-is-inflammation?-ecd=wnl_spr_040919&ctr=wnl-spr-040919_nsl-LeadModule_img&mb=U0Zs2w0NM%2fOpAorNWT5iYxXFE73IOX1cisubrdtf9Og%3d accessed April 11, 2019.

[11] https://www.sciencedirect.com/science/article/pii/S0969996119302463, accessed March 17, 2020.

[12] https://www.webmd.com/balance/guide/what-is-holistic-medicine#1,accessed April 17, 2019.

[13] Dr. Avery M. Jackson III, *The God Prescription: Our Heavenly Father's Plan for Spiritual, Mental, and Physical Health* (Kindle Edition), 1–2.

[14] https://www.circleofdocs.com/wp-content/uploads/2014/11/autonomic-nervous-system-diagram.gif

[15] Dr. Rodica Malos, *Find Your Peace: Supernatural Solutions Beyond Science for Fear, Anxiety, and Depression* (Lake Mary Florida: Siloam. Charisma Media/ Charisma House Book Group, 2020).

Chapter 32

[1] C. Faye, JC Mcgowan, CA Denny, DJ David, "Neurobiological Mechanisms of Stress Resilience and Implications for the Aged Population," *Current Neuropharmacology*, 16 (3) (March 5, 2018), 234–270.

[2] Dr. Rodica Malos, *Find Your Peace: Supernatural Solutions Beyond Science for Fear, Anxiety, and Depression* (Lake Mary Florida: Siloam. Charisma Media/ Charisma House Book Group, 2020), 267.

[3] BL Fredrickson, RW Levenson, "Positive Emotions Speed Recovery from the Cardiovascular Sequelae of Negative Emotions," *Cognition and Emotion*, 12 (2) (March 1, 1998), 191–220.

[4] https://www.ncbi.nlm.nih.gov/pmc/articles/PMC4406249, accessed January 22, 2020.

[5] C. Lange, E. Irle, "Enlarged amygdala volume and reduced hippocampal volume in young women with major depression," *Psychological Medicine*, 34 (6) (August 2004), 1059–1064.

[6] Greg Berglund, MD, MDiv, *This Mountain: You Shall Say to This Mountain, 'Move from Here to There'* (Xulon Press. Kindle Edition, 2017).

[7] Jonathan Cahn, *The Oracle* (Charisma House. Kindle Edition, 2019), 270.

About the Author

Born in Romania in a large family of eight siblings, Rodica Malos's family suffered under communist tyranny and oppression because of their strong Christian beliefs. Yet Rodica has never lost her faith in the power of the Word of God, especially its ability to promote physical and spiritual health.

Growing up in impoverished conditions and facing constant opposition because of her faith, Rodica persevered and, through hard work, achieved a high level of education. After graduating from the Academy of Economic Science in Bucharest, she worked as an economist for a large company until leaving the country.

Arriving in the United States in 1990 with no English skills or finances, initially, she earned a living doing janitorial work and as a caregiver for elderly nursing home patients. Thanks to saving and carefully budgeting her money, in 1992, she launched an at-home business offering foster care. Rodica also enrolled in health nursing and medical studies and eventually earned several degrees, including doctor of nursing practice from Oregon Health & Science University (OHSU).

Rodica worked in the health care field for about three decades. She and her husband, Stelica, as the founders and operators of Malos Adult Foster Homes, Tabor Crest Residential Care (memory care), and Tabor Crest II Memory Care provided physical, emotional, and spiritual care (including comfort care at the end of life) to elderly patients with multiple chronic conditions, including neurocognitive disorders and memory loss.

Since 1997, Dr. Malos has volunteered more than five thousand hours of her time to help the less fortunate. She has served as a registered nurse in community care and as a primary care provider at

Portland Adventist Community Service Health Clinic. With Agape Health Care, she has provided care for minorities and others lacking access to the health care system. She also organizes health fairs and free clinics in Portland and other countries.

Currently, Dr. Malos is working as a general practitioner/primary care provider at Good News Community Health Clinic in Portland, Oregon.

Married to Stelica since 1986, she and her husband have one daughter, Andreea, who also graduated from OHSU with a doctor of pharmacy degree.

Also, Dr. Rodica is an international speaker and organizes and speaks at medical and spiritual Christian conferences in USA and abroad. As a board member at Star of Hope International, she travels abroad and supports children with disabilities and their families financially, emotionally, and spiritually.

She is the author of *Find Your Peace: Supernatural Solutions Beyond Science for Fear, Anxiety, and Depression.* Her website is *www.rodicamalos.com.*

CPSIA information can be obtained
at www.ICGtesting.com
Printed in the USA
FSHW010100260121
78005FS